Date Due

OCT 28 60		
NOV 28 60		
JUL 3 1 61		
SEP 30 64		
RESERVE		
MAY 24 '67		
🄶🄱	PRINTED IN U. S. A.	

LISTENING TO MUSIC

ALSO BY WINTHROP SARGEANT

Jazz: Hot and Hybrid
Geniuses, Goddesses and People

Listening to Music

By Winthrop Sargeant

WITH DRAWINGS BY LASZLO

Dodd, Mead & Company

NEW YORK

1958

4 1035

Except for the Introduction, all of the material in
this book originally appeared in *The New Yorker*

Library of Congress Catalog Card Number: 58-8287

Printed in the United States of America
by The Cornwall Press, Inc., Cornwall, N. Y.

To Jane, my wife
and intrepid fellow listener

WITH RESPECT TO THE EXCERPTS from my published criticism that appear in this book, I should like to express acknowledgement of the scrupulous craftsmanship of the editors of *The New Yorker*, who have not only glued together my split infinitives, but have also assisted me greatly, from time to time, in clarifying my thought.

W.S.

HIGHLIGHTS OF MUSIC SEASONS

LISTENING TO MUSIC

INTRODUCTION

ANYONE WHO PUTS TOGETHER an anthology of anything so ephemeral as daily or weekly concert reviews is apt to be assailed by doubts as to the value of the undertaking. Each item thus republished has been originally designed as a report, or a mental reflection, on a specific musical happening still fresh in the minds of a great many readers. As an ingredient in a book it is likely to appear outdated and disconnected from its fellows, and the whole collection is apt to have the character of a pile of old bricks out of which one would like, somehow or other, to construct a wall. The wall, or its ideal lineaments may, however, be present in the mind of the author, and the patient reader may also discern it. What holds it together—if it may be said to hold together at all—is a consistent point of view on the part of the critic.

Consistency is, to my mind, one of the few positive virtues a critic may possess. One may not agree with the judgments it brings forth. They may be mistaken ones. Indeed, the history of music and of painting is filled with the names of very famous critics—Hanslick, Baudelaire (in his art criticism), and Ruskin come to mind—who were conspicuously wrong in some of their judgments, and who may even—as in the case of Hanslick—be remembered primarily for their errors, though they may still be read with a sense of stimulation.

No critic, as far as I am aware, has ever been an infallible oracle. The critic's function is not to lay down incontrovertible laws or pronounce absolute truths. It is to reflect his personal taste, for what it is worth, and to try to stimulate his readers into accepting or rejecting it according to their own lights. Thus, one reads criticism not primarily to learn objective facts about an artist or a work of art, but to have one's mind stirred up by personal insights and reactions which may throw a fresh light on the subject even though one may not necessarily be in sympathy with them. From this standpoint, the best critics may be said to be those with the strongest and most consistent prejudices, and, indeed, if you consult the general literature of criticism, I think you will find the theory borne out.

Music, in particular, is an art that invites intuitive and passionate reactions rather than cold-blooded appraisals. As that great, and eminently prejudiced, music critic Stendhal remarked in his "Life of Rossini": "In all the world there is no intolerance like that of a man of artistic sensibility. If ever you chance to meet, in artistic company, an individual who seems fair minded and reasonable, change the subject quickly; talk to him about history or about political economy, or about some related topic; for whereas there is every possibility that he may one day turn out to be a distinguished magistrate, a fine doctor, a good husband, an excellent academician, or indeed whatever you will, he can *never* become a true connoisseur of music or painting. Never."

The point of view of a critic who is reasonably consistent has, however, a certain logic about it. It can be defined and argued over, perhaps accepted as valid or rejected as false. But it represents a firm personal stand in a realm that, of course, admits of considerable controversy. Since the casual reader may not immediately discern such a point of view in the excerpts that make up this volume, I propose to give myself the luxury here of elaborating on the subject and a few adjoining ones.

Music, to begin with, is something that happens between three indispensable participants: the composer, the performer, and the audience. The first and second of these participants have long been regarded, quite justly, as the heroes of the art, and I shall discuss their place in its scheme presently. Meanwhile, however, let me, for a moment, consider the function of the audience, a group to which, as a critic, I belong, and one whose activities, I feel, often tend to be overlooked or minimized in talking or writing about the art.

There are good and bad audiences just as there are good and bad composers and performers, and a good audience is never a purely passive participant in music. The fundamental importance of the audience is obvious. Without it, a public art like music could not exist, any more than the art of literature could exist without readers. A good audience is musically literate. It understands, through long experience and perhaps through study, the language of music, and it is equipped for listening to, as distinct from merely hearing, what is set before it. It expresses its likes and dislikes through applause or the absence of applause, through going to hear music or staying away from it, and sometimes, I am happy to say, through honest expressions of hostility toward an artist it doesn't approve of. In the end, it is the audience which determines the value of an artist's work, though it may sometimes be capable of temporarily misjudging this value. Great periods of musical creation and performance are distin-

guished by great audiences as well as great composers and performers, and, in such periods, the rapport between these three
classes of participant is remarkably intimate. This sort of audience is highly cultivated, and may understand the language the
composer is using as well as the composer himself does. Through
its expressions of delight or disfavor, it may even influence the
tradition in which the composer expresses himself, and thus become a creative factor in the development of the art. Thus, in
the ideal musical milieu, which has at times been attained in
such eminently musical countries as Germany, Austria, and Italy,
the audience becomes a positive and very active element in musical creation—the lover, so to speak, to whom the composer
addresses his thoughts and to whom he must, if he is to be
successful as an artist, succeed in communicating them.

Our contemporary musical audience is, I think, on the whole,
a fairly good one. It is very large—much larger, for example,
than the audience that interests itself in the Broadway theatre.
In big cities like New York, Boston and Philadelphia, and in
many smaller ones, it attends a tremendous quantity of concerts
and opera performances, and does so with great devotion. It is,
as compared with other types of audience, a cultivated one, able
to distinguish good music from bad and capable of following,
and contributing to, a noble tradition. It has its faults. I am not
sure that it is quite as cultivated today as it was fifty years ago
when musical amateurs learned their music by performing a little themselves on such instruments as the piano and violin, instead of relying on the radio or the phonograph to perform it
for them at home. (The radio and the phonograph have undoubtedly enlarged the musical audience, but whether they have
deepened its perceptions is, I think, open to question.) The
contemporary audience is, moreover, in my experience, inclined
to be a shade too polite, and, at symphony concerts in particular,
is apt to abdicate its privilege and duty of expressing love or

hatred, in favor of listless applause over practically everything that it encounters.

There is, here and there, also to be found in this audience a superficial creature who might be designated as the parvenu highbrow—the man who thinks he likes Bartók because that is the chic thing to do, and who meanwhile finds, say, Verdi or Chopin boring. With all due respect to Bartók, who is an interesting composer, this man, in my opinion, is simply not sensitive to music, and will soon grow tired of the fashionable toy which is all that he perceives in Bartók. Fortunately he is in a minority. The majority of the contemporary musical audience consists of people who are vitally interested in the art, and I think that, on the whole, this group of educated listeners, despite its faults, may be regarded as the greatest single asset of our musical culture.

The performer, who displays his skills in person before this audience, is a very interesting figure, in some ways comparable to an actor who interprets a role in a play. He is both an artist and an athlete. His prowess in both fields is the product of years of meticulous training, and, if he is a fine performer, his knowledge of the traditions of his difficult craft, and of the music that he interprets, is profound. He has, in all probability, led a lonely childhood devoted to perfecting his skill, and his mature life is apt to be lived as much in railroad cars and aeroplanes as in concert halls. He is also a worker in a fearfully competitive field where his playing is ruthlessly analyzed by critics, audiences, managers and fellow artists, and the stature which these people accord him is likely to be a tribute to achievement of the most solid sort. These aspects of his career are, however, not of primary concern to the audience that listens to him. What the audience exacts, as he walks onto the stage, is a near-perfect communication of the composer's thoughts, and perhaps also a display of those feats of virtuosity and insight which good composers have provided for by their affectionate regard for his instrument and his function as a performer.

The performer is not, as may sometimes be supposed, a mere tool of the composer. On the contrary, the greatest composers (a good many of whom, it might be remarked, have been performers themselves) have always respected his art and its traditions, and have frequently altered and arranged their musical ideas to suit his particular talents and limitations. I need not adduce here such examples as Verdi's or Mozart's profound respect for the art of singing, or Chopin's for the art of piano playing, or Richard Strauss's engaging and uncanny faculty for writing in such a way that the horn players or oboists in an orchestra appear to be overflowing with personal exuberance as they go through their paces. These are tributes which the sensitive composer pays to the art of performance, recognizing it as the vehicle for the ultimate realization of his ideas—ideas which, like those of the playwright, are only fully embodied when they are set before an audience. Great music invariably reflects the tradition of performance. Indeed, there are many features in the composing style of nearly all of the great masters—cadenzas, pseudo recitatives, melodic ornamentations, and so on—that originated not as the inventions of composers but as elements of the performing tradition. So we may say, in this connection, even more emphatically than we did in discussing the contribution of the audience, that genuinely expressive music is to a certain extent a joint endeavor, and that while the composer creates a given composition, the language that he uses in doing so is a commonly understood medium to which the performer has contributed in no small part.

Judging performing artists is, for the experienced critic, a fairly exact proceeding. It is exact, at least, up to the point where the artist's personal gifts of inspiration and insight enter into the picture. The artist's mastery of the mechanics of his craft, or his lack of such mastery, is a matter of fact, not taste or opinion. A violinist or a singer may or may not play or sing in tune, for example, or a pianist's scales and arpeggios may or may not be evenly and precisely articulated, and in such matters there can be no question of doubt. These elements of his craft are purely technical. They belong to the athletic side of his art, and in this realm his prowess is as precisely measurable as that of any other type of athlete.

Considered merely as a branch of athletics, however, the performer's art is a rather complex and subtle affair involving the domination of his will and his intellect over the inert raw material with which he works—i.e. his instrument, his fingers, his lips in the case of a wind player and his larynx in the case of a singer. This raw material he must subdue by overcoming its awkward and inartistic tendencies, and by making it, through an elaborate system of habitual reflexes, into a vehicle which he manipulates almost unconsciously. Such mastery of the technical elements of his craft is, of course, taken for granted in the performance of a finished virtuoso or singer, though when it reaches an extraordinary degree of perfection it may be a source of amazement or pleasure in itself. The accurate marksmanship of a fine coloratura soprano, the fleet finger work of a master pianist, are exciting things to behold, and beyond these matters of mechanical speed and accuracy, there exist, in the athletic technique of a consummate virtuoso, certain other features of a subtler nature—the sense of force coupled with relaxation which gives a pianist's work a combined impression of power and ease, the feeling of limitless physical resource that a great singer may project to his audience by the combined power and ease with which he manipulates his voice, the variety of volume which permits an artist to achieve contrasts and climaxes of sound, the variety of tonal coloring and inflection by which he expresses shades of emotion, and, finally, though perhaps not most importantly, the purely sensuous beauty of the sounds themselves. All these things are to some extent a matter of talent and to some extent a matter of studied craftsmanship. They constitute, as I have said, the athletic facet of the performer's art, and they can be judged objectively with considerable precision.

A great performing artist is, however, not merely an athlete; he is also a projector, an interpreter—some will say a re-creator—of musical ideas. It is in his hands that the thought of a composer leaves the printed page and becomes embodied in sound, and at this point we arrive at another area of his art where questions of taste and opinion are apt to take precedence over matters of fact, though matters of fact are discernible here too. A performer may interpret a composer's work at a tempo that is, by common consensus, too fast or too slow; he may lose control of the work's formal structure, pulling it out of shape by emphasizing the wrong things, thundering away when he should be restrained, and misplacing his climaxes; he may oversentimentalize, or he may play or sing with undue coldness and dryness. Or, on the other hand, he may project the composition he is playing with complete mastery of its structure and meaning. These, and similar, faults and virtues of his playing may be regarded as belonging to the sphere of taste, but the taste is not necessarily personal. The common opinions held by generations of audiences, critics, and fellow artists bring them into a realm of definable laws which no artist is at liberty to defy. These laws relate to the accepted traditions of musical interpretation, and the most important of them are concerned with two quite definite departments of performing artistry: phrasing and the control of extended musical form.

Phrasing is to music what declamation is to the drama. It is the art of relative emphasis by which important notes are distinguished from less important ones, so that stresses and accents fall in their proper places and the meaning of a melody or a passage of music is made evident to the listener. It is quite comparable to the actor's art of speaking lines of monologue, stressing certain words in order to convey the meaning of a sentence. Though the composer's written score occasionally contains marks—accents, legato signs, and so on—that emphasize the cruder points of the phrasing he desires, the problems of correct phrasing are, in general, much too subtle to be indicated on the printed page. They are left to the performer's intuition and to his knowledge of musical tradition, and they are part of the living language of music, as opposed to the rather mechanical record of music which is conveyed by notes written on paper. In matters of phrasing, the composer is thus at the mercy of the performer, and, if he is a competent composer, he writes with a knowledge of the performing tradition in mind, secure in the faith that a fine performer will grasp and project those subtleties of his thought which his written notes only hint at. This faith, which is basic to the projection of all meaning in music, is a two-way affair. It exacts of the composer an intimate acquaintance with music as "spoken" by performing artists, and, from the performer, an intimate acquaintance with the meanings roughly indicated in music as written by the composer. In this matter the interdependence of the composer and the performer is profound, and the responsibility of both is correspondingly great. What I have spoken of as "the living language of music" is the province of the performer, and the composer who writes without reference to it is apt to convey nothing in the way of musical meaning. The performer, on the other hand, must be a master of his tradition, and must be able to vitalize the composer's written intentions with intuitive understanding and scrupulous care. Phrasing is one of the areas in which he exercises this faculty of intuition. It is the *sine qua non* of artistic musical performance. The intuitions of generations of performers have given it a body of commonly accepted laws, and a musical executant's artistry is judged to a great exent by his knowledge of these laws. A great performer is invariably a great master of musical phraseology, and this mastery is one of the outstanding things that distinguishes, say, a Gieseking, a Backhaus, a Toscanini, a Rethberg, a Casals, or an Eileen Farrell from the ordinary, more or less competent, artists in their respective fields.

What I have called "the control of extended musical form" is perhaps merely an extension of the problem of phrasing. It involves the artist's ability to place the ingredients of a composition's total dramatic continuity in proper, or meaningful, relation to each other, so that the work is built into an organic whole with all its contrasts and climaxes in just proportion. In music of any length and intellectual complexity, this is a very difficult thing to do, and great masters of the performing art, like the late Arturo Toscanini, owe much of their artistic stature to their formidable abilities in coping with the problem. A great symphony or concerto or opera is a close-knit dramatic unit stretching over a considerable period of time. It builds up to a climax, or to several climaxes, and its vast structure comes to an end with some sort of grand catharsis. To vitalize its over-all continuity, an artist must make use of conscious musical intelligence as well as intuition, keeping in mind the relations between future and past and giving each successive element of the work just the comparative emphasis that it requires in relation to what has gone before and is coming later. If he loosens his thunderbolts too early, his later climaxes will not appear climactic by contrast. Everything depends, here, on the exercise of conscious craftsmanship, deliberate timing and an acute sense of relative values. Masters of this particular phase of performing artistry are comparatively rare. Many well-known virtuosos and conductors lack the faculty required for the feat, or achieve it only intermittently or imperfectly. When a virtuoso or a conductor does achieve it in performance after performance, he may be regarded as one of the supreme artists in his field.

Beyond these measurable athletic points and traditional laws of fine interpretation, there lies, of course, a more elusive area which concerns the performer's personality and attributes of individual taste. Myra Hess and Sir Thomas Beecham, for example, perform Mozart more robustly and less meticulously than the late Artur Schnabel did, and you may have a preference for one style or the other, though both are admirable and equally correct. Some artists, like the late Ignaz Jan Paderewski or Josef Hofmann or Artur Rubinstein, bring to their performances not only a quality of personal flamboyance which is rather engaging in itself, but also a completely unanalyzable spell of magic capable of hypnotizing the auditor, and this spell may exist despite occasional imperfections in their playing. The quality of leadership, in a great conductor like Toscanini, may exert a comparable spell, and though one may be able to figure out to some extent how the trick is done, one is forced in the end to throw up one's hands and attribute it to the mysterious personal attribute of genius. In the field of opera singing, where the artist is required to project specific dramatic ideas as well as purely musical ones (expressing himself in both musical and dramatic departments mainly by vocal inflection), the contribution of personality is even more essential. Many a great Tosca or Carmen, for example, has been sung by a singer who would be incapable of the suavity and scrupulousness required in Mozart, and many a singer, finely schooled in the intricacies of the Mozart style, has failed in flamboyant roles like Tosca and Carmen.

Few artists, in fact, are equally at home in all types of music. Some, like Horowitz, can fascinate an audience with pure glitter of a steely sort; others, like Backhaus in Beethoven, by the profundity of their musical understanding; still others, like Fritz Kreisler (to those who remember him at his peak) or Maggie

Teyte, by qualities of charm almost unrelated to, or existing independently of, technical achievement. All these things are, as I have said, matters of personality, and, as such, not subject to rules and regulations. In assessing such things, the critic is no longer in a realm of artistic good and evil. Here, everything is a matter of taste and opinion. I might add, at this point, that the art of conducting—perhaps the most resplendent and glamorous one now practiced before the public—is concerned only with the facets of the performing art that I have described as relating to personality and the laws of interpretive tradition. The conductor, alone among performing artists, is not an athlete. His art does not involve a technique, and his feats are feats of pure musicianship and personality. Properly speaking, he is not a performing artist, but an overseer of performing artists.

Now let us get around to the composer, who is by tradition and common consent regarded as the great creative source of music, and whose works, if he is an important artist, live far beyond his own time. Today's composers are, I think, something of a problem. In his recently published book "The Agony of Modern Music," Henry Pleasants has suggested that the composer today is practicing, for his own exclusive benefit, a craft that has lost all meaning to its audience, and that he is, in fact, obsolete as an artist. I have never been able to bring myself into full agreement with this thesis. In the first place, I cannot conceive of the death of music as a creative art, since music has been created in some form or other from the beginning of history. In the second place, I can think of quite a number of contemporary composers whose work seems to me to have considerable vigor and meaning. Nevertheless, Mr. Pleasants' book does lay a finger on one of the persistent weaknesses of contemporary music, which, as a whole, seems to betray certain symptoms of severe illness. The illness seems to have set in at about the time of the First World War, and the main symptom is simply that very few works written by composers since that time have achieved the status of universally accepted masterpieces.

One must not, of course, generalize too hastily about what one calls "the contemporary composer." He comes in many models, ranging from the addicts of the twelve-tone system to conservatives of all shades including men like Vaughan Williams, William Walton, Ernest Bloch, Howard Hanson, and Vittorio Giannini. I should, offhand, hazard a guess that such music of permanent value as our period is producing will ultimately be discovered among the works of composers of the latter type, and I shall present my reasons for this guess presently. Meanwhile it is important to remember that nobody today is in a position to hear and judge all the work of the thousands of composers who are currently engaged in the task of putting music down on paper. It may quite conceivably happen that the great genius of twentieth-century music will turn out to be an obscure individual whose work is, at present, unperformed, or even somebody whose work the present musical world is taking for granted without paying any special heed to it.

There does exist, however, a formidable group of composers who, because of current fashion and the frequency with which their works are performed, have tended to set the tone of contemporary music and may be considered its most typical exponents, and it is with them that I am here concerned. Their work is characterized by certain definable formulas—most notably the methodical avoidance of such structural elements of the past as clear-cut tonality and the dynamic relation between consonance and dissonance. These composers are popularly regarded as the "progressives" of the art, and their various styles were for a long time referred to by the somewhat too inclusive term "modern music." For convenience, and despite the inaccuracy of the words, I shall refer to them here as "modern composers."

The "modern composer" is a product of the attempted revolution in musical technique that was initiated nearly fifty years ago by Stravinsky, Schoenberg, and the group known in Paris as "Les Six." The formulas with which these historically influential men replaced the conventions of classical and romantic music have since congealed into several easily recognized styles, and today one can detect the "modern composer" by merely listening to a few bars of his music. He is still the most widely performed of contemporary composers. Occasionally he comes up with some novel trick of technique, and very rarely, as in the case of the late Alban Berg, he may have something really interesting to say. The Russians, who officially disapprove of him, refer to him as a "formalist," by which they mean that he concerns himself with the purely abstract relationships between notes instead of with the musical meanings notes are intended to convey. I think that the Russian designation is an appropriate one, and, though I hate to agree with the Russians about anything, my position as a critic is antiformalist. In fact, I regard doctrinaire formalism as the curse of contemporary music, and I consider nearly all formalist music to be a waste of time, not only for its audience and its performers, but for its composers as well.

I would not be so vehement on this subject were it not for the enormous prestige that the "modern composer" still enjoys. He and his fellows, at the moment, are, in fact, the leading academicians of the art. They serve on the advisory boards of foundations and publishing houses. They hold chairs of musical pedagogy at leading universities and schools of music, where they teach other people to be formalists. In these powerful positions, they tend to dictate musical fashion. The young composer who wants to achieve success is bound, first, to study with them and, second, to write the kind of music they like if he is to receive the prizes, fellowships and publishing contracts which, unfortunately, he has to depend on for his main source of economic support. Thus, formalism tends to perpetuate itself, and perhaps the most interesting feature of the process is that the musical audience, for whom the composer presumably writes, has virtually nothing to do with it. Whether it likes or dislikes the music is irrelevant. The music is composed, not for audiences, but for other formalist composers.

This situation is, I think, unhealthy to say the least, and certainly unprecedented in the history of music. It is what Mr. Pleasants referred to when he said that the contemporary composer has lost contact with his audience, and is perpetuating an outworn tradition purely for his own benefit. Actually, the judgment of talent and ability among composers should never be, and in healthy periods of creation never has been, left in the hands of fellow composers. Nor, for that matter, have many of the great composers of the past been pupils of other composers. In general, the great masters have been either self-taught or have been pupils of professional pedagogues who have trained them in such rudiments of the musical language as are embodied in conventional harmony, counterpoint, fugue, and so on. A composer, especially a composer with eccentric doctrines and mannerisms, is apt to be a poor teacher of his craft. His pupils will tend to imitate his own style and to be deficient in their understanding of the basic techniques of their art.

This lack of understanding of basic technique, and accompanying tendency to ape mannerisms, is very widespread in contemporary music—so widespread that one can often detect, instantly, in the work of younger composers, the superficial features of something that might be called "the foundation style," a dreary routine of academic formulas that is guaranteed to win fellowships and prizes, but that shows little or no comprehension of the difficult problem of conveying some sort of musical message to an audience. I have found, as a rule, that the contemporary music in which I have detected sparks of originality and

substance has been written by composers like Gershwin and Paul
Creston who were self-taught, or by composers like Samuel
Barber and Gian-Carlo Menotti who studied with conventional
pedagogues, and this coincidence is, to my mind, no accident.
One of the main troubles with formalism is that it has become
the most narrow and hidebound of artistic dogmas. Today, in
formalist circles, the young composer who forgets himself so far
as to write a do-mi-sol chord is subject to a degree of academic
disapproval far exceeding that with which nineteenth-century
professors viewed those who disregarded the famous prohibition
against consecutive fifths.

In its development from the early revolutionary ideas of
Schoenberg, Stravinsky, and the other fathers of "modern music," formalism has, as I have noted, congealed into a dogma, and
this dogma has been supported by a number of aesthetic notions
which, to my mind, reflect a basic misapprehension as to the
nature of music. These notions express themselves easily in the
form of slogans, and some of the more important and widely
circulated of them can be conveniently itemized here along with
the objections to them:

*Music of originality involves a revolution against the conven-
tions of the past.* This notion was perhaps more popular in the
1920s, when Marxist ideas had given the word "revolution" an
exciting ring, than it is today. There has, as a matter of fact,
been no perceptible revolution in formalist technique since about
1911 when the first examples of the genre were created. Moreover, revolution, as it applies to the basic tradition of the art, is
an aesthetic impossibility—a point which I hope to prove presently. What an attempt at revolution arrives at is simply not
music.

*The history of music is one of continuous progress in technical
matters.* This is, on the face of it, an absurdity. Music, of
course, changes in style from period to period, but it does not

progress in any clear evolutionary line. During some periods, some aspects of music have tended toward greater or lesser complexity, but there is no more reason to assume that the art of music has "progressed" since, say, Monteverdi, than there is to assume that the art of narrative has "progressed" since Homer.

Experimentation in technique is one of the composer's most important functions. This idea has been borrowed from the laboratories of the scientists, and the position has even been held that the primary purpose of the composer is to invent and discover new sounds or new arrangements of sound. The position results from two outrageous misconceptions about the nature of music: 1) that music is in some way analogous to a science; 2) that music consists of mere sounds, rather than of meanings conveyed through a commonly understood language of sound. A composer may, doubtless, experiment to some extent in an attempt to convey new meanings within the framework of the language. But if he experiments merely with sounds for their own sake, as many formalists have done, he involves himself in something that has no relevance whatever to the art of music.

Important music is difficult to understand at first hearing. This may be true as regards some complex forms of important music. But it is certainly not true of the work of the formalists, whose formulas are, by now, quite transparent to any educated listener, and are, in fact, far simpler than, say, the intricate counterpoint of Bach or the complicated palette of chromatic harmonies used by the nineteenth-century Romantics. The corollary—that music which is difficult to understand is likely to be important—is, of course, dubious to say the least.

A composer should compose for future generations. This idea is a holdover from the Romantic era. It was extremely popular at the time of Richard Wagner, a composer who, paradoxically, was esteemed by his contemporaries even more unreservedly than he is today. We are now in the position of a "future gen-

eration" in respect to the atonal compositions of Arnold Schoenberg, who held the theory, and I cannot say that these
compositions are any more popular with audiences today than
they were with the audiences who first heard them. To my
mind, it is a pretty good rule of thumb that a composer who
cannot convey anything to his own generation is not likely to
convey anything to future generations either.

Great music must express its time. I suppose there is something to this, inasmuch as all genuine music inevitably contains
certain elements of style that we recognize as belonging to a
period. I doubt, however, whether any really important composer has ever been conscious of expressing his "time." A composer who sets out deliberately to "express his time" is faced
with certain very perplexing problems, not the least of which is
to determine what he means by his "time." The word is, of
course, so vague as to be practically devoid of meaning. I doubt
whether any composer is in the Olympian position to give any
precise definition of what his "time" really is. Jazz and popular
Broadway tunes may, I suppose, be said to express their time in
the sense that they belong to it and are eagerly listened to by
contemporary audiences. I must say that I find the whole concept of a composer's "time" quite baffling as well as aesthetically
unfruitful. I suspect that what the contemporary composer
really means when he says he must express his time is that he
must be in fashion. And experience has led me to doubt the
importance of a composer who is merely fashionable. A good
composer will doubtless be influenced by the time in which he
lives, but, from his own point of view, expressing his "time"
would not seem to be nearly as important as expressing himself.

*The technique of composition always moves in the direction
of increasing dissonance. A dissonance is merely a combination
of tones that audiences have not yet learned to recognize as a
consonance. Today's dissonances will therefore be regarded as*

*consonances by future audiences, whose ears will have become
more educated.* This theory is not only not borne out by history
(Schubert was not, for example, a more dissonant composer
than Monteverdi); it reflects an almost childish naïveté concerning the nature of dissonance. Dissonance is, of course, one of
the most important ingredients of musical style, and a great deal
of the propulsive power of all fine music depends on the dynamic relationship between consonance and dissonance. Dissonance is, in the language of the psychologist, the main
"affective" device used in music, and its resolution to consonance
is one of those mechanisms by which a composer induces suspense followed by catharsis. Dissonance, however, has nothing
to do with relative pleasantness or unpleasantness of sound. It
exists only in relation to consonance, and is quite meaningless
without the latter. The word "dissonance," as employed in the
above slogan, means simply cacophony, or unpleasant sound, or
noise, which is a very different thing from dissonance. The
atonal works of composers like Schoenberg or Roger Sessions, for
example, may be cacophonous, but they cannot properly be said
to contain any dissonances. This is because they are written in
an artificial idiom where the opposition between consonance and
dissonance does not exist.

*All arts in a given period have comparable goals. Modern
music is something like modern art. It is moving in the direction
of abstraction and distortion.* This is a tempting thesis in view
of the great success and popularity of masters like Picasso and
Braque. But, to my mind, its effect on contemporary music has
been disastrous. The arts of music and painting are really not
very much alike, and analogies between them are apt to be very
misleading. Music cannot move in the direction of abstraction,
for the simple reason that it has been an "abstract," or non-representational art from the very beginning. The invention of the
camera, which did so much to remove literal representation from

its former documentary function in painting, is an event without any parallel in the musical field. Even distortion, in music—if it can be said to exist at all—is not a distortion of observed phenomena of the real world. The vast differences between the arts of painting and music, which involve distinctions between the eye and the ear, between space and time, between the perceptions and temperaments of painters and musicians, and so on, might easily be the subject of a book. One of the main differences, which is of particular use to this discussion, is that the creation of a painter is a hand-made object in which every feature may be subject to the individual will of the artist, whereas the creation of a composer is a sort of blueprint from which the performer extracts and projects meaning according to a traditional system of principles which is, or should be, well understood by both. Music can be said to exist only when it sounds, and the mechanisms for translating it from print into sound involve complex conventions which are by no means the creation of any single artist.

This brings me back to my starting point—that music is something which takes place between three indispensable participants, of whom the composer is only one. The intercommunication between these three participants is based inevitably on a tradition. Now, the word "tradition," which I have been using rather frequently, has, for some time, had a somewhat negative or unpleasant connotation in fashionable artistic circles. It has been popularly associated with the practices of the mere imitator or the academician, and, to many, it has become simply an ugly word. This, however, is a perversion of its true meaning. In music, because of the art's peculiar dependence on a commonly understood system of communication, tradition is indispensable. It is to music precisely what language is to literature, and just as literature without language would be meaningless, so music without tradition is also meaningless. A composer may further, or expand, the musical tradition, and many have done so, but he cannot revolt against it or create his own individual tradition any more than a writer can revolt against his language or create an entirely new language of his own. If he attempts to do so, he winds up in a sterile exercise which has nothing to do with the conveyance of meaning.

Here, I feel, is where the formalist composer has run off the track. He has conceived music as an arbitrary relation between formal elements without regard to their traditional meanings, and he is in the position of a writer who throws over the traditional meanings of words and devotes himself to constructing an individual variety of gibberish by putting letters together in new relationships. Because language is more widely understood than musical tradition, the writer who does this (There were a few who did it in Paris in the 1920s under the aegis of the Dadaist literary magazine *Transition*.) is quickly detected and recognized as an eccentric practitioner of a not-very-rewarding typographical game. Music, however, is, to most people, a rather mysterious art, and the formalist's revolt against tradition has not been so easily detectable. The audience, however, has had its intuitive reactions to the phenomenon, and has, as a rule, disliked formalist music. It has, I think, been quite correct in these reactions, since formalist music does not convey musical meaning.

By "musical meaning," I do not, of course, mean the sort of meaning that is conveyed by words. If musical meaning were the same thing as conceptual meaning, there would be no reason for music to exist as a separate art. Musical meaning is a very difficult thing to describe, and the critic who writes for popular consumption is often at a loss for terms that come anywhere near defining it. Its ingredients may, however, be pinned down, and for the intrepid reader who is interested in the subject, I can highly recommend that admirable, if difficult, treatise "Emotion and Meaning in Music" by Leonard Meyer, a book which covers its ins and outs with extraordinary comprehensiveness.

It is not necessary to define musical meaning in order to understand it, however. It is something that can be found in jazz, folk music, and virtually every popular song as well as in the masterpieces of symphonic and operatic music where it appears in more intricately developed form. It is what grips, charms, cajoles or awes the mind of the listener. It is the thing that the average auditor refers to when he describes a composition as "inspired." It has little or nothing to do with the mere sensual impressions that sounds produce on the ear or with the purely calligraphic relations between notes written on paper. It is something conveyed to the mind, as distinct from the senses, of the listener, and any perceptive music-lover can recognize it instantly. This recognition is an awareness that the composer is "saying something" that lies beyond mere sounds and mere formulas for the arrangements of notes. And, in "saying something," the composer makes use of a language, or a tradition, by which notes are given widely accepted significances.

Musical traditions differ somewhat, though they all involve systems of tonality and of consonance and dissonance which may be regarded as basic to Western music. There is, for example, the Italian operatic tradition, grounded in Mediterranean folk music and the art of *bel canto*. There is the Austro-German symphonic tradition which is, as a whole, more intricate and is devoted to the manipulation of themes, though, at bottom, it is a development of the Italian and Germanic musical languages. Popular music also has its traditions, or dialects of tradition, which range from the Moorish-Iberian idiom of Spanish Flamenco music to such things as the language of jazz, that of the Anglo-Celtic ballad which survives in Hillbilly music, that of the Lutheran chorale, that of the revivalist hymn and so on.

It may, I think, be laid down as a rule that any music which conveys meaning speaks the language of some tradition or other. The most imposing and artistically elaborate of these traditions, up to now, have, of course, been the tradition of the Austro-German symphony and that of the Italian opera, and it may be that these are on the decline and are shortly to be superseded, though even this is a debatable point. The French, though they have, from time to time, produced musicians of great importance, have never had a very strong musical tradition of their own, and it may be for this reason that so much contemporary formalist music has appeared under French auspices. Like the Russians, the English and ourselves, they have tended to adopt their musically meaningful traditions, perhaps with slight alterations, from the Germans and the Italians, and much of the finest French music (certain compositions by a few highly individual composers like Berlioz and Debussy notwithstanding) has been the product of this adoption.

Now, when one surveys the field of contemporary music, seeking to distinguish the meaningful from the meaningless, one finds, as might be expected, that meaningful compositions invariably embody a tradition. The reason why Carlisle Floyd's "Susannah" is a better opera than Aaron Copland's "The Tender Land," for example, is not that Mr. Floyd is a better technician than Mr. Copland, for, in some respects, he is not as good a one. The reason, apart from imponderables such as relative talent, lies in the fact that Mr. Floyd has written eloquently within the framework of a tradition—in this case the tradition of rural American folk music and hymn singing—and has succeeded in developing this tradition in accordance with the conventions of opera, without distorting its fundamental system of meaning. Mr. Copland, on the other hand, has used a few folk-music mannerisms as decorative effects, but the structural features of his score, in "The Tender Land," have no relevance to any tradition whatever. They simply follow a formalist pattern which Mr.

Copland himself has invented, and hence have no accepted frame of reference. Mr. Copland's "El Salon Mexico," to take another example, has more musical meaning than his purely formalistic "Short Symphony," because it reflects to some extent the tradition of Mexican folk music. George Gershwin's opera "Porgy and Bess" owes its meaning to the musical language of the American Negro which he has modified for his purposes by mixing it with the musical language of Broadway. Gian-Carlo Menotti still employs the strong and eloquent tradition of Italian opera. Paul Creston owes his distinguished stature as a symphonist to the fact that his music, though individual in style, is securely grounded in the Austro-German tradition of symphonic music, and the same can be said for Shostakovich and Prokofieff, as regards their more expressive and less formalistic works. Roy Harris' Third Symphony is quite meaningful in those passages in which he speaks the language of symphonic tradition, and quite meaningless in those in which he does not speak it. And so on.

"Speaking the language" of a tradition does not, of course, necessarily guarantee the quality of a composer's music. A great deal of trivial, vulgar, and imitative music speaks the language of tradition. But speaking the languages does guarantee the conveyance of meaning, and, in my opinion, it is better to write music which may be trivial and vulgar than to write music which is meaningless.

Formalism, as I have said, results from a misconception about the aesthetic nature of music, and it is a curious commentary on the aesthetic confusion of our time that this misconception exists in the minds of composers—men who might be expected to understand more about music than anybody else does. It is, I am convinced, a passing phenomenon—the product of a generation of muddled thinking which we are only at present beginning to unravel. Already, some composers who were once formalists have begun to question or abandon the method—among them Poulenc, George Antheil, and that refreshingly exuberant antiformalist Carl Orff. Meanwhile, however, doctrinaire formalism persists in the work of the twelve-tone composers and in much of the output of such celebrated figures as Stravinsky, though it might be remarked that Stravinsky—at his best an extremely clever composer of widely eclectic tendencies—has often rejected pure formalism (in parts of "The Rake's Progress" for instance) in favor of some archaic tradition or other. In the end, the case against formalism rests simply on the fact that it is boring—and to be boring is perhaps the only cardinal sin of which an artist can be capable.

FALL SEASON, 1949

November 5, 1949

AT A RECENT Philharmonic-Symphony concert, Leopold Stokowski paid his respects, rather casually, to Arnold Schoenberg, whose seventy-fifth birthday occurred this year, by sandwiching a snippet from his great cantata "Gurre-Lieder," along with a short work by Heitor Villa-Lobos, between some extremely uninspired performances of music by Wagner and Beethoven. The snippet was the episode known as the "Song of the Wood Dove," which requires only a small segment of the four-hundred-man ensemble necessary for the full work and is therefore, naturally, much easier to do. It was heartening to hear even this fragment of a very impressive composition that has not been performed here in its entirety since Stokowski himself did it at the Metropolitan Opera House in 1932. One of the most satisfying features of the performance was the singing of the American mezzo-soprano Martha Lipton, who gave the difficult solo part both the requisite volume of sound and the appropriate sense of tragic dignity.

Various critics have written a good deal about the Wagnerian character of this work, but I find the "Song of the Wood Dove" much more akin to the music of Gustav Mahler in its gloomy, soul-searching, and subjective passion. Actually, it is contemporary with Mahler's later symphonies and, like Mahler's music, reflects the Vienna of Sigmund Freud and the Expressionist painters—a period when the great romantic tradition flared into a last, poignantly poetic flame, during the final years of the Hapsburg Empire. Schoenberg's writing here has qualities of magic and mystery that have all but disappeared from today's music, and probes far deeper into the human psyche than anything written by his equally famous contemporary Igor Stravinsky.

The Schoenberg represented in this work is the Schoenberg of about 1900, familiar elsewhere only in the lovely sextet "Verklärte Nacht," which is now practically a popular classic. It is one of the enigmas of our time that a composer of such obvious originality and communicative power should subsequently have slipped into a realm of cryptic technical ideas where, for nearly forty years, he has produced nothing that seems to have any meaning for the musical public. This technical realm is, of course, the one known to musicians as "atonality," and is detected by the average concertgoer through certain unmistakable features—mainly a cacophony so methodical and absolute that nothing identifiable in the way of a melody or a concord ever interrupts its monotonous flow.

The continuing public apathy toward Schoenberg's later work is commonly explained by two theories, one popular among his supporters, the other among his detractors. The first is that the music is ahead of its time, and that the public has just not yet learned to like it. The second is that the music is simply bad or meaningless music. The first of these theories has lately begun to lose some of its force, inasmuch as Schoenberg's earliest essays in atonality are now nearly forty years old and show no more signs of ingratiating themselves with the public than they did when they were first performed. I am afraid that I incline toward the second theory. It presupposes that a composer of great ability may become the victim of a confused and fruitless aesthetic idea. This is a view that I have not accepted lightly, but it is the theory I favor, nevertheless.

It is not difficult to discover behind the aesthetics of atonality the presence of one of those philosophies of historical determinism that have been so dear to the academic German mind from the time of Hegel and Karl Marx to that of Oswald Spengler. Atonality is, as its apologists have frequently pointed out, the logical continuation of a historical trend in nineteenth-century German music. This trend was quite clearly toward the increasing use of dissonance and toward the gradual elimination of the classical canons governing the relationship of keys. Stated simply, this means that Beethoven used more dissonances and more freedom in mixing keys than Mozart, and that Wagner used more dissonances and more freedom in mixing keys than Beethoven.

If the trend were pursued to its ultimate conclusion, one would arrive at a type of music in which everything was dissonance and the relation between one key and another became blurred to such an extent that one had no identifiable key at all. This conclusion has been, in fact, reached in Schoenberg's music. Having lost the subtle principle of opposing consonance and dissonance, upon which all classical and romantic music had been based, atonality moved into a realm of pure, unrelieved dissonance. This was, by the logic of historical determinism, the only conceivable direction in which the music of the future could move, and if the musical public didn't like it, so much the worse for them. You couldn't stop Schoenberg because you couldn't stop history.

Now, the logic of this development looks unassailable as long as you accept its deterministic frame. But once you step outside it, a number of objections arise. Music, in the first place, is not a vast, self-contained, historically conditioned organism evolving through the ages independently of the wills of the people who create it. It is something created by individual composers, who are, I trust, men of reasonably free will and who are at liberty to compose any kind of music they like, whether it fits into some academic historical scheme or not. Secondly, the atonalists, in projecting their theoretical extension of nineteenth-century trends to a point where the opposition between consonance and dissonance disappeared, threw overboard music's main propulsive principle. Consonance and dissonance have occupied a place in the narrative form of music not very different from that occupied by good and evil, or by catharsis and suspense, in literary narrative.

Moreover, all theories of historical determinism, whether political or musical, tend to overlook the fact that the future is never entirely predictable. There is always the chance that they may turn out to be dead wrong. The theory of atonality thus appears to be suspect on grounds of common sense, and since the music that proceeds from it seems to convey nothing to the majority of music-lovers, it is not illogical to conclude that it represents an aesthetic blind alley that is being bypassed by the actual course of history.

But right or wrong, Arnold Schoenberg, who now lives on the outskirts of Hollywood, has stuck uncompromisingly to the atonal idea, stubbornly certain that history will someday vindicate him. Whatever one may think of the importance of his present work, it is still a fact that the Schoenberg who composed the "Gurre-Lieder" deserves our respect as one of the last great creative figures of the romantic movement.

December 17, 1949

LEONARD BERNSTEIN, having pretty well established by now that he is a *Wunderkind*, could be expected, one of these days, to move on to the status of mature artist. The change, if it came about, would be perceptible first not in his conducting of complex modern scores, in which his ability to deal accurately with a great quantity and variety of notes has been his most impressive accomplishment, but in the conducting of simple classics, in which taste is just as important as accuracy.

His appearances with the Boston Symphony at Carnegie Hall last week showed, I am afraid, that he has not yet made the transition. His performance Saturday afternoon of Olivier Messiaen's intricate new "Turangalîla" Symphony had the efficiency that one has learned to count on from him in contemporary music, but his earlier concert, devoted to familiar compositions by Mozart and Brahms, was an exhibition of slapdash energy rather than of musical insight.

Mr. Bernstein proved that he is capable of leaving his personal stamp on the playing of the Boston Symphony, but the result of this influence was that the most refined and delicately adjusted of all our orchestras actually played somewhat coarsely. Mozart's "Haffner" Symphony was little more than a succession of hard-driven rhythms. The same composer's B-Flat-Major Piano Concerto, which Mr. Bernstein conducted while playing the piano part himself, sounded, in general, as if it were still being rehearsed.

Mr. Bernstein's baton technique, which encompasses an enormous range of lunges, head shakings, shoulder shrugs, and other theatrical devices, seems designed mainly to impress his audience, and exists in a choreographic world of its own, almost completely detached from the orchestra's playing. This histrionic art reached its apogee in his interpretation of Brahms' Second Symphony, in which he exhibited most of the visual phenomena, and brought forth some of the musical qualities, associated with Al Jolson's interpretation of "Mammy."

The Messiaen symphony, hailed recently by Serge Koussevitsky as one of the milestones of contemporary music, at least had the virtue of not boring its audience, though its ten movements took almost an hour and a half to perform. In fact, certain of the movements revived among the New York symphonic public the custom of hissing and booing as well as applauding—a development that I am delighted to report. Its title, "Turangalîla," according to a program note, is a poetic word, in an unspecified Indian language, meaning "love song," and love is its subject. To this subject, Mr. Messiaen has brought one of the most elaborate repertoires of curious noises that have been displayed in symphonic music since Stravinsky's "Le Sacre du Printemps." The orchestra twittered, jangled, and thudded with an almost stupefying variety of novel sound effects.

Love is, of course, a highly individual emotion. At times, Mr. Messiaen's conception of it suggested the methodical demolition of a warehouse full of cutlery. At others, it was expressed in an idiom that, for unadulterated sentiment, outdid the most plangent orchestrations of André Kostelanetz. There are, no doubt, a good many concertgoers who, like me, favor the idea of getting a little love back into contemporary music, but Mr. Messiaen's colossal gesture in this direction is too special to be what I have in mind. Following its final burst of clangor ("An exuberant and brilliant coda ends the work in a delirium of love and passion," Mr. Messiaen explained in the program), the composer came onstage to accept the audience's applause.

WHEN DIMITRI MITROPOULOS took over the conductorship of the New York Philharmonic-Symphony last week, he brought with him not only his usual virtuosity but a program of some interest. The interest lay principally in two large and unfamiliar works—a new Concerto for Piano and Orchestra by Ernst Křenek and the seldom performed "Faust" Symphony by Franz Liszt. Like Mr. Bernstein, Mr. Mitropoulos appeared as his own piano soloist, but, unlike Mr. Bernstein, he justified his double capacity of pianist and conductor beyond the obvious point of saving money on soloists.

The Křenek concerto is a dry, satirical work of no particular pretensions and no particular attractions, but Mr. Mitropoulos played and conducted it brilliantly, giving its percussive, atonal phrases a great deal of momentum, and gravely rising from the keyboard, when required, to pluck the piano strings with his fingers, according to Mr. Křenek's unconventional specifications.

Liszt's huge "Faust" Symphony received a bravura performance that squeezed out every ounce of its impetuous rhetoric. Though it was pleasant to hear this composition again, it is easy to see why it has never attained a permanent hold on the affections of the musical public. Aside from the second movement, which is supposed to depict the character of Gretchen and has some moments of good, sentimental melody, it is strictly a period piece, full of bombast and weighted down with a kind of pseudo-philosophical upholstery that strikes the present-day listener as merely quaint.

December 24, 1949

As a musical instrument, the violin has its limitations. To begin with, it is incomplete. Except in a handful of musical works, like the Bach solo-violin sonatas, it needs an orchestra or, at the very least, a piano to back it up. The number of great concertos written for it hardly exceeds a dozen, and the number of great sonatas in which it shares honors with the piano or the harpsichord is not very much bigger.

The violin is, moreover, one of the most awkward of all musical instruments, in that its bow is an unevenly balanced affair that, unless firmly controlled, plays louder at the heel than it does at the point, and hence has a tendency to distort, with all sorts of inappropriate swoops and swells, the niceties of musical phrasing. A good violinist (and by this I mean a musical violinist) should be judged to a large extent, I believe, by the skill with which he defeats this tendency and forces his instrument to conform to the principles of fine melodic style. Unfortunately, there are very few good violinists.

In general, our particular generation of violin playing has been dominated by what might be called the glamour violinist. I use this term because to me it conveys the quality of surface finish (comparable to the faultless makeup of the female movie star) that is characteristic of the type. Mr. Heifetz and Mr. Elman, for example, have developed luscious tone and accurate agility of the left hand to a point of perfection probably unmatched in the history of the instrument. Yet I do not find them interesting violinists. The reason is that, for all their cosmetic glitter, they almost never interpret music with a real understanding of its deeper dramatic and emotional content. They shine magnificently in showy concertos by such composers as Tchaikovsky and Glazunov, but the purity and subtlety of style required in a simple Mozart sonata seem to be beyond them.

There exist, of course, plenty of unglamorous but musically sensitive violinists, many of whom are members of string quartets, concertmasters of symphony orchestras, and so on. The trouble with these men is that they lack the individuality, dash, and brilliance of the true virtuoso. In surveying the subject of contemporary performance on stringed instruments, one is led to the conclusion that the only entirely satisfying artist in the field is not a violinist but the cellist Pablo Casals.

All this is by way of a preamble to a discussion of Joseph Szigeti's recent performance, with the New York Philharmonic-Symphony, of the Alban Berg Concerto for Violin and Orchestra and the Bach G-Minor Concerto.

Mr. Szigeti is not a glamour violinist. He is a large man who crouches over his violin, and he occasionally draws from it sounds that scratch and whistle. He lacks the formidable and immaculate polish of Mr. Heifetz. But he is, despite his mechanical faults, my favorite violinist. He never allows the unwieldiness of the bow to interfere with the justness of his phrasing. He never wallows in beautiful tone for the sake of beautiful tone. He is always intent on communicating the inner substance of the music he interprets, and he accomplishes this task with the most scrupulous regard for emphasis and other subtleties of melodic contour. When listening to him, one can forget that one is listening to a violin and listen to the music.

Nothing could have offered a more convincing test of Mr. Szigeti's qualities than the juxtaposition on the program of Bach's serenely classical concerto and Berg's modern, expressionist score. Mr. Szigeti's playing in the first work was here and there a little thin in tone, but he gave both pieces performances of great musical insight, providing each with its own spectrum of musical coloring and making evident the two centuries of change in violin style that separate them. Dimitri Mitropoulos, who conducted, kept the Philharmonic players in unusually intimate rapport with Mr. Szigeti, and the result of this collaboration was, in the case of the Berg concerto, among the most memorable events the musical season has thus far offered.

The Berg violin concerto is, I think, one of the few important symphonic compositions written since the First World War. Finished in 1935, just before Berg's death in Vienna, it has most of the technical features of the atonal style that was popular there at the time, but, unlike most atonal music, it seems to have a sense of poetry that lies beyond its interest as a mere collection of notes. The lack of propulsion that is characteristic of atonality has been compensated for here by a gloomy and intensely dramatic atmosphere that gives the work continuous momentum and excitement. A good deal of this atmosphere is created by Berg's uncanny artistry as an orchestrator and by a stream of dour romantic passion that breaks through the abstract formality of the idiom and brings it to life. Berg has proved in this work that a composer of sufficient genius can make even atonality convey a human message.

SEASON OF 1953-1954

LÁSZLÓ

GOTTFRIED VON EINEM's opera "The Trial," which received its
first American performance at the City Center last week, proved
to be a pretty dreary business all around. This prevailing dreari-
ness was due not so much to the quality of its ingredients as to
two monumental errors in casting. Franz Kafka's morbidly entertaining novel, a work that in unadulterated form has, of
course, its claim to distinction, was dreadfully miscast as an opera
libretto, and Mr. von Einem, a composer of some obvious talent,
was miscast as the man to set Mr. Kafka's shifting emotional
subtleties to music. Things got so bad midway through the performance that I found myself alternately wishing that Mr. von
Einem's music would keep quiet so that I could follow Mr.
Kafka's train of thought and wishing that somebody would remove Mr. Kafka's dramatic ideas so that I could listen to Mr.

43

von Einem's rather lusty, extroverted, and in every other way inappropriate music.

My sense of dismay was only compounded by the heroic efforts of the New York City Opera Company, which, with the help of Otto Preminger as director, had given this curious concoction a truly magnificent production. Rouben Ter-Arutunian's weird, constructivist scenery had all the requisite moodiness that Mr. von Einem's music lacked. The costumes and even the makeup, inspired by that dismal, grotesque Central European era portrayed in the early drawings of George Grosz, were designed with a sharp eye that is too seldom brought to bear on operatic stagecraft hereabouts. All this admirable ingenuity and taste was worthy of something better.

In discussing the unsuitability of Kakfa's novel as operatic material, one is naturally led to a consideration of similar uses of similar material that are bedevilling a good deal of contemporary opera. It is easy to say that "The Trial" is too subtle and too devoid of clear-cut action for operatic treatment. But the fundamental difficulty, I feel, involves something that it has in common with the librettos of such celebrated recent operatic efforts as Stravinsky's "The Rake's Progress" and Benjamin Britten's "Peter Grimes": an utterly frustrated approach to the thing that has always been opera's great subject—namely, sex.

I need not point out that there are virtually no sexless operas in the classical repertory. (The prepubescent fairy-tale opera "Hansel and Gretel" is the only exception I can think of at the moment.) Sex is what limbers up the vocal cords of tenors and sopranos, what leads to suicides and murders on the operatic stage, and what causes operatic audiences to applaud and weep. It is apparently a subject worth singing about, and opera's attitude toward it has always been straightforward and passionate.

Within the past generation, however, fashions seem to have changed. An increasing number of operas have been devoted to roughly the following propositions: first, that sex is just too horrible to be borne (Alban Berg's "Wozzeck"); second, that sex is not necessarily even relevant to opera (Virgil Thomson's "Four Saints in Three Acts" and "The Mother of Us All"); third, that sex is ridiculous (Stravinsky's "Mavra," which I shall return to presently); fourth, that sex is an aberration, leading not to the boudoir but to the booby hatch (Stravinsky's "The Rake's Progress"). In line with this tendency, we have been presented with a series of operatic heroes who are fumbling, hagridden neurotics and a series of operatic heroines who are either dreamworld phantoms or malignant trollops. The music that is written to express the emotions of these curious characters is usually either a grinding cacophony indicating the hero's unhappiness or a lot of satirical fluff that tries to pretend that the whole thing is intended as fun, which is clearly not the case.

Only rarely does anything singable emerge in this strange and eminently unoperatic world, and no wonder, for of all the mental states that might conduce to song, frustration is the least fruitful. One is led to the discouraging conclusion that most of our leading operatic composers just don't believe in love any more. I am aware that some deep Hegelian thinking could blame all this squarely on the Zeitgeist and conclude that in our era the emotions of civilized men have simply become too rarefied for operatic purposes.

But let us not be overhasty in accepting this theory. The fact is that in the less lofty world of the Broadway musical show boys still meet and lose girls in a reasonably enchanting atmosphere, expressing themselves meanwhile in melodies that are often beautiful and usually singable. "Oklahoma!" and "Pal Joey" are not as complicated intellectually as "The Trial," but in some ways they are closer than "The Trial" is to being good opera.

THE OTHER HAPPENING of the week that seemed to me of interest was the concert by the Little Orchestra Society, with Thomas Scherman conducting. Mr. Scherman and his associates led off with a generally acceptable performance of Giovanni Pergolesi's "Stabat Mater" and continued with two very dissimilar items, the Second Symphony of the American composer Paul Creston and a revival, in concert form, of Stravinsky's seldom performed one-act comic opera "Mavra."

"Mavra" was, I believe, first introduced to the world as an interlude in a Diaghilev ballet program at the Paris Opéra in the early twenties. It has a tenuous little plot concerning a lover disguised as a maid, lasts about twenty minutes, and is obviously intended as a delightful trifle. I did not find it particularly delightful. It dates from Stravinsky's spoofing period, and most of the spoofing seems to consist of making a perfectly good operatic cast look ludicrous and making a perfectly good orchestra sound as much as possible like a street band. In my opinion, we have outgrown it and could well afford to let it rest on the library shelves.

Paul Creston's Second Symphony, which I had never heard before, is a different matter. I found it a very distinguished work, in which a fine feeling for symphonic structure is combined with real originality and vigor. Unlike Mr. Stravinsky, Mr. Creston uses no tricks. His style is modern without being doctrinaire, emotionally alive without being vulgar or derivative. He writes with the utmost clarity and wit, and with a compelling forcefulness that never allows one's interest to flag. His symphony struck me as one of the most authentic things of its kind that I had ever heard from the pen of a contemporary American composer. I should like very much to hear it again.

November 14, 1953

I MUST CONFESS, I am afraid, to a growing impatience with some of the compositions of the great Ludwig van Beethoven. If the reader considers this statement an unpardonable blasphemy, I suggest that he turn to another page and read something else; I intend to get this out of my system.

The compositions to which I refer all belong to what is generally known as Beethoven's "third," or "final," period, and are talked and written about, as a rule, with hushed reverence. I have been listening to them respectfully for years. They include certain movements from string quartets and piano sonatas which sounded to me somewhat diffuse and aimless on first acquaintance but which I long assumed to contain profundities that I had not yet penetrated. They also include the last movement of that sacrosanct item, the Ninth Symphony. This movement, to be perfectly honest, has always seemed to me to consist of a lot of banging and shouting, introduced by a baritone recitative that borders on the fatuous, surrounding a text (Schiller's "Ode to

Joy") that is bad poetry and adolescent philosophy, and pervaded throughout by an atmosphere of self-conscious nobility and uplift that I find highly irritating. Moreover, its orchestration is generally muddy, its vocal writing is painfully awkward, and some of its martial tunes remind me uncomfortably of the earnest tooting of a German street band. It contains, of course, some passages of genuinely exalted music, in particular the frightfully taxing phrases allotted to the unaccompanied quartet of vocal soloists, but these are infrequent, and require a great deal of unpleasant and all but superhuman effort to make their beauty clear to an audience.

Nearly everthing I have said about the last movement of the Ninth applies even more strongly to Beethoven's Missa Solemnis, which Dimitri Mitropoulos performed at a recent Philharmonic concert. It is obviously a work full of lofty intentions, and its traditional Latin text is several grades above Schiller's pompous platitudinizing as a work of literature. But what strikes the ear is a confusing body of singularly ugly sound, whose dominant characteristic seems to be an unremitting sense of strain. One finds oneself struggling along with fiddlers and double-bass players to negotiate growling tremolos that owe their interest only to the energy that is being expended on them. One suffers with the soloists and the chorus in their heroic attempts to convey whatever message there is without literally wearing out their vocal cords. And when it all finishes up with a passage that is so inconsequential as to seem almost absent-minded, one leaves the hall wondering whether it has really been worth the effort.

I am aware that the thing one is supposed to admire in works of this sort is what is usually referred to as Beethoven's "magnificent conception"—something that presumably existed in the mind of the Master, which was soaring beyond anything expressible by mere singers and orchestra musicians. One way to get closer to this "conception" is to do what several people in the audience did the other night—bring along an orchestra score and bury yourself in it, digging out fascinating details that are seen but not heard. I am also aware that certain supremely gifted conductors, notably Toscanini, are able to smelt out more shining metal from the rocky ore of the Missa Solemnis than others; as a smelter, Mr. Mitropoulos seemed to be practically lost among the slag.

My main quarrel, however, is with the work itself. It may be that a mind as great as Beethoven's sometimes finds the art of music an insufficient vehicle for its thoughts. But from that point on, what it expresses is likely to strain the limits of musical communication.

November 28, 1953

IN MOUNTING THE NEW production of Gounod's "Faust," which opened the Metropolitan Opera season last week, Rolf Gérard, its scenic designer, seemed to be torn between two somewhat disparate ideas. The first was to present the opera as a period piece, with costumes and props evoking the France of Gounod's era—that of Louis Philippe and Napoleon III. The second was to heighten the air of mystery and doom that attaches to the Faust legend. The first idea led—rather happily, I thought—to a Devil in a tailcoat and a top hat, some mid-nineteenth-century-*pompier* soldier uniforms, and a waltz scene with a delightfully Gallic bandstand. The second led to a lot of moonlight and murk.

It would be easy to criticize Mr. Gérard for the resulting conflict in moods if it were not for the fact that it had been dumped squarely in his lap by Charles Gounod himself. This conflict has always been inherent in the opera, which seeks to combine Goethe's highly mystical and sometimes sinister dramatic ideas with a large number of dear old tunes that are about as mystical and sinister as the Empress Eugénie's celebrated hats. As it was, I found Mr. Gérard's scenery a generally handsome contribution, and a welcome change from the Met's threadbare medieval set, which was nearly ready for the scrap heap anyhow. About his costumes for Faust and Marguerite, I was not so pleased. They seemed unnecessarily drab, and succeeded only in making their wearers look as middle-aged and unromantic as possible.

On the musical side, things were more consistent and, on the whole, more gratifying. Pierre Monteux's guidance from the orchestra pit was not exactly impassioned, but it was genuinely affectionate. Jussi Bjoerling and Victoria de los Angeles, as Faust and Marguerite, sang with considerable elegance. Nicola Rossi-Lemeni, who was making his début as Mephistopheles, pranced about the stage with a creditable amount of vigor. His interpretation of the role was not an especially subtle one from either the dramatic or the vocal standpoint, and his voice seemed somewhat coarse and heavy at times, but his impressive stage presence and the gusto with which he tore into the role did a good deal to redeem his lack of polish.

The Met's refurbished opener, then, contained a few things that were both new and good, enabling it to take a decent place in the long series of "Faust"s that has been continuing for nearly a century and will probably continue as long as opera is performed. The secret of this remarkable vitality has always baffled me slightly, for "Faust" is certainly neither a dramatic nor a musical masterpiece. I think that the secret may lie simply in the fact that it is one of the most operatic of all operas, and by this I mean that in writing it Gounod never forgot that the main thing in opera is neither drama, as such, nor even music, but the beauty of the human voice. As a work of art, "Faust" has very little to recommend it except its wonderful singability, but this quality alone, in the curious aesthetic world of opera, evidently entitles it to immortality.

December 5, 1953

In attending the first two weeks of the Metropolitan's season, I found two productions that I can recommend as deeply enjoyable experiences. These are the current "Le Nozze di Figaro" and "La Forza del Destino." I have one qualification about the former: I wish that the set designer, Horace Armistead, had touched up the old "Figaro" scenery, which was very presentable, instead of cluttering the stage with some rather

41035

fussy new screens and props, which have a makeshift appearance and sometimes get in the way of the action. But aside from this, I thought that the initial performance of the Mozart comedy was wholly delightful. Two important new sopranos appeared in it—Lisa Della Casa, who looked very pretty and sang the role of the Countess with lovely tone, and Irmgard Seefried, whose Susanna was a masterpiece of assurance and cultivated musical style. Fritz Stiedry, in the orchestra pit, held the whole thing together with both precision and spirit.

"Figaro" is, of course, one of those rare operas that even the most exacting operagoer need never apologize for liking. Its warm humanity, infinite sophistication, and magnificent musical craftsmanship make it one of the great exceptions in an art form in which imperfection of some sort is usually taken for granted. It was good to hear it again, and to hear it so excellently performed.

"La Forza del Destino" is not a perfect opera, but it was enjoyable for other reasons. One of these was the lusty enthusiasm with which a superb group of singers sang its fine old melodies; another was the inimitable vigor and spontaneity of the melodies themselves. There was not an Italian in the cast, but several of the Metropolitan's best Italian-style artists, including Richard Tucker, Zinka Milanov and Jerome Hines, gave it as authentic and heartfelt a reading as one would be likely to hear anywhere. Mr. Stiedry again showed, as he did in "Figaro," that he is the most nearly indispensable member of the Metropolitan's conducting staff. And, beyond and above all this, there was the wonderful, inexhaustible musical fecundity of Giuseppe Verdi, a composer who seems to me to grow in stature every time I hear him, and this in spite of a degree of familiarity with his music that, in the case of most composers, would have tired me long ago.

Part of Verdi's vitality undoubtedly lies in the more or less imponderable factor known as genius, but a big part also lies in his unaffected and eminently civilized attitude toward the aesthetics of music, and this part, I feel, could be studied today with immense profit by anyone interested in the art. He seems to have understood, or taken for granted, a fact that Søren Kierkegaard (not a bad music critic, by the way) years ago pointed out —that music is the language of passion—and he seems never to have been led away from this basic definition into trying to make music something that it is not. His subject matter consists of love, hate, and kindred emotions, and he never distracts your attention from these by means of elaborate technique or by otherwise obtruding his ego into the picture.

Verdi's technique is, in fact, so simple and so artfully subordinated to his subject that you almost feel you might have thought up his melodies yourself—until you try. Everywhere his music bespeaks a deep love and respect for his materials—the voices of those who sing his operas. And, finally, he is one of the most truly original of all composers, not because he makes use of self-conscious mannerisms or artificial tricks but because every tune and chord reflects the thinking of a profound and unique musical mind. "La Forza del Destino" is not his greatest work, but it is great music and great opera.

December 19, 1953

THERE ARE, of course, two ways of looking of Mozart's "Don Giovanni." It can be regarded as a comedy about a devil of a fellow who seduces an amazing number of women and ends up being rather quaintly hurled into Hell by an animated piece of sculpture. This view makes the opera a moderately amusing period piece, in which the death of the hero is not really taken seriously but assumes a childlike quality, like the deaths of bad little boys in fairy tales who get eaten by hobgoblins. It also entails a fairly embarrassing inconsistency, in that the supposed comedy begins with a particularly violent and brutal murder and involves a lot of earnest, vengeful, and heart-rending emotions on the part of several of its characters.

The other way of looking at "Don Giovanni" is to consider it a tragedy, in which the hero's amorous peccadilloes are merely part of the background of his character, and the main plot revolves around a sinister tale of crime and punishment. This view has the advantage of consistency and makes Don Giovanni himself a figure of epic grandeur. I think it is the one that Mozart had in mind, though, it is true, some of the more trivial details of the Lorenzo Da Ponte libretto seem to contradict it.

Seen from this standpoint, Don Giovanni is, like Faust or Don Quixote, one of the great mythical archetypes of dramatic literature. He is the embodiment of all human arrogance—a man who has placed himself above God and moral law, the ultimate hedonist, who does not even stop at murder in the pursuit of his overmastering desires. He represents uncontrolled passion, with all its vigor and beauty, sweeping like a whirlwind through the lives of the more ordinary people who surround him, and this gives him an air of magnificence. He is so magnificent, in fact, that his death cannot fittingly be brought about by the little human beings who have sworn vengeance against him. He dies not because he has been a naughty boy with the women but because he has, in a supreme bid for power, defied God Himself. And so his doom is consummated by supernatural means, at the hands of a walking marble statue, the monument of the man he killed in his careless quest of pleasure. Thus, "Don Giovanni" is, in a sense, a theological essay, dealing profoundly with basic problems of good and evil. It is only by looking at it in this way that one can get the opera into focus, realize why Mozart lavished his most wonderful musical and psychological talents on it, and understand the dramatic power that has made it universally recognized as the greatest opera ever written.

The ideal performance of "Don Giovanni" would be one in which, by the most skillful direction, its comic moments were held in proper subordination while the great drama of Don Giovanni's crime and doom was given the center of the stage. I have seen very few performances that attained this ideal, and none of them has been at the Metropolitan Opera House. The tradition at the Met has been inclined toward the first of the above-mentioned conceptions, in which the mildly amusing clowning of Leporello and the somewhat coy vicissitudes of Don Giovanni's love life take precedence over the opera's deeper meaning.

When the Metropolitan presented a restaged version of the opera last week, I thought for a few moments that this new version might have finally come to grips with the real dramatic problem. It had some stunning things in it. I have never seen a better staging of the duel that results in the Commendatore's death in the first act, and Don Giovanni's own death in the last act was, barring some rather hesitant flashes of lightning, as impressive as it should be. But in between, I am afraid, it was the same old Metropolitan "Don Giovanni," and from the purely vocal point of view it was not the equal of several performances of the work that have been given during the past decade.

One of the best features of this "Don Giovanni" was provided by Max Rudolf, who conducted it with control and fine musical insight. Nicola Rossi-Lemeni, who was singing the part of Don Giovanni for the first time here, was a considerable disappointment. He sang somewhat heavily, and his dramatic conception of the role was arch and foppish, rather than heroic and elegant. As a result, he failed to dominate the performance, and "Don Giovanni" without a dominating Don is like the proverbial "Hamlet" without its Prince.

The Metropolitan's new scenery, in which a single constructivist set does duty throughout, made it appear that Don Giovanni inhabited a rather weird region resembling the driveway in front of a stylish tropical tourist hotel. This did not disturb me unduly, as I had always considered him a myth existing outside the realities of time and space anyhow, and a good myth can be presented in various fashions.

What did disturb me, aside from a few faults of individual singers, was the way the myth got lost in the clutter of rather unfunny clowning and snickering that is so apt to submerge it. I do not, for example, like to see Leporello, after his scream of terror at the approach of the walking statue, spoil the mood of the scene by describing it to Don Giovanni with gestures that cause the audience to burst into giggles. Leporello at this point is really a very awed man, and his audience should be awed, too.

"Don Giovanni," properly performed, is in fact a very awesome opera, and, of course, a very great work of art.

December 26, 1953

I HAVE SOMETIMES been inclined to take a slightly defensive position against the vogue Hector Berlioz's music is having among intellectual concertgoers. To be sure, I always find the music interesting to listen to, because of the highly individual and striking way in which Berlioz orchestrated and otherwise manipulated his material; practically all his work I am familiar with shows the mark of a restless and daring musical intelligence, and this is something that certainly cannot be said of the mediocre composers.

On the other hand, I often find that the creative essence upon which this intelligence is exercised is somewhat tawdry and theatrical. This is true, it seems to me, of many of his most popular works, including the symphony "Harold in Italy" and the "Fantastic Symphony." The famous "March to the Scaffold" in the latter work, for example, strikes me as pure fustian—an appropriate accompaniment for some melodramatic stage spectacle, perhaps, but outrageously cheap when considered as a symphonic movement. In other words, Berlioz to me is not one of the greatest composers who have ever lived. The quality of his inspiration is too uneven.

Yet, having expressed these qualifications about Berlioz's work in general, I find myself wanting to take them all back in the case of one composition of his, which was performed one evening last week by the Little Orchestra Society, under Thomas Scherman. This is the oratorio "L'Enfance du Christ," a work I had never heard before, and one in which the tricky, flamboyant side of Berlioz's genius is submerged in music of the most profound and enchanting sort. Here, for once, Berlioz was not seeking to astound his listeners with batteries of kettledrums and feats of ingenuity. The only concession to this theatrical instinct was a chorus of angels—situated, apparently, somewhere in the second balcony—and what it sang was supremely beautiful.

"L'Enfance du Christ," which simply and eloquently relates the incidents of the Flight into Egypt, is one of the most moving things in symphonic and choral literature. Listening to it, I was able to forget that awful "March to the Scaffold" and to realize anew that, at his very best, Berlioz occasionally reaches the heights of great musical inspiration.

January 16, 1954

IF FRANZ LISZT'S "Totentanz," which was recently resurrected by the Little Orchestra Society with Claudio Arrau as piano soloist, were a painting instead of a musical composition, it would probably occupy a dignified position in one of the back rooms of some vast museum, where it would be catalogued as an interesting example of grotesque genre art. And those who like this sort of thing would be free to pause before it while the others passed on to contemplate more important and rewarding items.

As a matter of fact, the "Totentanz" does have a certain quaint historical and biographical interest. It reflects the ultra-romantic era when fashionable Europe was under the sway of Goethe's Mephistopheles, when diabolism was chic, and when that old musical mountebank Liszt, with his long hair and clerical collar, was slightly shocking a delighted public by giving out veiled hints that he was in league with the powers of darkness.

Today, of course, it is obvious that the brew Liszt was stirring up in his witch's cauldron was really just goulash after all, and that the "Totentanz," in particular, is one of the most awful bits of musical rubbish ever set down on paper. But the point I am trying to make is a different one. It is that the "Totentanz," like many compositions that periodically invade the standard repertory and then disappear, is a once-fashionable trifle, and that the rather austere art of symphonic music is less hospitable to such trifles than most other arts are.

There are several good reasons for this. Like the drama, symphonic music is an art that incorporates the skills of many other people besides the man who creates it. The average symphonic performance demands the contributions of roughly a hundred artists who have spent most of a lifetime perfecting their craft, and to waste or disparage these contributions is to be guilty of extremely bad taste. Moreover, the man who goes to listen to a symphonic concert is in a position somewhat different from the man who saunters casually through an art gallery or leafs through a book of poetry. While a painter or a poet may dash off a spontaneous little thing, involving only himself and some canvas and brushes or pencil and paper, and not even demand that you look at his product unless you are so inclined, the symphonic composer has roused two or three thousand people from a comfortable dinner and trapped them in a concert hall, from which they can escape only by the unpleasant expedient of getting up and walking out during the performance. His responsibilities are correspondingly grave. What he presents to his audience should be worthy of the attention his hundred-odd fellow-artists must give it, and of the time a large number of people spend in listening to it. Artless spontaneity, delightful kidding, and coy fooling around are just not part of his medium. He deliberately accepts a big challenge, and unless he meets it, his offering is merely an impertinence.

Actually, I found the solemn melodramatics of the "Totentanz" somewhat amusing, though I shall be happy not to hear it again for a long time.

LÁSZLÓ

January 23, 1954

MOUSSORGSKY'S "Boris Godunov," as anyone who looks up its history can learn, exists only as a magnificent dramatic idea for which a gifted but technically ill-equipped composer wrote some rather disjointed music, parts of it so inspired as to rank among the greatest moments in operatic literature but most of it so awkwardly put together as to be virtually unperformable. Actually, the so-called original "Boris Godunov" that is so often talked about is a sort of half-realized myth—fragments of a massive and noble tapestry that must be stitched together somehow by somebody if it is to make an intelligible whole.

The tremendous task of editing "Boris," which has been essayed by various people, is a very important one, for the composition, despite its technical flaws, is a tremendous piece of artistic pageantry, and its central theme—the gradual crumbling of a human mind under the strain of guilt and fear—definitely belongs among the world's great dramatic subjects. The standard editing job is, of course, that of Rimski-Korsakov, who handled it with high professional competence—brightening Moussorgsky's rather muddy orchestration and touching up the sequence of dramatic episodes—and laid himself open to a lot of criticism for making the thing too slick. Since Rimski-Korsakov did his version, there have been a number of attempts to get closer to the crude monumentality of Moussorgsky's original conception, and these attempts have concerned themselves—I think rightly—with preserving the extreme individuality of Moussorgsky's musical thought, even though it conflicted violently at times with the traditions of what most people think of as opera.

A week ago the Metropolitan Opera presented, with some additional alterations, the original—or more approximately original—"Boris" that it staged for the first time last season. This version is the work of Karol Rathaus, a modern composer, who has conscientiously stuck closer to the more primitive aspects of the Moussorgsky manuscript. The result is extremely interesting. A couple of Moussorgsky's scenes have been reinstated, and the opera ends not with the surefire dramatic climax of Boris's death but with the scene in the Forest of Kromy, where the Simpleton wails his unforgettable little song suggesting the eternal suffering and patience of peasant Russia. This is both more subtle and more quietly moving than the standard ending. Elsewhere, in spots, the new version seems less effective—notably in the famous coronation scene, which Rimski-Korsakov made into a stunning spectacle and which is now so cluttered with the noise of church bells that its musical content is practically indiscernible.

The opera was performed in English, for the very good reason that the Met hasn't enough Russian-speaking singers to do it in the original language. The translation used, which is the work of John Gutman, is generally trite and pompous, but this fact was almost unnoticeable, because most of the words issued from the mouths of singers who obviously couldn't sing English, either. To this rule, there were two outstanding exceptions: Charles Kullman, who sang the role of Shuiski with immaculate enunciation and great dramatic subtlety, and Mildred Miller, who did similarly well with the minor role of Boris's son. The other performances, barring the problem of language, were generally creditable. Nicola Rossi-Lemeni turned in his best characterization to date as Boris, singing the role with fervor and acting with unmistakable sincerity and considerable spirit, and Salvatore Baccaloni clowned with reasonable persuasiveness as the drunken mendicant Varlaam.

A perfect "Boris" is, I suppose, an impossibility. The Met's new production is, I think, a courageous and absorbing experiment, which, despite its faults, is something well worth going to hear.

January 30, 1954

THE NEW YORK DÉBUT of the well-known Dutch conductor Eduard van Beinum, which took place last week when he appeared with the Philadelphia Orchestra, was, I think, an event of considerable importance. At any rate, it is many years since I have watched the manipulations of a new conductor with comparable excitement or been so certain from what I heard that I was being introduced to the work of a superlative performer in this rather elusive art.

Mr. van Beinum evidently combines a meticulous regard for workmanship, such as characterized the conducting of his countryman Willem Mengelberg, with a great deal of dash and fire. The other night, his musical taste, as exhibited in Haydn's Symphony No. 96, was impeccable, and his sense of proportion in dealing with the long lines and accumulating climaxes of Anton Bruckner's difficult Seventh Symphony was masterly. What impressed me most about his conducting, however, was the dynamic energy he appeared to infuse into the most obscure nooks and crannies of the orchestral apparatus. He seemed to be in direct control of more musical detail than any conductor in recent memory except Toscanini. This gave his interpretations a wonderful sensitiveness and pliancy, and produced the impression that conducting an orchestra was to him as intimate a process as molding a handful of clay.

Aside from Mr. van Beinum's remarkable achievements, the main interest of the evening for me lay in the Bruckner symphony, a work that, though relatively popular as symphonies by this composer go, is still so seldom performed here that it is unfamiliar to most concert audiences. For some odd reason, Anton Bruckner, who was born before Beethoven died and was still writing eloquent and profound music in the final decades of the last century, has remained a "controversial" composer, and even at this late date it is fashionable to apologize, as the Philadelphia Orchestra's program notes did the other night, for certain weaknesses his music is supposed to have—notably a tendency toward long-windedness and diffuse structure.

As far as I am concerned, this controversy has itself become a tiresome tradition. I find Bruckner neither long-winded nor diffuse. I find him a symphonist of the very noblest stature, quite comparable to Beethoven and Mozart and vastly superior to Brahms. I will admit only that his music is a little difficult to grasp on first hearing, and even for this I think there are good reasons. In order to help elucidate them, I should like to relate an experience I've had with his work, which may prove helpful to anyone interested in understanding it better.

For a number of years, I was about as well acquainted as the average music lover with Bruckner's symphonies. I got from them a vague impression of monumentality, together with a feeling that they were rather repetitious and that their themes were often rather trite. My opportunities for hearing them were so infrequent that I could scarcely tell one from another; they all seemed very much alike—great slabs of somewhat Wagnerian music, singularly lacking in distinguishing features. I was, however, conscious that there was more in them than at once met the ear, and I was also conscious that the logic of their massive structure, if there was any, eluded me. I determined to find out whether or not I really liked Bruckner, so I bought several phonograph records of the symphonies and began to study them, playing each movement over and over, until I could identify every motive and perceive exactly how it fitted into Bruckner's over-all scheme.

This modest research proved a revelation to me. I came to see that in my casual listening to a Bruckner symphony in the concert hall I had been in the position of a man standing near the foot of a colossal statue, able to discern certain interesting details but having no idea whatever of the extent and proportions of the whole. It was necessary to approach the thing from several angles before its total meaning became apparent. Such study might, of course, have been accomplished in the concert hall if I had been able to hear Bruckner's symphonies as often as I am able to hear those of, for example, Beethoven or Brahms. But the once every three years or so that I had the opportunity to hear a repetition of any given Bruckner symphony was not sufficient to produce any real understanding.

I am convinced that Bruckner is one of those very rare composers who require repeated hearings to be appreciated. I am also convinced now that he is the towering symphonic figure of the latter half of the nineteenth century, and the successor of Beethoven in the development of his complex art.

On close acquaintance, Bruckner's symphonies reveal a sort of simple lyricism that is far more nearly akin to the music of Schubert than it is to that of his contemporary Richard Wagner. This is coupled with an intricate technique of symphonic development by which he, like Beethoven, builds a gigantic structure out of simple ingredients. His technique of development, in which he contracts, extends, reverses, and inverts his material, is actually very lucid, and is the most absorbing aspect of his work intellectually.

Beyond these technical matters, however, lies the poetic and inspirational side of Bruckner—the broad, sweeping themes, the knotty little themes, the themes that are contrapuntal aggregations of themes, the rather baroque climaxes, the magical and highly original touches of orchestral color, the iridescent web of subtly changing chromatic harmonies. No one since Beethoven, to my knowledge, has written slow movements of comparable grandeur, and no one else except Beethoven has written true scherzos of the vigorous, propulsive type. (The scherzos of Schubert and Brahms are merely waltzes or folk songs.) Few composers of any era have been as straightforward in their communication of musical ideas—as willing to place those ideas candidly before the listener without attempting to baffle or impress him with self-conscious feats of style. In this respect, Bruckner is a little like Verdi; what he says is of such immediate consequence that the method of saying it takes second place.

But I have still not quite explained why I think Bruckner is one of the greatest of all symphonists. Perhaps the ultimate answer is to be found in the position his music occupies in the scale of emotional values—in the sort of scale, that is, that measures the shades of difference between the epic and the trivial.

Here I find Bruckner writing on a plane of the utmost nobility, saying profound and simple things in a profound and simple manner, with a serene, affirmative faith in God and humanity that makes each of his symphonies a deeply moving experience.

February 6, 1954

Igor Stravinsky's opera "The Rake's Progress" turned up again one evening last week at the Metropolitan and gave many New York operagoers, including me, a chance to form some second thoughts about it. Its composer is, of course, one of the most celebrated figures in contemporary music, and a man whose remarkable feats in certain branches of the art entitle him to respect. After taking these points into consideration, and listening to it all over again with painstaking attention, however, I can only conclude that my first thoughts on the subject were correct and that it is not, in fact, much of an opera.

For one thing, W. H. Auden and Chester Kallman, the authors of its drama, seem to have set themselves the impossible task of proving that the death in a madhouse of a lonely and erotically somewhat bizarre hero is a gay and amusing spectacle.

As a matter of fact, the experiences of this hero, Tom Rakewell, are anything but rakish. They constitute a kind of psychopathic case history, the prevailing morbidness of which contrasts in extremely bad taste with the atmosphere of horseplay that surrounds it. The result is neither farce nor tragedy but an uneasy and painful attempt to combine the two. Any sympathy one might feel for the harassed characters is effectively forestalled by the authors, who seem bent on demonstrating from the start that they themselves have no sympathy for them. This sort of treatment doesn't make for convincing operatic drama, or, for that matter, convincing drama of any kind.

For another thing, the music that Stravinsky has written for this strange concoction is decidedly artificial, satirical in its treatment of emotion, and full of self-conscious tricks—a combination of qualities that might be quite appropriate to a dashing bit of musical millinery but that, spread over a long evening of opera, strains one's patience to the point of boredom. It is not that the music is in any way inferior Stravinsky, for there are passages in the "Rake" that are as provocative and ingenious as anything he has written. The trouble is, rather, that the fashionable, witty, and essentially satirical idiom to which Stravinsky has devoted his career is altogether out of place in serious opera. To me, the conspicuous flaws of the "Rake" served only to confirm something that I had long thought to be true of Stravinsky; namely, that for all his eminence in the contemporary scene, he is a very specialized and limited kind of composer.

Despite a lot of high-sounding aesthetic mumbo-jumbo on the part of Stravinsky enthusiasts (and a certain amount of similar mumbo-jumbo on the part of Stravinsky himself), I have never been able to see that his music is in any sense profound. His art is a light, sometimes diverting, and basically decorative one, which stands in relation to the more serious branches of music somewhat as the art of scenic design stands in relation to the art of painting. He will be remembered, I think, mainly as a superb creator of flashy and adroit musical backdrops for the ballet —which is what most of his greatest works ("The Firebird," "Petrouchka," "Le Sacre du Printemps," "Orpheus," and so on) have been written for.

Stravinsky is one of the most resourceful technicians in the history of music, and a supreme master of the use of artifice. His style is remarkably lucid and easily grasped, and this is one respect in which he is clearly superior to many of his contemporaries. When one considers him as a major composer of emotionally meaningful music, however, I think one is placing him in a category where he does not belong. I do not know of a single Stravinsky work (and this includes such avowedly serious compositions as the "Symphony of Psalms") that succeeds in conveying any very deep human message, and I know of few that even make the attempt.

Moreover, notwithstanding his mastery of exotic and provocative mannerisms, I do not find him a particularly original composer. The arresting dissonances, the nimble tricks of orchestration, the witty phraseological distortions are all pure Stravinsky, but when one looks beneath them for the musical substance, one finds that it is usually borrowed from somewhere else—from Russian folk music, from African tribal chants, from street-band music, from Pergolesi or Bellini or Handel. A great deal of his work consists of clever satire on the styles of eighteenth- and nineteenth-century composers. This, of course, is no crime, and the satire is often highly amusing. But the nature of this satirical spirit is basically critical rather than creative; it produces an aesthetic commentary on music rather than a human commentary on life, and thus limits Stravinsky to a sophisticated and entertaining but not very serious world of ideas.

In "The Rake's Progress," Stravinsky has borrowed largely from Rossini and Handel—composers of originality, whose methods of expressing emotion as very familiar to us. And it is interesting to note that in the few passages of the opera expressing any emotion at all, the emotion is expressed in Rossini's or Handel's language, not in Stravinsky's. Throughout the score, Stravinsky has made his presence felt by his handling of dissonance and orchestral coloring, and by the characteristic twists he gives his Rossinian and Handelian phrases, but the curious fact remains that the parts of the "Rake" that are human and emotional are not Stravinsky, and that the parts that are Stravinsky are not human and emotional.

There are many reasons why "The Rake's Progress" is a poor opera, and not all of them have to do with Stravinsky. But I have yet to be convinced that, even with the finest possible dramatic material at his disposal, Stravinsky is a composer of sufficient depth and originality to write a good one.

February 20, 1954

WITH THE POSSIBLE exception of Richard Wagner, the most unfashionable composers of the moment among intellectual concertgoers seem to be Jean Sibelius and Richard Strauss. The feeling against their music, which one can hear expressed at nearly any cocktail party, is not shared by the general musical public, with whom they have always been reasonably popular, and I can explain it only in terms of a very doctrinaire attitude that regards "romanticism" as a sin.

As it happens, I myself have never shared this feeling, and though I can find fault with certain details of certain of their compositions, I have never really been able to understand the blanket condemnation of their work that I so frequently hear aired by my more sophisticated friends. On the contrary, it seems to me that each of these composers had (I use the past tense because Sibelius, though living, hasn't turned out a note in almost twenty-five years) qualities that are found only in very important composers—qualities that, by the way, are not very common today: Each was the possessor of an individual style whose originality sprang from personal, rather than eclectic, sources; each wrote music that has an emotional content as well as an intellectual form; and each was a master of the structural problems involved in writing music that is in the true sense symphonic.

Last week, Pierre Monteux conducted the Boston Symphony in one of the most eloquent performances of Sibelius's Second Symphony that I have ever heard. The following evening Dimitri Mitropoulos and the New York Philharmonic performed with equal eloquence an entire program devoted to less well-known compositions by Strauss. I found both these events of interest not only because I enjoyed the music but because they gave me the opportunity to test again my impressions of the composers in question.

Aside from the similarities that I have pointed out, the two are, of course, quite different. Sibelius's Second Symphony, which is early and very typical Sibelius, has a monumental quality that has always reminded me of heroic landscape. It ex-

presses a passion for the grandeur of nature and the open air
that is quintessentially Finnish. I do not find it particularly
civilized music. The emotions it expresses are not complex or
very deeply human. Sexual passion is not among them. They
are, in general, the emotions of a man who has found serenity
and affirmation in contemplating the drama of the world of
natural forces. Thus their range is somewhat limited. But
within this range Sibelius has found room for a kind of poetry
that is all his own—the poetry of elemental cataclysms and of interminable northern forests, and the echoes of an epic national
folklore. He expresses this poetry unaffectedly and with vigor,
and I, for one, find his rather austere, moody kind of nature
drama moving and frequently impressive.

Strauss, on the other hand, is a distinctly urban type. His
music contains both sex and humor. At its worst, it sometimes
verges on vulgarity, but it is so endlessly exuberant and so dashing in its audacious virtuosity that one easily forgives these
lapses. I have always been a little irritated, for example, by the
crude, if clever, touches of realism in the "Sinfonia Domestica,"
and by the shameless way Strauss has of parading his own not
too interesting autobiographical experiences in this work.

But the other night I forgot about all this and listened to the
"Sinfonia Domestica" as music pure and simple. Considered
from this point of view, it has moments of great magic. Its
orchestration is almost unbelievably brilliant and lucid—the sort
of orchestration that is so effective and so lovingly written for
the instruments that it makes you feel the players themselves are
enjoying the spectacular tasks the composer has set them. At
the present time, not much music is written that is deliberately
designed to show off the marvellous potentialities of voices and
instruments, though this sort of writing was a commonplace with
most of the great classical and romantic composers of symphony
and opera. And beyond this technical point lies another reason

for Strauss's importance—his unabashed emotionalism. He is not afraid to have emotions, to express them, and to let you share them for what they are worth.

I am aware that nowadays it is not considered the thing to draw attention, as I have, to the emotional content of a musical composition. Nowadays the curious idea is very popular that music is somehow an "abstract" art, consisting of aural sensations and mathematical relationships—purely a matter of "form," without any content except what naïve listeners read into it. I admit that it is hard to pin down the content of great music—that its exact content is open to varying interpretations. But to assume therefore that great music has no content whatever is to my mind arrant nonsense, and this nonsense, I believe, is responsible for a great deal of the confused thinking that currently bedevils musical aesthetics.

Music is, of course, an elusive art, and most of the aesthetic thinking that surrounds it is borrowed by analogy from other arts. One speaks of musical "form" and musical "architecture" as if one were speaking of sculpture or building, and this is apt to be misleading. At the risk of confusing things even further, I should like to suggest another analogy—one that I find is far more fruitful. This is that if music is like any other art, it is like the drama—so like it, in fact, that it may be regarded as a purely aural branch of it. A symphony is something that is written to be performed before an audience by artists who are in somewhat the position of actors. Like a drama, it involves stretches of time, it contains conflicting and otherwise interesting emotions, it builds up suspense to climaxes, and it ends, if it is a good symphony, in some sort of catharsis. To apply to it notions of abstract form and color derived from such static visual arts as painting and architecture is, I submit, a mistake. Yet a lot of contemporary music has been influenced by this mistake.

To me, the important thing about a great piece of music is

that it moves and pulsates with emotion. And here is where I get back to Sibelius and Strauss. Their music moves, and it is clearly dramatic. This is one reason I feel that both of them are composers of consequence.

March 6, 1954

THE LATE BÉLA BARTÓK was a composer of rather complex music, which defies classification in any obvious technical category such as atonality. It is perhaps because of this that his music is often difficult to understand on first hearing, and seems to improve with repetition. I have always found, however, that at a certain point it seems to stop improving, and that this point is somewhat short of the standard of really great music; when one has it all figured out, Bartók's art is basically of the sort that titillates the ear and stimulates the nerves but leaves the emotional regions of the psyche untouched.

I saw no reason to revise this estimate last week when, on separate evenings, I listened to the Concerto for Orchestra, which was brilliantly played by the Minneapolis Symphony under Antal Dorati, and the Music for Strings, Percussion and Celesta, which was played with equal brilliance by the New York Philharmonic under Guido Cantelli. Both works (of the two, I prefer the former—mainly, I think, because it is louder and more dramatic and has a kind of propulsiveness that I find exciting) contain fascinating ingenuities of style but neither makes an impression that goes beyond the purely sensual pleasure of experiencing bizarre and colorful combinations of sound. Bartók's Violin Concerto, which was performed a few weeks ago by the Boston Symphony, with Pierre Monteux conducting and Tossy Spivakovsky as soloist, affects me in very much the same way. Even Mr. Monteux's perceptive conducting and Mr. Spivakovsky's impressive virtuosity failed to make anything more of the concerto than what is usually described as an "interesting" composition.

Quite aside from the Bartók works, both of last week's symphonic concerts were worthy of attention. The Minneapolis Symphony, which was making its first appearance here in six years, proved to be an extraordinarily well-drilled and competent orchestra, clearly entitled to a place among the finest organizations in the country, and its conductor, Mr. Dorati, whom I was watching for the first time, seemed to me an artist who shines to advantage in flamboyant, tense, and technically complicated music. Whether he would be similarly at ease with more serene and measured compositions, I have no way of judging. He conducted a suite of three symphonic pieces from Alban Berg's opera "Lulu" very eloquently, and I discovered, as I have in the past, that this music has compelling emotional power, despite the rather neurotic air of moody pessimism that pervades it. Mr. Cantelli, who was leading the Philharmonic for the first time this season and who is another conductor I had never seen before, appears, like Mr. Dorati, to be an expert technician and a specialist in flamboyance and high tension. I did not altogether like his performance of Brahms' First Symphony, for, though in its

way it was well controlled and well proportioned, it struck me as
hurried and lacking in the sort of majestic gravity that a really
fine Brahms performance should have.

March 20, 1954

DESPITE SOME FAULTS, most of which had to do with insuffi-
ciently inspired orchestra playing, the most enjoyable event of
the past week was, I thought, the performance by Thomas
Scherman's Little Orchestra Society of Richard Strauss's miniature opera "Ariadne auf Naxos." The main reason for this
enjoyment was the score itself, which contains some of the
ripest, most ebullient, and most delightfully affectionate music
Strauss ever wrote.

In "Ariadne auf Naxos" Strauss displays over and over again
the rare faculty for dealing with the human and psychological
side of musical theatre that characterizes his finest work. His
musicians and singers are treated not as a mere palette of interesting colors to be used in painting a musical picture but as a
group of human beings whose talents and enthusiasms are chal-
lenged and stimulated to a point where the whole performance

becomes an engaging little circus full of prancing sopranos and bouncing French-horn players, with Strauss himself standing by like a benign ringmaster to provide delectable hoops and hurdles for everybody in the tent.

I have touched on this quality of Strauss's writing previously. It goes beyond what is ordinarily thought of as "orchestration"— the art of getting the specific sounds you may want out of a group of performers—and invades a different dimension, in which the composer's love of the performing art causes him to treat the executors of his music with a special sort of gallantry. Strauss writes not so much for voices and oboes as for the eager and gifted people who want to do amazing and charming things with voices and oboes, and the joy he generates in the process is largely responsible for the unique brilliance and heartening humanity that seem to bubble over the footlights in so many of his compositions.

I do not mean to imply by this that Strauss is a particularly deep composer, in the sense that Bach and Beethoven and Bruckner are deep composers. There is very little spirituality, and often a touch of vulgarity, in his music. But this tender awareness of the role of the performing artist, which implies a profound understanding of the communicative and coöperative nature of music, makes him a composer of remarkable insight.

"Ariadne," a comic-heroic little opera that mixes Greek gods, *commedia dell' arte* characters, and Hapsburg gaiety in a really witty satire on the nature of love, is a perfect vehicle for this peculiarly Straussian gift. I did not think that Mr. Scherman made the most of the graceful orchestral athletics Strauss had placed at his disposal, but there were features of the performance that compensated for this shortcoming. Most notable among them was the singing of Mattiwilda Dobbs, a young American Negro sporano, new hereabouts, who tackled the showy and

formidably difficult soubrette role of Zerbinetta with such ease
and such cultivated style that she almost stopped the show. Miss
Dobbs' feat, which encompassed great appeal as an actress as
well as great agility as a singer, unquestionably entitled her to a
place among the ablest coloratura sopranos heard here in recent
years. The production as a whole, presented without scenery
and with the singers in evening dress instead of in costume, was
extraordinarily tasteful, and in some ways seemed more effective
than a number of performances I have seen with full stage para-
phernalia, for on the operatic stage "Ariadne" is so lacking in
dramatic incident that it often appears somewhat static.

April 3, 1954

THERE ARE MANY reasons why I resent Richard Wagner's "Parsifal," not the least of them the fact that during the first act I invariably suffer from indigestion, as a result of wolfing my dinner
in order to arrive at the opera house at the barbarous hour of
seven-fifteen. In this uncomfortable state, I find myself presented with a long and rather tedious spectacle—containing, it is
true, some patches of lovely music—which apparently leaves my

co-auditors in a sort of mystical trance. Tradition, established when the opera was first performed at Bayreuth, forbids applause, and those uninformed listeners who break into a spontaneous handclap or two are immediately shamed with pious shushes. It seems to be assumed, for the moment, that one is not in an opera house at all but in some hallowed, churchlike environment, listening to a vast sermon. And it never seems to occur to anybody that this sermon, for all its pretensions, is spiritually a pretty dubious affair.

Last week I went dutifully to the Metropolitan Opera House to hear "Parsifal" again, and again I found myself wondering what all this high-pressure holiness was really about. I have no particular quarrel with the music. It is dignified, passionate, and, in passages like the "Good Friday Spell," truly moving. But the spectacle as a whole has always struck me as slightly obscene. This, I think, is because its ponderous ecclesiastical to-do is concerned not so much with the Holy Grail as with the subject of sex.

The opera's central theme is, of course, chastity. Sex is "Parsifal's" Devil, and what suspense the opera contains arises from the heroic and more or less successful battles waged by the knights of the Holy Grail to preserve their virtue from contamination at the hands of an evil magician who runs what can be described without much exaggeration as a very fancy bawdy-house next door to their castle. I have somehow never been able to glow with satisfaction over the incorruptible purity that permits Parsifal to withstand the temptations of this strange establishment. I have never felt that Amfortas's one lapse from the straight and narrow path was a sufficient sin to produce by way of retribution an unhealable wound that causes him to groan through two and a half acts.

For me, the only human being in the cast is the magician.

Klingsor. He obviously thinks the knights of the Grail are a terribly stuffy lot, and I am afraid I agree with him. It is not that I object to religion as a subject for operatic drama; I just feel that the religious issues discussed in a four-and-a-half-hour essay on the subject should be a little more basic, or if they are not more basic, that they should be treated with a little less pomposity.

Granted, it is a terrific job to stage this peculiar Wagnerian monument in a manner that does not burlesque it, and the Metropolitan cannot be blamed if its temptresses in the second act looked about as seductive as the hostesses at some turn-of-the-century Bavarian beer picnic. Even after making these allowances, however, the performance was singularly dreary.

RICHARD STRAUSS's "Salome," which opened the spring season of opera at the New York City Center, also pits sex against religion, but it does it convincingly and without sanctimoniousness. Its drama is, of course, both unpleasant and gripping, and the evil, iridescent music that Strauss wrote for it makes it a masterpiece of psychological melodrama. I thought the City Center's production of it quite effective. The orchestra, under Joseph Rosenstock's direction, played the score with a great deal of eloquence, and nearly all the roles were adequately sung and acted, in spite of the fact that most of the singers were tackling them for the first time. Phyllis Curtin, a young American soprano whom I had never heard before, proved to be the handsomest Salome I have ever seen, and her "Dance of the Seven Veils" was unusually presentable. Her acting appeared to me a bit spotty, at times conveying the psychotic passion the role calls for and at others lapsing into the demeanor of a well-brought-up American girl. Her characterization will undoubtedly improve with time. From the vocal point of view, she started rather coldly, but by the end of the evening she had revealed a voice of considerable emotional range and power.

April 10, 1954

AARON COPLAND's opera "The Tender Land," which was given its première by the New York City Opera Company last week, is about a young girl on an isolated Midwestern farm who falls in love with a rather serious and likable hobo. Her family disapproves; the hobo himself, after some soul-searching, decides to move on; and the girl, having had her first glimpse of broader horizons, leaves home to try her luck in the big, wide world.

This little plot, which, except for its setting, is not entirely unlike that of Charpentier's "Louise," is obviously suitable for opera. But, for a number of reasons, "The Tender Land" does not quite come off. Chief among these, in my opinion, is the fact that Mr. Copland's musical style—a deft fusion of ingredients assembled from Debussy and Satie, and of desiccated elements of American folk music—seems incapable of suggesting the passionate and poetic feelings of his characters. Nowhere is this weakness more evident than in the opera's love scenes, which, had they contained less self-conscious workmanship and more spontaneous melody, might have been extremely effective. As it was, I found myself wishing that Mr. Copland would for once let himself go, forget about his technique, and give his singers something romantic to sing—for the situation the opera describes is a romantic one. But Mr. Copland, like many a composer of his generation, is such an embattled anti-romanticist that the very idiom in which he writes lacks the machinery for communicating this sort of emotion.

The production given the opera was in every way resourceful and pleasing. Oliver Smith's scenery, evidently inspired by certain features of Grant Wood's paintings, caught the lonely, austere atmosphere of the Great Plains admirably. Among the singers, Norman Treigle, who sang the role of the girl's rather crusty grandfather, turned in a particularly arresting characterization and showed that he has a voice of very promising quality. The most remarkable thing about the performance for me, however, was the conducting of the young American maestro Thomas Schippers, who had presided excellently over several previous opera productions at the City Center and who whipped this one into efficient shape indeed. Mr. Schippers seems to combine taste and energy with the rare faculty of conveying musical ideas by means of gesture that is the indispensable talent of the born conductor.

"The Tender Land" was followed by Gian-Carlo Menotti's little Christmas opera, "Amahl and the Night Visitors," which has been performed before but which I had never heard. I did not like it as well as some of his earlier operas—notably "The Medium." I thought it a shade arch and sentimental, and it was somewhat difficult for me to reconcile the three wise kings' buffoonery with the seriousness of their sacred mission in bearing gifts to the infant Jesus. It is, however, an unpretentious work with a few charming moments, and it shows throughout the facility for musical theatre that distinguishes Menotti's operatic output. Its music is sometimes rather trivial, but the opera is far better written for voices than Copland's, and far more compelling from a dramatic standpoint. I might add that Mr. Menotti, who writes his own librettos, is a much more skilled craftsman in fitting words to music than the librettist of "The Tender Land." "Amahl" does not face up to any such emotional challenges as are involved in the Copland work, but such small challenges as it does face up to are met, on the whole, with grace and fluency.

FOR ME, the most memorable performance of the week was the piano recital by the seventy-year-old German pianist Wilhelm Backhaus, who had not appeared in New York for twenty-eight years. Like many people who follow musical happenings here and abroad, I had been aware of Mr. Backhaus's towering European reputation and had heard a number of fine recordings of his that have been available locally. But I was not prepared for the unique artistry he exhibited in this program, which consisted of five Beethoven sonatas. In fact, I left the hall convinced that I had never in my life heard Beethoven's music so magnificently, sensitively, and authoritatively performed.

Mr. Backhaus is technically such a master that he overcomes the knottiest mechanical problems with no effort at all, and in such a manner as to leave his audience almost unconscious of his tremendous feats of virtuosity. But all his technique is merely a means dedicated to the conveyance of deep and subtle musical nuances. Perhaps the greatest achievement of the evening was his lucid and wonderfully revealing performance of the difficult Sonata in C Minor, Opus 111, but the delicate insight with which he did the gay and seldom performed little

Sonata in G Major, Opus 79, was in its way equally unforgettable. His playing, in general, had both suavity and a rocklike
substantiality. It showed an inspired comprehension of the most
elusive and fragile details of Beethoven's musical thought and an
incomparably sure sense of the dramatic values the sonatas contain. Mr. Backhaus's concert was, I thought, one of the outstanding happenings of the current musical season.

May 15, 1954

FROM A HISTORICAL point of view, the most important event of
the past musical season was, I suppose, the retirement of Arturo
Toscanini. It has brought to a close a period of approximately
a quarter of a century that will no doubt be known in the annals
of American symphonic music as the Toscanini era.

The powers that enabled this distinguished Italian artist to
dominate the musical scene as completely as he did were, of
course, altogether extraordinary—so extraordinary, in fact, that
it would be easy to lump them all under the heading of "genius"
and let it go at that. But the analysis of the personal and the
artistic elements that contributed to Toscanini's genius has al-

ways been a fascinating problem to me, and I am going to allow myself the luxury of a few retrospective comments on the matter.

The great artistic integrity and the spirit of dedication that Toscanini brought to every moment of his work can, I think, be set aside from this discussion. These were qualities of attitude rather than of method, and the Maestro's attitude toward his art was, of course, to a very uncommon extent one of "infinite pains." The art on which these infinite pains were expended, however, has always seemed to me to spring from two phenomena that were unusually well developed in his personality: first, his outstanding musical intelligence, and second, the uncanny faculty he had for forcing those who worked with him to give substance to the insights of that intelligence. The first included his tremendously thorough comprehension of the scores he conducted, and the wonderful sense of proportion that permitted him to achieve both perfection of detail and absolute mastery of the larger dramatic continuity of a composition. The second included those more functional and practical talents by which he controlled an orchestra or a group of singers and seemed to make them into the responsive tools of his artistic imagination.

It was the first phenomenon that provided the musical taste in his works—a taste that was always fastidious, sometimes limited by considerations of temperament, but invariably lucid and eloquent to a degree matched by few of his contemporaries. The second phenomenon—the source of the electrifying enthusiasm and the almost hypnotic control of the human materials that were features of practically all his performances—was, however, the more mysterious one. Toscanini not only conducted everything as if his life depended on its perfection but seemed able to infuse this psychology of crisis into the minds of everyone who worked with him, and this was the particular gift that made him unique among conductors. His methods of accomplishing this—

the lashing beat of the baton, the fits of temper, the scoldings and imprecations, the incantatory crooning, and the cajolery and wheedling—have elicited no end of fairly amusing journalistic comment for years. The amazing thing about them is that they worked with complete efficiency, and that the result was always a triumph of inspiration.

The mentality behind this impressive functional gift had, of course, its own set of predilections. No conductor performs all kinds of music equally well; Toscanini performed more kinds of music remarkably well than most other conductors. Nevertheless, there were kinds of music in which he was not especially at home, and there were other kinds of music to which his peculiar temperament brought a rather specialized sort of interpretation. His talents shone in the direction of brilliance, clarity, and galvanic energy, and he tended to impart these qualities to all his work, even when he was dealing with music of a relaxed and contemplative type. The symphonies of composers like Bruckner and Mahler eluded him; his approach to Brahms lacked a breadth that one can find in the interpretations of other conductors, and even his Beethoven performances, though magnificent in their way, were sometimes too driven and sleek for my taste. I remember an old recording he once did for Victor of the Blue Danube Waltz that was so metronomically exact and so relentlessly dynamic as to make it appear that that poetic river was overflowing with Vesuvian lava. Often, too, the somewhat imperious Toscanini approach deprived singers of a certain leeway for the expression of their own individuality. His recent recording of Verdi's "Otello," for example, is a superb piece of conducting craftsmanship, but its hard-driving intensity, in my opinion, sometimes obscures the tender human emotion the score contains. I am conscious that in making these criticisms I am pointing out minor flaws in the work of a great master, but they are, to me, still flaws.

The Toscanini era was remarkable for, among other things, the effect it had on our other symphonic maestros, since he was the most widely imitated conductor of his time. In some respects, his influence was admirable. His sincere devotion to the essentials of his craft did away once and for all with a rather hammy and visually self-conscious tradition of showmanship that had been fairly common among conductors in America before he arrived on the scene. In some other respects, his influence, through no fault of his own, was less happy. A good many lesser conductors laid hold of his most obvious peculiarities of style—particularly his unswerving tempos and his tendency toward speed—and made them into fetishes, with the result that restlessness and a sort of chromium-plated brilliance became the prevailing goals of American symphonic performance. Had these lesser conductors possessed the wonderful faculty for elasticity with which Toscanini enlivened his rigid and speedy tempos, this development might have been more fruitful. But they did not possess it, and the effect, on the whole, was to make bare metronomic precision into a prime canon of musical taste.

Toscanini's retirement means, of course, the loss of a superlative artist and a public idol. But it does not mean that superlative artistry in this field is about to disappear from our musical life. Even during the period when he reigned undisputed over American symphonic music, there were other conductors—notably Wilhelm Furtwängler, whom political considerations prevented from appearing on this side of the Atlantic—who were artists of very nearly comparable stature. Recent guest appearances here by such conductors as Eduard van Beinum have suggested that Europe is by no means barren of younger maestros with extraordinary qualifications, and we may have been somewhat inclined to overlook the contributions of such familiar top-rank figures as Georg Szell, Bruno Walter, and Pierre Monteux. Still, there was that old electric excitement that Toscanini alone seemed able to give a symphonic performance— and I, among so many others, shall deeply miss it.

SEASON OF 1954-1955

October 9, 1954

ONE THING that has always struck me about the melodies of the great Giuseppe Verdi is their absolute indestructibility. They can be badly sung, badly played—they can even be whistled, or performed on a hand organ—and still retain a certain amount of their beauty. This attribute must, I suppose, indicate something about the sturdiness of the classical principles on which they are built. Their significance seems to lie wholly in the evocative character of their structural line—a peculiarity somewhat analogous to narrative power in writing and draftsmanship in painting. Harmonic and contrapuntal ingenuity, subtle contrasts in tone color, thematic development, and all the other methods more cerebral composers use in creating musical interest are almost irrelevant in Verdi's case, though he employs them occasionally.

The kernel of Verdi's musical thought is always expressed in unadorned melody—melody that is so vigorous and clean in its logical form that it needs no intellectual trimmings to make its message felt. There is something quintessentially musical about this characteristic of Verdi's style, for the quintessence of music is, after all, melody. There have been numerous celebrated melodists in the history of music, of course—Chopin, Tchaikovsky, Rossini, and Bellini come immediately to mind—and their tunes, like those of many present-day popular composers, would probably survive performance on a hand organ, too. The big difference between their music and Verdi's, however, is to be found in the enormous emotional scope and variety of his melodic thought. Verdi's melodies sound like popular tunes, but their range of human feeling encompasses nearly every shade of fundamental emotion.

I was reminded again of all this while listening to the performance of "Aïda" with which the New York City Opera opened its fall season last week at the City Center. The production, limited by a small stage, too few supernumeraries for its grandiose triumphal scene, and a cast of singers notable for earnest intentions rather than brilliant artistry, was certainly not up to the grander standards of grand opera. It was, moreover, so inadequately rehearsed that a few details, particularly some offstage choruses, failed to reach the ear at all. Nevertheless, the vitality and passion of the old Verdi score made themselves felt, and the total experience, though rather sketchy, was not without its enjoyable moments. Under the circumstances, the best scenes were the ones that made the smallest demands on the City Center's rather rudimentary capacities for pageantry, and one of these—the scene on the banks of the Nile—was performed with reasonable conviction.

October 23, 1954

It is, I think, too frequently forgotten nowadays that a symphony is a large orchestral work that achieves its effect not through decorative, impressionistic sounds but through certain intellectual musical principles involving the statement and manipulation of themes. It makes an appeal to the ear, of course, as does all music worthy of the name. But it differs from most ballet music and other descriptive music in that it goes beyond mere aural sensation and enlists the mind of the listener, which becomes engrossed in the drama of its architectural form.

The capacity for writing fine symphonies has always been a rather rare one, and the past forty years or so seem to have been extremely poor in composers with this capacity—mainly, I should say, because composers have been too preoccupied with novel and striking sound effects to devote themselves to the more rigorous intellectual demands of the symphony. There has been a tendency, too, to drop overboard, as unfashionable, the technique of development and the contrast of tonalities on which the noble art of symphonic writing depends for its propulsion and what might be called its narrative power.

The Tenth, and latest, Symphony of Dimitri Shostakovich, which was introduced to this country with considerable fanfare by the New York Philharmonic-Symphony, was attended by a note in the program in which the composer stated that his aim in writing it was to express the "thoughts and aspirations of our contemporaries"—particularly, the program went on to say, the thoughts "of people who ardently love peace, who resist the drift to war, who regard man's mission on earth to be creative, not destructive." I am afraid that I regard these sentiments as pure poppycock in their bearing on his symphony, not only because of their political flavor but also because such concrete, propagandistic ideas are simply inexpressible in musical terms. Having made this observation, however, I am happy to report that the work itself is a symphony in the true sense of the word, and, by the standards of the day, a very impressive one indeed.

It is impressive for the vigor and freshness of its thought, which is neither academic nor doctrinaire in the modern manner, and for the originality of its material, which now and then recalls such composers as Sibelius and Prokofieff without being in any way imitative of them. Parts of it—notably the second movement, which bristles with woodwind cascades that veritably yelp with exuberance—are a little on the noisy side. Other parts— the third movement especially—are quieter, quite charming, and somewhat pastoral in feeling. Here and there are to be found the reminiscences of Rimski-Korsakov's mannerisms in "Le Coq d'Or" that seem to be standard attributes of modern Russian music. But, for all its length—and it is a fairly lengthy work— it never bores its audience, and there isn't a moment of muddled musical thinking in it.

To me, though, the most impressive thing about it is that, like any good symphony, it achieves its aims chiefly through the interest of its melodic and structural features. In listening to it, one realized anew what a wonderful thing tonality is, and what tremendous resources have been lost to a whole generation of twelve-tone, and otherwise atonal, composers in abandoning it. I do not mean to imply that the Shostakovich symphony is, in any sense, a traditional composition. As a matter of fact, I was somewhat surprised, in view of what one has recently heard about the conservatism of Russian official taste, by its bumptious modernity. It is, however, modern in the best meaning of the term—modern, that is, in spirit rather than in formula.

To my mind, the Tenth takes its place beside the finest of Shostakovich's past symphonies, among which I would include the First and the Fifth. It lacks, perhaps, the tragic emotional power that one finds in the work of the great nineteenth-century symphonists and that was still echoed in the twentieth-century symphonies of Gustav Mahler. But this is, after all, something we have long been accustomed to do without. As the harsh, bright, and nervous symphonies of the present era go, the Tenth is, in my opinion, a work of great distinction. The performance, under Dimitri Mitropoulos, was altogether brilliant and, I am sure, delineated the complex details of the new symphony with the utmost clarity.

THE FIRST PUBLIC New York appearance of the famous Concertgebouw Orchestra of Amsterdam took place last week in an atmosphere of international friendliness, launched by what seemed to me the finest performance of "The Star-Spangled Banner" I have ever heard. The conductor was Eduard van Beinum, an artist who was well received here last winter as guest conductor of the Philadelphia Orchestra, and the program contained a varied assortment of items that had obviously been chosen to demonstrate what the visiting orchestra could do. What it did was show us that the lush and vigorous approach of our own American orchestras is by no means the only way to produce fine symphonic music.

Man for man, the Concertgebouw Orchestra does not show

quite the virtuosity and competitive drive that characterize our finest symphonic organizations. But there is about its playing a mellow and well-aged quality that our own orchestras seldom achieve. Its instrumentalists play with, rather than against, one another, and its ensemble is close to perfection. It also exhibits a subtle variety of tone color, ranging from dry understatement (something not often heard here) to richness and brilliance when richness and brilliance are required. I do not know exactly why it should give such an impression of age and maturity, since it is actually nowhere near as old an organization as our own Philharmonic, but it does, and with this impression comes an atmosphere of relaxation and meticulous attention to finespun detail that results in admirable lucidity.

The one contemporary composition on the program, a Symphony No. 2 by the Dutch composer Henk Badings, I found a bore, but Weber's "Der Freischütz" Overture and Ravel's "Daphnis et Chloé Suite, No. 2" were given a jewellike polish and sparkle. The evening ended with Brahms' First Symphony, done without heroics and with extraordinary balance and poise.

October 30, 1954

SOME YEARS AGO, I saw a movie called, I believe, "Pépé le Moko," in which a murder was committed while a broken-down player piano thumped out a particularly racy and lightheaded tune. The scene has always stuck in my mind as an especially gripping bit of melodrama, because of the way it set off the serious business of death against a background of frivolity, thereby making death itself doubly poignant and horrifying. This trick of depicting murder to the accompaniment of trivial music is also to be found now and then in opera, though it is not by any means the rule there. The rule is, of course, for the orchestra and the protagonists to groan and wail in an attempt to underline the dreadfulness of what is taking place on the stage, and generally, I suppose, this is the appropriate thing for them to do.

Certain theatrically gifted composers, however, have used the "Pépé le Moko" method, and have been rewarded in nearly every instance I can think of with an unforgettable moment of operatic drama. One such moment occurs in Verdi's "Rigoletto," when the aging jester, carrying the body of his dying daughter in a sack on his back, hears the voice of the man whose corpse he thinks is in the sack singing the notably tawdry strains of "La donna è mobile" offstage. Another such moment is the murder of Carmen, a passionate, bloodthirsty affair that takes place against the bright, martial music emanating from the bull ring.

The incongruity in each case intensifies the dramatic action almost incredibly, suggesting, as it does, both the awful irrevocability of death and the potential joy of the life that is being snuffed out before the eyes of the audience. The very triviality of the music is an important ingredient of the mixture, for it indicates that the death is not a heroic one but merely the extinction of a rather pathetic human being who asked little more of life than the shimmering and inexpensive dream of happiness evoked by the melody. In these moments, the curious art of opera demonstrates one of its numerous paradoxes—that great dramatic climaxes can sometimes be reached more effectively through music that is intrinsically cheap and shallow than through music that is profound.

Jacques Offenbach's durable opera "The Tales of Hoffmann" also contains one of these moments, in a scene so haunting that I have made two trips to the New York City Center in the past two weeks just to witness it. As far as I am concerned, "The Tales of Hoffmann" is otherwise a somewhat dreary and dated thing, with a first act that is a trifle silly and a third act that is more than a trifle boring. But sandwiched in between the two is the famous "Barcarolle" scene, laid in Venice, and here, accompanied by one of Offenbach's most sensuous and cajoling tunes, there is a bit of bloodshed that I shall always rank as my favorite operatic murder.

The murderer is, of course, Hoffmann, and his victim is the gloomy, passionate character known, rather unhappily perhaps, as Schlemil. The cause of the murder is a woman of easy virtue named Giulietta, with whom both men are in love, and the scene is dominated by a third man—a formidably diabolical and cynical fellow named Dapertutto—who eggs the two on to fight and, in the end, laughingly keeps the girl under his thumb. Dapertutto is a realist, and he certainly succeeds in proving that romanticism doesn't pay, especially when it is a question of women of easy virtue.

But it is not this fairly commonplace moral that gives the situation its magic. Instead, it is Offenbach's frivolous tune, coming from the Venetian lagoon offstage, which embodies the yearning of Hoffmann and Schlemil and seems to mock the sordid events we are witnessing. In an extra stroke of theatrical genius, Offenbach has given his three principal male characters spoken lines that sound rather harsh, flat, and desperate in contrast to the happy tune issuing from the distant gondolas. Although the whole thing is a trick of stagecraft, it rarely fails in effect, and it is, I think, the main reason this overstuffed old opera has survived as long as it has.

There were several additional points of interest in last week's performance. For one thing, it showed that "The Tales of Hoffmann" is still one of the best and most lavish productions currently being offered at the City Center. For another, Frances Yeend, one of the company's better dramatic sopranos, appeared in all three of the opera's feminine roles—a tour de force that is successfully attempted only by very gifted singers, since it requires coloratura and lyric resources that few dramatic sopranos possess. Though Miss Yeend did remarkably well, I did not think she quite brought it off. She seemed far more at home in her accustomed role of Giulietta than with the cold, rippling cascades of notes that fell to her lot as Olympia, the mechanical doll of the first act. The remaining roles were, for the most part, excellently sung. They included a ringing and youthful performance of Hoffmann by Robert Rounseville, and a notable one by Walter Cassel, who, aside from a faulty high note at the end of his main aria, proved to be as impressive a Dapertutto as I have heard anywhere.

November 13, 1954

DIMITRI MITROPOULOS, whose striking appearance on the podium often suggests a Byzantine monk frantically engaged in shaking Martinis, is, I think, a conductor of considerable stature. His virtues lie in the way he is able to make an orchestra play exactly as he wants it to and in the enthusiasm he seems able to generate in presenting music of a passionate or exuberant character.

Mitropoulos is, however, a conductor of the inspirational, rather than the methodical, type, and the quality of his performances appears to depend to a great extent on impulses of the moment. I have heard him do things by Strauss, Rachmaninoff, and certain contemporary composers with unforgettable brilliance; I have also heard him bludgeon his way through a composition, throwing its most delicate nuances out of kilter and drawing about as rough a sound from his orchestra as I have ever encountered. The latter phenomenon is, I am afraid, most apt to occur when he undertakes music of a serene, formal variety—music that depends for its effect not so much on energy and vigor as on elegance and poise.

The New York Philharmonic-Symphony recently provided an unusually good example of both his virtues and his defects. In presenting Schumann's familiar Symphony No. 2 in C Major, Mr. Mitropoulos seemed to be at his worst. Exaggerated accents and eccentric tempos made the symphony sound more like some particularly boisterous Slavic rhapsody than the masterpiece of German Romanticism that it is. I looked in vain for the limpid and sensuous tone in the strings that this symphony requires to assert its full magic. Its rapid passages struck me as generally indistinct and muddy, and I thought its adagio—perhaps the greatest single movement Schumann ever wrote—was done with remarkable disregard for the subtleties of its soaring melodic line. After the Schumann work was over, however, Mr. Mitropoulos turned his attention to what were apparently more congenial tasks, and succeeded in finishing off his program with quite a demonstration of virtuosity.

The compositions that called forth this demonstration were Prokofieff's Second Piano Concerto, which is not often performed and which I believe I was hearing for the first time, and a new suite of Greek dances by a countryman of Mr. Mitropoulos's named Nicholas Skalkotas. The soloist in the former work was the Italian artist Pietro Scarpini, who was making his American début and who proved to be a pianist of prodigious muscular and technical powers. The concerto is an early work, antedating the "Scythian Suite" and the "Classical Symphony," and I found its rather bumptious and primitive idiom—what we think of as the typical Prokofieff style had not yet congealed—fairly exhilarating. Mr. Mitropoulos and Mr. Scarpini evidently found the concerto exhilarating, too, for they performed it with enormous dedication and an incredible display of pyrotechnics.

I wish it hadn't been followed by Mr. Skalkotas's "Greek Dances," for by the time they arrived I was pretty well worn out by the sound of bass drums and cymbals. But Mr. Mitropoulos was not worn out at all, and he gave this score, which to my mind was a moderately interesting and somewhat explosive essay in transcribed folk music, a generally thundering interpretation.

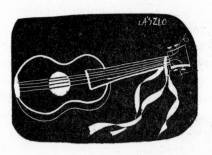

December 4, 1954

To ME, the most interesting musical experience of the season thus far was the first New York performance of the curious and altogether enchanting work called "Carmina Burana," by the Bavarian composer Carl Orff. Its performance involved the services of the Boston University Chorus and Orchestra and the Boys Choir of St. Thomas Episcopal Church, plus some really spirited conducting by Leopold Stokowski.

As you probably have heard, Mr. Orff is almost sixty years old, has been quietly composing in Munich for more than a generation, and is the author of a large number of works, including an opera, several ballets, some music for the theatre, and some choral items similar to "Carmina Burana." To judge by the

"Carmina," which was written twenty years ago and is, unfortunately, the only large work of his to have been performed hereabouts, Mr. Orff is one of the most original and spontaneous of living composers.

The work possesses both vigor and infectious charm—qualities that, heaven knows, are rare enough in contemporary music. It consists of a tightly joined series of songs, sung in medieval Latin and equally medieval German, the lines of which were selected from a collection of secular poetry discovered in 1803 in the archives of an old Bavarian Benedictine monastery. The poetry is the work of various university students, vagabond minstrels, and unfrocked priests of the Middle Ages, and it sings, in a very unmonastic way, the delights of spring, drink, and love. There is a dirgelike lament bewailing the ruthless turning of Fortune's wheel, a song sung by a drunken abbot, several items celebrating the power of the sexual urge, and even a song by a roast swan who regrets his transfer from the pond to the platter. Mr. Orff's sympathy and skill in setting both the Latin and the ancient German languages to music are such that all this emerges as freshly and cajolingly as if it had been written yesterday instead of in the era of the Gothic cathedrals.

The music with which Mr. Orff has clothed these ancient ditties is totally different from any other contemporary music I have heard. If it has any antecedents, they will be found, I think, in the unabashed melody of Verdi, the jinglelike musical stanzas of Moussorgsky, and the nostalgic little tunes in Mahler's symphonies. But this music is simpler in style than the work of any of these three composers. Mr. Orff sometimes strums his orchestra as if it were a giant banjo. His melodies can be whistled and have a way of sticking indelibly in the memory. His harmonies are so elementary that most of them could be reproduced by alternately sucking and blowing on a harmonica. He does not disdain oom-pah accompaniments, and he does not distort them with funny noises to assure you that his intention is satirical. He uses them, like Verdi, perfectly seriously, and if there is any satire connected with them, it is of the happiest and most affectionate sort. The writing, in general, is almost without what one ordinarily thinks of as technique. Yet there is nothing banal or trivial about it, and it everywhere reveals the mind of an extremely sophisticated musician—a master at concealing his art to the point where only its essential message is evident to the listener.

The fundamental features of Orff's style, as I discovered after listening a few times to the recording of "Carmina Burana," which I went straight out and bought the day after the concert, are its reliance on powerful, propulsive rhythm and on something that has been rigorously tabooed in most of the "progressive" music of the past forty years—namely, tonality. This is not, however, the sort of changing and iridescent tonality that appears in the work of the romantic composers but, rather, the simple, insistent tonality characteristic of folk music. The reappearance of this phenomenon in music of an aggressive, modern sort comes to one, in this age of musical artifice, like a breath of fresh air. It is as though Mr. Orff had decided to discard with one sweep both the academic formulas of the twelve-tone composers and the fashionable and effete furniture that has cluttered French and French-influenced music since the time of Satie, and then begin over again with the primary elements of the art. The result is a highly individual and striking musical idiom, and I suspect that it may give Mr. Orff a place as one of the few really revolutionary composers of the past generation.

This somewhat primitive idiom of Mr. Orff's has, of course, its limitations. "Carmina Burana" is essentially a picaresque composition—a chain of little incidents rather than an organized whole—and his style lacks the beams and braces of intellectual development necessary for the construction of such big and close-knit forms as the symphony. But so, for that matter, does the style of Stravinsky, and so, for that matter, did the easy and lucid styles of Giuseppe Verdi and of countless Italian opera composers who preceded him. While "Carmina Burana" is anything but an intellectually complex work, it does something that few compositions of the present era succeed in doing: it speaks from the heart and the viscera instead of from the frontal lobe of the brain.

December 11, 1954

THERE ARE VERY few living violinists I would willingly cross the street to hear except in the line of duty. Violinists in general, I find, are poor musicians who love to wallow in the sound of their own lush tone, fleet fingerwork, and rhetorical heroics. Only truly exceptional ones have the musical sensibility required to perform a classical phrase with any elegance whatever, and as for the violin itself, no instrument, except possibly the saxophone, lends itself so easily to mawkish vulgarity.

The art of violin playing, moreover, coincides at only a few points with the art of music. These points are to be found in compositions that demand refined musical interpretation rather than displays of agility—in such masterpieces, that is, as have been written for the instrument, and they are not numerous. The bulk of the violin repertory consists of showpieces of purely athletic interest; the majority of the people who play them are exhibitionistic craftsmen whose mental equipment, insofar as it finds expression in musical terms, seldom seems to surpass that of a gypsy; and the people who go to listen to them constitute, as a rule, a specialized audience, somewhat similar to that which attends concerts by Neapolitan tenors. This audience is concerned not with music but with the violin.

In view of these somewhat depressing facts, the rare occasion on which a violin is played as a musical instrument becomes one for real rejoicing. Last week the New York Philharmonic-Symphony, under George Szell, devoted the major part of its program to a couple of violin concertos in which Nathan Milstein appeared as soloist. Though I have listened to Mr. Milstein off and on ever since his début here about a quarter of a century ago, I had not heard him for a number of years, and I remembered him as an exceedingly brilliant technician but otherwise a fairly ordinary violinist.

I was not prepared for the solid and sober artistry and the genuine musical insight Milstein revealed last week, and I can only conclude that the past decade or so has seen an extraordinary development in his artistic capacities. I was not surprised by his nearly flawless accuracy or by the air of complete security with which he attacked the technical problems of the music, since these are virtues he has possessed for a long time. But I was both surprised and impressed by the modest dignity and the understanding of inflection with which he undertook his tasks. The works he played were Bach's A-Minor Concerto for Violin and Strings and Max Bruch's rather florid Concerto No. 1 in G Minor. Mr. Milstein performed the Bach concerto with an exquisite sense of classical line, giving every phrase its proper emphasis, and he played the other composition with the combination of eloquence and poise that indicates the true virtuoso.

December 25, 1954

THAT SOMETIMES erratic but nearly always astonishing conductor Dimitri Mitropoulos showed up in the pit of the Metropolitan Opera House one evening last week and churned Richard Strauss's "Salome" into what, from the orchestral point of view, seemed to me the finest performance of this highly orchestral opera I have ever heard. Not only did Mr. Mitropoulos appear to be in command of every slightest inflection and dramatic twist of Strauss's boiling and steaming score but he succeeded in rousing the Metropolitan's orchestra out of its usual state of routine efficiency and making it play with all the enthusiasm and brilliance of which it is capable.

This gratifying feat was, of course, not entirely unexpected, for Mr. Mitropoulos has shown many times in the past that he has a particular feeling for Strauss's music, and he has also shown the special qualities of personal leadership and inspirational dash that are bound to shine with considerable effect in an opera house. I wish the Metropolitan had more conductors of his calibre. No amount of fine singing can give an opera finish and dramatic continuity unless the man in the orchestra pit drives and guides it with real authority and control, and this is what Mr. Mitropoulos did.

The performance had its other points, good and bad. The new and widely heralded Salome of Christel Goltz was certainly as wild and uninhibited a one as I have ever encountered. The sheer physical stamina with which Miss Goltz pranced and wriggled about the stage was, I suppose, impressive, and I frequently found myself out of breath just from watching her. Her singing was generally loud and expressive. The trouble was that her conception of Strauss's psychotic heroine lacked any sense of psychological progression. From the moment she appeared on the stage, and long before her consuming passion for John the Baptist was supposed to develop, she seemed to be in a state that could have been calmed only by a strait jacket. From this point, there was obviously no place she could go in the direction of hysteria. Miss Goltz continued to claw the air like a maddened tigress; she rolled halfway across the stage from the top of John the Baptist's cistern, and at the end she seemed to be chewing the great prophet's head to bits beneath the silken robe that she had mercifully thrown over herself and it. But all the stops had been pulled long before, and each successive scene proved only that even violence, if pursued unremittingly, can become monotonous.

"Salome" is by no means my favorite opera; indeed, to me the most pleasant thing about going to it is the pristine freshness that the night air on Broadway has when one leaves the auditorium. Still, it is, in its way, a masterpiece of mood, and deserves the sort of production that will enhance its atmosphere of murk and terror. I did not think that the details of the Met's staging were altogether satisfactory. For one thing, the scimitar carried by the slave on his journey into the cistern to behead John the Baptist was patently a cardboard affair that couldn't have cleaved a piece of well-aged Camembert; for another, the Baptist's head, on its silver platter, looked disconcertingly like one of those masks made of carved coconut that are sold to tourists on Caribbean cruises. Not that I am a stickler for realism in this grisly melodrama, but "Salome" makes its effect through horror, and if I have to witness horror, I like to have it convincing.

LAST WEEK provided one of those rare full-length performances of Berlioz's cantata "The Damnation of Faust." I had not heard such a performance in many years, and had nearly forgotten how little justice is done to the work by the comparatively trivial snatches of its score that are frequently given on symphony programs. The regimental resources that it requires brought out most of the New York Philharmonic, the chorus of the Schola Cantorum, the Choir Boys of St. Thomas's Church, and the soloists Jennie Tourel, Jon Crain, Martial Singher, and Norman Treigle. Robert Lawrence, who, among other things, was once dance critic of the *Herald Tribune,* conducted it with care and sometimes with eloquence.

I am not, as I think I have noted in these pages before, an unqualified Berlioz enthusiast. At his greatest, however, I find him a composer of quite wonderful freshness and originality, and the complete "Damnation" is certainly the greatest work of his that I am acquainted with. Like all his music, it has patches of theatricality, patches of magnificent orchestration, and patches of curiously eclectic melodic inspiration. But in this work the theatricality is so effective, and the sweep of the dramatic idea that lies behind it is so grand, that I was shaken out of the mood of critical detachment that his music usually arouses in me. "The

Damnation of Faust" struck me on this occasion as a vast mosaic made up of gleaming scraps of melody and strange nuggets of orchestral and choral color, rather Byzantine both in its exoticism and in its spirit of monumentality. It is possible that I have been underestimating Berlioz. If, as his fervent admirers claim, he has written works of comparable nobility, I should very much like to hear them.

January 8, 1955

GIAN-CARLO MENOTTI's opera "The Saint of Bleecker Street" is about a young Italian-American girl, named Annina, who lives in Manhattan's Little Italy and whose exemplary piety, rewarded early in the story by the appearance of miraculous stigmata, causes her neighbors to regard her as a saint. By the time the final curtain falls, Annina has realized her fondest desire, which is to become a nun, and has died shortly thereafter, but before these happenings take place, a good many complications arise.

The complications involve her brother, a rather belligerent and greatly mixed-up young man who is torn between a number of irreconcilable emotions, including a pathological devotion to his sister and a furious resentment against the Church, which makes him try to thwart her at every turn on her Heavenward path. His emotions also include a lukewarm passion for a woman of easy virtue called Desideria, whom he kills at the end of the second act because she questions, as well she might, the purity of his feeling for his sister. In the end, a broken man and a fugitive from justice, he is still clutching at the heroine as she departs for a better world.

As can be seen from this somewhat simplified sketch, Mr. Menotti's plot, which I shall return to presently, contains a good deal of love, hate, jealousy, death, and other standard ingredients of operatic stagecraft, and he has set it to music of conventional full-blown operatic eloquence and sometimes of almost Wagnerian intensity.

"The Saint of Bleecker Street" is easily the most ambitious undertaking of the sort that Menotti has attempted up to now, and since he is far and away the most skillful craftsman among those who are at present devoting themselves to the writing of opera in English, it has its moments of effective theatre. Sometimes the secrets of this effectiveness are borrowed. The religious procession that closes the first act is almost a replica of the procession that closes the first act of "Tosca"; the chord that announces the death of the wayward Desideria in Act II is the exact chord with which Puccini announces the death of Mimi in "La Bohème." But Mr. Menotti has done his borrowing wisely, and his work is a genuine opera, obviously written by a man who knows what opera is—a sort of knowledge that is by no means widespread among today's composers. Mr. Menotti uses a musical idiom that, though not strikingly original, is capable of expressing the emotions of his characters; he writes well for the human voice; he knows how to choose melodies that go nicely with words; he has a remarkable instinct for melodramatic effect. All these virtues of craftsmanship should have combined to produce a work of real dramatic force, but—to my mind, at least—they have not, and the trouble seems to be a certain cloudiness in Mr. Menotti's approach to the problems of human behavior.

It was, I suspect, Mr. Menotti's intention to make his pious heroine a figure of some grandeur, and to show through her actions the triumph of faith over sin. Her important position in the plot and the amount of soulful ecclesiastical music that surrounds her main scenes would, at any rate, lead one to this conclusion. There is nothing in the opera, however, that indicates exactly why she deserves to be blessed with the unusual amount of sanctity she seems to possess, and since her overpowering holiness causes no end of havoc among the other characters of the drama, one's sympathy naturally tends to drift from her to her more sinful and more human associates.

Piety is, of course, generally regarded as a virtue, but, as Wagner long ago demonstrated in "Parsifal," it is not the most dynamic theme on which to build an operatic drama. In fact, the history of successful operatic dramaturgy, as exemplified in such familiar items as "Salome," "Manon," "Faust," and "La Forza del Destino," seems to prove that in opera, religion is most effective when it is used as a noble backdrop against which misguided human beings play with passionate and irreligious emotions—a proceeding that invariably ends in their infinite discomfiture and usually ends in their death. There must, I think, be some basic wisdom in this tradition. In any case, Annina, with all her visions and all the psalm singing that surrounds her, has too few human frailties to make a convincing heroine, and in her relation to the other principals she often comes close to being an unctuous nuisance. Her brother is not much help, either, since his frantic efforts to woo her away from her churchly destiny show him to have a mind that is unbalanced, to say the least.

"The Saint of Bleecker Street," in my opinion, has only one major character capable of arousing any great sympathy, and that is the rather sluttish villainess Desideria, who, unlike the others, is capable of normal passions, and dies expressing them. As might be expected, her big scene in Act II is the most moving thing in the opera; this is so, I think, mainly because, for once, somebody is singing about an understandable and fairly universal form of emotion.

Gloria Lane, as Desideria, stopped the show in the second act, not only because she is obviously a young singer who has extraordinary dramatic and vocal gifts but also because the role had this earthy reality. Virginia Copeland sang beautifully as Annina, and David Poleri did as well as anyone could with the conflicting impulses that fell to his lot as her brother. The work was given an extremely handsome production under the composer's direction. An orchestra of sixty men played the score with great virtuosity, and Thomas Schippers conducted it brilliantly.

January 22, 1955

SINCE THE PREMIÈRE a couple of weeks ago of Gian-Carlo Menotti's "The Saint of Bleecker Street," there has been a good
deal of writing in the papers to the effect that it is unfair to
criticize Mr. Menotti's work as a drama because, after all, it is
an opera, and, as everybody is presumed to know, in opera the
music is the thing and the drama is nearly always terrible anyhow.

I should like to file an emphatic dissent from this theory,
which seems to me to reflect an ignorance of the operatic art that
I find much too widespread. I myself took issue with certain
dramatic aspects of "The Saint of Bleecker Street" because I
have great respect both for the art and for Mr. Menotti's extraordinary talents as a practitioner of it, and because I felt that
some of the dramatic elements that formed an integral part of
the show did not quite come up to expectations. It never occurred to me that the art of operatic composition consists of
pouring music over a play as one would pour gravy over a dumpling, and that as long as the gravy is good the dumpling doesn't
matter. The appearance of this odd notion in the public prints
set me to thinking about operatic drama in general, and the conclusions my thoughts have led to are that opera is most certainly

a branch of the drama, and that operatic drama, on the whole, is much better drama than some people are willing to concede. I know, in fact, of only a few successful operas that do not stand up excellently from the dramatic point of view.

Operatic drama differs, of course, from "legitimate" drama in that it conveys through music all the poetic and psychological subtleties the latter conveys through language. It also differs in that its performing artists do their acting to a great extent through their voices, according to the well-established traditions of a rather specialized vocal art. Here, however, the dissimilarity between the two theatrical forms ceases, and in all other ways opera is drama as one sees it anywhere in the theatre, subject to the same laws and standards as the product of any playwright. It is true that most of the currently popular operatic repertory seems a little old-fashioned from the theatrical standpoint, since a good deal of it constitutes a sort of museum of eighteenth- and nineteenth-century drama, in which plots by such varied playwrights as Goethe, Scribe, Beaumarchais, Oscar Wilde, Victor Hugo, and Dumas *fils* survive in musically embalmed form. Still, most of this drama is expertly and effectively written, with clear motivation, convincing conflicts, and sharply drawn characters, and I think that some of opera's remarkable power of survival is due to these virtues. Certainly, characters like Rigoletto, Violetta in "La Traviata," Carmen, Figaro, and the unfortunate hero of "Pagliacci" owe their rather impressive stature as theatrical archetypes as much to their clear-cut dramatic personalities as to the music that surrounds them and emphasizes their emotions.

Mozart's "Don Giovanni," which had its first performance of the season at the Metropolitan Opera House last week, is perhaps the supreme example of the delineation of human psychology through the combined arts of music and drama, and I know of few theatrical works in any form that surpass it in subtlety and grandeur. Its music is, of course, the work of a master, and contains many passages that can stand alone as wonderful instances of pure melodic inspiration. But the full meaning of "Don Giovanni" can be apprehended only in the opera house, and this, I think, is because every note of it has reference to the tragedy of crime and punishment that is unfolding on the stage and underlines some psychological point in the lives and personalities of the characters who take part in that tragedy. Operatic literature contains few examples that come as near to perfection, and this fine old work still stands as just about the final demonstration of what a great mind—great in human perception and dramatic skill as well as musical imagination—can accomplish in the medium.

I must say that the performance accorded this towering masterpiece the other night left some things to be desired. The orchestra's playing and some of the vocal ensembles—especially the trio preceding the serenade—struck me as somewhat slipshod; the singing of Margaret Harshaw, as Donna Anna, lacked the requisite agility; and the yellowish costume, with a helmet that cast a veil of shadow over the face, worn by Luben Vichey, as the Commendatore, in the last act, made him look more like a khaki-clad beekeeper than a marble statue of a Spanish nobleman.

Nevertheless, the staging was, on the whole, better than last year's. The statue had a marble horse to sit on, which enhanced his dignity no end, and the awkwardness of the Met's inexpensive constructivist set was somewhat minimized by various drapes and props. Lucine Amara brought a new sense of passion and brilliance to the role of Donna Elvira, and sang, in general, very well. The most notable performances of the evening, however, were the agreeably unclownish Leporello of Fernando Corena; the admirable Don Ottavio of Cesare Valletti, which, vocally, recalled the effortless elegance of John McCormack; and the Don

Giovanni of George London. Mr. London's interpretation of the role is obviously so conscientious and carefully studied that it has an air of self-conscious deliberateness about it, but it is a very distinguished interpretation, for all that.

January 29, 1955

I CONFESS to a considerable amount of satisfaction in noting the recent climb of certain young American conductors to positions of prominence. This satisfaction, I suppose, arises from the fact that, as a simple patriot, I like to see my countrymen stepping into the front rank of a resplendent and dictatorial profession that in the United States has heretofore been almost exclusively the province of Europeans.

Leonard Bernstein, who led the Symphony of the Air in a program of contemporary music last week, has demonstrated over the past few years that, from the point of view of pure technique, he is one of the most gifted of currently active symphonic maestros. Thomas Schippers, whose engagement by the Metropolitan Opera House was announced last week, has appeared here primarily as an operatic conductor, and his work in this field, with the New York City Opera and in the Broadway production of "The Saint of Bleecker Street," has invariably been done with brilliance. I am not sure, as yet, whether either of these young men will develop into what might be regarded as a mature artist, but both of them seem to possess a mastery of the conducting craft that can be judged by the highest standards.

In making this distinction between the art and the craft of conducting, I am, I think, pointing out two fairly well-defined areas that, between them, encompass the total talents of the ideal maestro. There are, among conductors, great artists—Bruno Walter is an example—whose craftsmanship at times leaves something to be desired. There are also magnificent craftsmen who are not particularly gifted artists. And occasionally, of course, one comes across a real genius, like Toscanini, in whom both the art and the craft have been developed to an almost incredible degree.

Curiously, the craft of this peculiar and elusive profession is more difficult to describe than the art. It involves a mysterious gift known among musicians as "beat," which enables its possessor to convey subtle musical impulses to an orchestra by means of gesture and which is apparently as inborn as the natural grace of a dancer. Of course, it also involves such scholarly accomplishments as a thorough knowledge of scores and awareness of the potentialities of instruments and voices. And it involves the quality of personal magnetism—something that is possessed by generals and politicians as well as conductors, and that can generate enthusiasm toward the realization of a common purpose.

Beyond all these functional attributes, however, lies what I have termed the art of conducting, and this art, to my mind, involves the elements of taste, the sense of musical proportion, and the authority that permit a fine interpretive musician to make evident the essential meaning of such varied types of great music as he chooses to present.

Leonard Bernstein has shown since the very beginning of his career an uncanny facility in the craft of conducting. As to his mastery of the art, I am not quite so certain. I have found his performances of intricate modern scores generally lucid and eloquent; I have found some of his attempts to solve the far more difficult problem of performing the classics with poise and insight somewhat unsatisfactory, largely because of a tendency toward sensationalism and theatricality. For a time, he displayed exhibitionistic mannerisms that suggested he was enacting the stellar role in a public crucifixion, and that, while not entirely alien to his notoriously flamboyant métier, still seemed a little excessive.

At last week's concert, I am happy to report, these mannerisms were held to a minimum, and the program, which consisted for the most part of the sort of complex contemporary music he does best, was, on the whole, magnificently presented. I enjoyed his very dramatic performance of Prokofieff's Fifth Symphony, which I regard as one of the more worth-while works in this form turned out in recent years, and I thought he did well by Aaron Copland's slight but pleasing "Appalachian Spring." Hindemith's Concerto for Clarinet and Orchestra, which was being given its New York première, was presented conscientiously and clearly, though I felt that Benny Goodman's playing of the solo part was a bit dry and lacking in nuance. The work itself seemed to me to contain a few passages of genuine inspiration imbedded in acres of ingenious but rather tiresome musical carpentry.

February 5, 1955

VINCENZO BELLINI's rather special place in the history of music is apt to be forgotten by operatic audiences simply because his operas are so seldom performed nowadays, and the reason they are so seldom performed is that there are at present very few singers who are capable of meeting the exacting demands of his vocal writing. This is a deplorable situation, for Bellini was certainly one of the greatest melodists who have ever lived, and his three finest works—"Norma," "I Puritani," and "La Sonnambula"—realize the ideals of Italian opera with a degree of purity probably unmatched by any other composer.

It is, in fact, this very purity of Bellini's aesthetic approach that stands in the way of his being currently successful. Bellini conceived opera as a medium that makes its appeal almost exclusively through beautiful singing, and he wrote for the greatest singers of his day, exploiting the most delicate and the most spectacular capacities of the human voice with unique subtlety and eloquence. He was to the voice what his contemporary and admirer, Frédéric Chopin, was to the piano. His sense of classic melodic line was, like Chopin's, both scrupulously refined and vigorously evocative, and his art consisted, to a large extent, of eliminating from his canvas everything but the precise and elegant quality of what might be called his musical draftsmanship. He was never guilty of excess or vulgarity. Though, like most Italians of his period, he wrote floridly for the voice, his elaborate musical ornamentations always formed an integral part of his melody and were never tacked on for mere show. Bellini's style may not have encompassed the dramatic depth, the human insight, or the technical complexity that other great composers have brought to opera, but in its own particular way it is unsurpassed anywhere in music.

In presenting "La Sonnambula" in concert form last week, the American Opera Society, an organization that is to be generally commended for its enterprise, undertook a task of staggering difficulty, and, within certain limitations, succeeded in carrying it out. The limitations were, of course, vocal. Strictly speaking, there was only one singer in the cast—Cesare Siepi—who would have proved entirely adequate to the requirements of his role had the opera been produced in the grand manner and in a large opera house. Despite this handicap, the American Opera Society so skillfully balanced and adjusted the material at its disposal that "La Sonnambula" became a remarkably pleasant musical experience.

The most admirable of the evening's technical triumphs was the singing of Laurel Hurley, who undertook the terrifyingly difficult role of Amina. Miss Hurley certainly does not possess the ample and infinitely flexible voice Bellini had in mind when he wrote the part. Her voice was nevertheless sufficiently ample to fill Town Hall, even when she sang—as she often did—in a safe mezza-voce. And the neat craftsmanship with which she manipulated her limited resources was a continuous joy to witness. From the musical, as distinct from vocal, point of view, her performance was a very brilliant one indeed.

Arnold U. Gamson conducted the production with spirit, and the remaining roles were sung, on the whole, with grace and accuracy. I left the hall feeling that perhaps this sort of thing is the best present-day answer to the problem of putting on Bellini. The small-scale performance had the virtues of coherence and musical precision and was in many ways more satisfying than some indifferently sung versions of Bellini operas that I have encountered in bigger and more pretentious surroundings.

February 12, 1955

I AM UNABLE to see much sense in the Metropolitan Opera's current ban on solo curtain calls, since it deprives both artists and audience of some simple and perfectly harmless pleasure. The abolition of this traditional ceremony struck me as a particular pity the other night when the new Italian soprano Renata Tebaldi, having made a considerable impression as Desdemona in Verdi's "Otello," was hauled before the curtain at least a score of times by Mario Del Monaco and Leonard Warren, two familiar and able singers who were evidently sharing her applause with some reluctance, since it was obvious that she, as a successful newcomer, was the sole and proper center of attention. I bring the matter up purely as a point of etiquette, however, for my own reactions to Miss Tebaldi's performance, while pleasurable for the most part, were somewhat more restrained than those of the rest of her public.

Miss Tebaldi is an extremely handsome woman with a large voice of rich emotional power, and hence a very valuable addition to the Metropolitan's roster. She was at her best in the love music of the first act, which she sang with both passion and poetic feeling. And her singing also had appealing moments in the remaining three acts. To my mind, though, her performance as a whole relied a little too heavily on impulsive and rather arbitrary vocal mannerisms, which sometimes marred the classical simplicity of Verdi's long and noble melodic phrases. This was, I thought, especially true of the "Ave Maria," in the last act, which she sang with a great deal of fervor but without the poise and artful naïveté that would have given it unforgettable magic. I must point out, though, that I am comparing her with the most distinguished Desdemonas I have ever heard—notably, the magnificent and musically flawless one Elisabeth Rethberg used to sing decades ago. By these standards, Miss Tebaldi's Desdemona was not a great one. But it had a pleasingly lush and impassioned quality, nevertheless.

"Otello" is, of course, one of opera's supreme masterpieces— I think perhaps the finest and most dramatically moving work in the form written during the entire nineteenth century—and any reasonably good performance of it is bound to leave an audience deeply impressed. Since last week's performance was reasonably good, I enjoyed it, even though I was conscious of its flaws. Mr. Del Monaco, as Otello, has improved his dramatic characterization enormously since he first appeared here in the part several years ago. He has the loud and ringing voice that is the basic requisite of the role, and from the very first difficult notes that follow his entrance, he sang with admirable assurance. But the tenderness that should have added depth to his monologue in Act III and to the final moments of the drama—a quality on which, naturally, a large part of Otello's conflict depends— seemed to elude him totally. He made Otello a violent and masculine figure, but not the torn and heartbroken man he must be if the tragedy is to achieve its full effect.

I have somewhat similar objections to the Iago of Mr. Warren —a very familiar interpretation, which I have witnessed many times and in which I have found certain consistent weaknesses. Considered purely as a singer, Mr. Warren is, I think, one of the most scrupulous and refined operatic baritones now appearing before the public. The other night, he sang his notes with immense polish and subtlety, but over and over again I found myself praying that he would, for once, risk an element of harshness that might have added to the drama, even if it destroyed, for the moment, the pure, velvet quality of his tone. As a piece of acting, his Iago comes near to being a complete travesty. It contains not a single touch of oiliness or evil. It is, on the contrary, a curiously benign and fatherly affair, somehow suggesting that the character is a good-natured bumbler, rather than a ruthless villain.

Fritz Stiedry's handling of the great and passionate score was not all it should have been, either. It lacked pace and tension. For one thing, the growling and intensely dramatic phrases in the double basses that announce Otello's stealthy entrance into the bedroom in the last act sounded so diffident and creaky that they nearly wrecked the atmosphere of one of the opera's most crucial scenes. I have seen more felicitous jobs of staging, too, than the one provided by Dino Yannopoulos. In particular, I do not see what is to be gained by having Desdemona sing her "Ave Maria" beside the bed instead of before the altar, where it is usually sung, or by placing her bed parallel to the footlights

in such a way that her dying moments are obscured by the writh-
ings of Otello.

I note at this point that I have found a good many faults with
the Met's current production. "Otello" is, however, such a
superb piece of musical theatre that, despite some disappointing
details, the production was well worth going to hear.

February 26, 1955

I OFTEN WONDER whether music has quite as much to do with
history as the Teutonic professors of Hegelian dialectic claim.
Their notions of historical determinism—which, I understand,
are also at least in part responsible for the delights of Marxism—
have certainly created a good deal of mischief in the musical
field lately. Within my own memory, the late Arnold Schoenberg, a composer of some moderate gifts, marched over the cliff,
like the good but unintelligent German soldier whose officer
had yelled "*Vorwärts!*," into the meaningless mumbo-jumbo of
atonality, and he did so, I am convinced, not because he liked
atonality but because he conceived the move to be a fulfillment
of his duty to history. Even today I come across people who say,

in extenuation of some contemporary composer's perfectly dreadful effusion, "Sure it sounds terrible, but, after all, there is no other direction in which the music can *go*."

Now, I should like to state as my personal opinion, for what it is worth, that music is not *going* anywhere, and that its qualities as art are to be judged not by their conformity to some imaginary historical process but by the talent and inspiration that individual composers have put into it. The present situation is a little like the one that might obtain in the art of writing if some relentlessly knot-headed pedant, having discovered that Hemingway writes shorter sentences than Henry James did, found in this fact the basis of a great historical trend and decreed that sentences must consequently get shorter and shorter in the interest of artistic progress.

My analogy is not really so far-fetched. This is, I think, almost exactly what happened to Schoenberg and a whole generation of his followers. In a more widely understood art like literature, this sort of thing would have been laughed out of existence almost before it got started. After all, nobody speaks of "modern" literature in the sense that people have for at least thirty years spoken of "modern" music, or pretends that the technical fundamentals of the art of writing have changed, in any very radical way, since the time of Homer. But to the average listener, music is, unfortunately, a rather mysterious art, with a mathematically complicated technique, and technicians sometimes make cryptic statements about it that cannot always be checked by the nonprofessionals who form its rightful audience. Under the circumstances, it is easy for the professionals to lose touch with the ordinary communicative purposes of their art and reduce it to a sterile demonstration of some theory or other.

If you ask why I have chosen to embark on this rather elaborate and possibly boring lecture about aesthetics, I can only say that I was reminded of the problem while listening to two operatic performances last week. One of them was the American Opera Society's performance of Gluck's "Iphigénie en Tauride" at Town Hall; the other was the production of Puccini's "Tosca" at the Metropolitan Opera House. The former composition is, of course, one of the oldest works that can be considered part of the current standard repertoire, and the latter, written about a century and a quarter later, is one of the more recent universally popular operas.

There are, obviously, considerable differences between the two works, not the least of which is in the quality of their music, Gluck's being altogether magnificent and Puccini's merely deft and effective. "Iphigénie en Tauride" has the purity and formality of the best eighteenth-century opera, and "Tosca" the brutal realism and highly charged sexuality characteristic of much of the Italian opera that was written at the close of the nineteenth; from these facts, I suppose, the professors of history can draw appropriate conclusions. But despite the long lapse of time that occurred between the composition of these two operas, I can discover only a few superficial technical differences between the respective approaches of Gluck and Puccini, and I prefer to attribute these differences to the personal temperament and style of the two composers rather than to some dreary theory of musical evolution. Puccini, a sensible Italian who probably never even heard of Hegel, used the same general palette of consonance and dissonance and showed the same regard for haunting and singable melody that Gluck did, and if his "Tosca" is not the musical masterpiece that the Gluck opera is, the reason is to be found, I think, not in the technique but in the fact that Gluck was the greater genius.

"Iphigénie en Tauride," in a modest concert performance under the baton of Arnold U. Gamson, turned out, in fact, to be one of the more worth-while musical offerings of the current season, and in listening to it I wondered why it is so seldom tackled by our large opera companies. It has a great deal more dramatic interest than the same composer's more popular "Orfeo et Euridice," which I understand is shortly to be revived by the Metropolitan, and its impassioned classical melodies are as great as any that have been written. The quality of the singing the other night was not always as spectacular as it might have been, and the French enunciation of some of the cast was a little ragged. But the essentials of the drama were, on the whole, convincingly conveyed, and so were the essentials of the music. The finest performance of the evening, to my mind, was that of Leopold Simoneau, who evidently knows his French and sang the role of Pylade with elegance.

The performance accorded "Tosca" was another matter. The production was a last-minute substitute for "Aïda," which had been hastily withdrawn because of the illness of Renata Tebaldi, the scheduled Aïda, and it had had practically no rehearsal. As a result, smoothness and polish were hardly to be expected. And though the experience of the leading singers kept things going remarkably well, the dramatic side of the spectacle occasionally verged on uncontrolled hysteria. The most notable event of the evening was Zinka Milanov's first New York appearance as Tosca. I am sorry that it had to occur under such trying conditions. Miss Milanov, nevertheless, sang quite beautifully, and she acted with at least the passionate sincerity that she has brought to other roles in the past. George London, as usual, succeeded in making Scarpia into an imposing figure, and Giuseppe Campora sang suitably enough as Cavaradossi.

March 12,1955

THE BERLIN Philharmonic Orchestra appeared recently in Carnegie Hall, under the direction of the Austrian conductor Herbert von Karajan, adding another gesture to the resumption of normal musical relations between the United States and Central Europe. Whether one likes or dislikes certain other aspects of the German mentality, it is a fact that the Germans and Austrians invented the art of symphonic music, gave the world an overwhelming proportion of its masterpieces, and still retain many of the noble traditions that are a part of their proper performance. It was interesting the other night to study the effect of these traditions on the playing of an exceedingly good and quite typically German orchestra.

The Berlin Philharmonic is a somewhat different mechanism from the symphony orchestras that we are accustomed to. Its string tone is dull by American standards, possessing neither the elegant transparency of the Boston Symphony nor the glow and brilliance characteristic of the Philadelphia Orchestra, and its wind soloists lack the individual virtuosity of those in the great American orchestras. But its members have a commendable knack of subordinating themselves as parts of the total ensemble, and the over-all effect is one of extreme solidity and painstaking teamwork.

While listening, I was struck over and over again by the admirable unanimity with which the cellos, basses, and heavier brass instruments attacked their entrances, providing a grand and substantial foundation for the upper parts of the musical edifice. I also admired the exactitude and authority with which the inner voices of the various scores emerged—all of them carefully calculated and fitted into the performances with expert joinery. Here and there I noticed peculiarities that are found only in German orchestras; the first oboe had that somewhat rough, reedy quality Germans esteem in this instrument, and the brasses, as is often the case in Germany, were inclined to sacrifice suavity and brilliant articulation in favor of large and impressive tone. There is in the sound of this orchestra a certain rather agreeable ruggedness that I had not heard in a concert hall for a long time. There is also a curiously impersonal atmosphere about its playing, as if it were a huge organ, instead of an aggregation of virtuosos. Everywhere, I noticed evidences of great earnestness and absolute dedication to a common purpose. The Berlin Philharmonic may not be the most scintillating orchestra in the world, but it is, nonetheless, in its thorough and sober way, a magnificent instrument.

The program chosen for the occasion was quite conventional, and consisted—appropriately, I suppose—of the sort of music that would show off the orchestra to best advantage. Mr. von Karajan, a slim and fastidious-looking man, whose appearance on the podium reminded me of old photographs of the great Arthur Nikisch, conducted it with immaculate taste, a minimum of unnecessary motion, an obvious command of musical proportion, and a sense of dramatic climax that immediately proclaimed him an artist of the first rank. Haydn's "London" Symphony and

Beethoven's well-worn Fifth were given authoritative and vigorous readings.

To me, however, the most arresting performance of the evening was that of the Prelude and the Liebestod from Wagner's "Tristan and Isolde," which Mr. von Karajan seemed to have a special feeling for and which he conducted with an altogether extraordinary mastery of what, in the dreadfully inadequate language of music criticism, I am obliged to refer to as its long architectural lines. The enthusiasm of the audience at the close of the program was so vociferous that the Overture and Bacchanale from "Tannhäuser" were added as an encore.

HAVING HEARD Mr. von Karajan's version of the "Tristan" excerpts, several nights later I found myself at the Metropolitan listening to the entire opera, under the baton of Rudolph Kempe. I did not think Mr. Kempe's mastery of architectural line quite up to Mr. von Karajan's, but he provided a generally clear and lively rendition of the long, ponderously passionate work, which, as usual, had its moments of wonderful poetic eloquence and its moments of heavy tedium. From the vocal point of view, the evening was remarkable mainly for the excellence of the singers who undertook the lesser roles. Astrid Varnay sang the part of Isolde very energetically and with some beauty of tone but without the simplicity and grandeur required for a really great performance. Set Svanholm's Tristan was, I thought, simply inadequate. He often resorted to shouting in an effort to make himself heard over the orchestral brass, and his rather strange dramatic impersonation suggested, somehow, that he was manfully staving off an attack of epilepsy.

It is perhaps unfair to recall, in connection with this presentation, what is beginning to look like a golden age of Wagnerian opera at the Metropolitan—the period, fifteen or so years ago, when singers like Kirsten Flagstad and Lauritz Melchior and conductors like Artur Bodanzky made nearly every Wagner production an unforgettable experience. Such periods, of course, come and go in the history of the best opera houses. It may be that the present era is fairly poor in first-rank Wagnerian singers, or it may be that the Metropolitan's management, having deduced that Wagner is no longer as popular as he used to be, is picking and choosing its finest singers mainly with an eye to other parts of the repertory. In any case, the fact is that the Metropolitan's best current productions are operas by Mozart and Strauss, and certain items in the Italian and French categories, and that the Wagnerian music drama is no longer one of its strongest suits.

I do not offer this observation as a complaint. I am by no means a starry-eyed Wagnerian. Still, I think that Wagner's greatest works—and "Tristan" is surely the greatest of them all—deserve a better break than they are getting at the moment. Perhaps we shall have to await a new generation of singers, or perhaps the trouble is that history is moving on, and that the herculean machinery of Wagnerian opera has fallen out of fashion.

March 19, 1955

THERE WAS A TIME, about ten years ago, when a performance of Mozart's "Don Giovanni" at the Metropolitan Opera House was practically unthinkable without Mr. Ezio Pinza, whose magnificent voice, dashing figure, and considerable theatrical urbanity gave the title role what most people then regarded as its definitive interpretation.

Since then, by one of those unpredictable dispensations of nature that affect the world of opera much as bumper crops affect agriculture, the Metropolitan has become the possessor of an extraordinary number of good Don Giovannis—not all equal to Mr. Pinza, perhaps, but each gifted with particular virtues that have illuminated slightly different facets of this complex and difficult part. There is, for example, the carefully studied, highly conscious, and intellectual interpretation by Mr. George London, which is a pleasure to witness, partly because one can admire the deft and deliberate craftsmanship that lies behind every note and every gesture. At the opposite pole, there is the wholly intuitive, tasteful, and engaging interpretation by Mr. Cesare Siepi, which, in elegance of musical style and pure beauty of tone, sometimes surpasses, I think, even Mr. Pinza's.

Last week a brand-new Don Giovanni was added to the list

in the person of Mr. Jerome Hines, a young American basso whose admirable vocal equipment and conscientious artistry had already attracted a good deal of notice in other roles. To me, Mr. Hines' Don Giovanni was the most exciting operatic event of the week—not entirely because of what it was (although that was very good indeed) but also because of what, in the process of mellowing and polishing, it gives promise of becoming. Mr. Hines, who is in the neighborhood of six feet four and looks like an El Greco grandee, is, I imagine, one of the handsomest singers ever to undertake the role. He also has a voice of rich color and ample power, which he uses intelligently. His dramatic interpretation is as yet a bit too unrestrained and, in spots, rather self-consciously boyish for a Spanish aristocrat whose charm must not outweigh a steely streak of cynicism. His singing, too, for all the native beauty of his voice, could have been improved here and there by more fastidious attention to the subtleties of Mozart's classical phrasing. Even so, what faults his performance had were easily attributable to the conditions normally attending an underrehearsed Metropolitan début, and in listening to him I couldn't help feeling that I had possibly participated in an occasion of some historic importance. I shall watch his future appearances in the role with great interest.

The rest of the production reflected a combination of artistic gallantry and economic insufficiency that, I fear, has become fairly prevalent at the Metropolitan. As far as the quality of its cast was concerned, this was a very fine "Don Giovanni" indeed —as fine a one as you would be likely to hear at any opera house in the world. The shortcomings of the evening were due almost entirely to the absence of things that a little extra money could buy: a more impressive and less awkward set, a suit of armor for the Commendatore that would seem less in danger of succumbing to the ravages of decomposition, and more time for rehearsals, which might have smoothed out and unified the opera's action, to the immense benefit of all the characterizations, including Mr. Hines' Don Giovanni.

Still, I am often struck by what the Metropolitan manages to accomplish within the limitations of its budget. In Salzburg or Vienna, where this kind of opera is given with more polish than we are accustomed to, twenty or thirty rehearsals would very likely have preceded the production. From what I know of the Met, I am almost sure that last week's "Don Giovanni" was put on after a quick run-through in some odd attic of the old building, and with no general stage rehearsal at all.

April 2, 1955

WHEN I WENT to hear the American Opera Society's production of Claudio Monteverdi's three-hundred-year-old opera "The Coronation of Poppea," I was prepared for one of those moderately entertaining adventures in musical antiquarianism that so often seem to prove that music composed before the time of Bach is properly the affair of scholars and has little more than a remote documentary interest for present-day audiences. By the time I left, however, my evidently rather careless notion of musical history had been somewhat jolted.

"The Coronation of Poppea" is not a quaint, archaic museum piece. It is, on the contrary, as gripping a musical drama as I have ever heard, and its performance struck me as one of the most exciting operatic events of the current musical season. In listening to it, I was forced hastily to revise several misconceptions I had entertained concerning what is often referred to as "preclassical" music. Apparently, an operatic genius was at work in Venice during the first half of the seventeenth century, writing music of enormous fire and passion and wedding it to drama with a deft theatrical sense that suggests the era of Giuseppe Verdi, who, of course, lived some two hundred years later.

This ancient opera seems far more modern, for example, than the comparatively formal and stilted eighteenth-century operas of Gluck, which are usually regarded as the oldest works in the form that are fit for regular consumption today. "The Coronation of Poppea" has, in fact, very little classical formality about it. It deals with elemental emotions—jealousy, illicit love, envy, ambition—and depicts them with an intensity that I had thought was the exclusive province of the nineteenth-century romantics. Clearly, the art of laying hold of an operatic audience and forcing it to weep and shudder over the fate of believable human characters is older than I had suspected.

The amazing thing about "The Coronation of Poppea" is not so much the quality of its music—though this is everywhere strikingly noble and poetic—as the way the music underlines, and becomes an integral part of, the dramatic action. The plot concerns an incident in Roman history in which the Emperor Nero steals the wife of his friend Ottone—a conniving, passionate, and unprincipled woman named Poppea—and, despite the objections of his wise counsellor Seneca, marries her and crowns her Empress of Rome. By the time he has carried out his plan, he has caused the banishment of his legal wife, Octavia, the suicide of Seneca, and the attempted murder of Poppea by her jealous husband.

As can be seen from this sketchy outline, Monteverdi's plot is rich in the raging passions that have always been associated with effective Italian opera, and he has illuminated them with melodies and orchestral commentary that delineate uncannily the individual personalities and white-hot feelings of his protagonists. From the purely technical point of view, his score bristles with astonishing dramatic effects. Shivering tremolos and abrupt, startling transitions that one ordinarily thinks of as belonging to a far later period emphasize and give suspense to the opera's points of crisis. The moody scene in which Ottone reluctantly contemplates murdering his wife contains some magical harmonic devices that, as far as I am aware, did not appear in opera again until the late nineteenth century, and even then not with such telling effect.

One of Monteverdi's tricks of style—the use of the stark minor chord to sharpen moments of extreme dramatic tension— seemed to me particularly prophetic. A few months ago, in reviewing "The Saint of Bleecker Street," I accused Gian-Carlo Menotti of swiping this trick from Puccini, who had used it to announce the death of Mimi in "La Bohème." I guess I shall have to withdraw my accusation—at least in regard to the source of the trick. Monteverdi was curdling blood with it in 1642.

"The Coronation of Poppea" was sung in Chester Kallman's excellent English translation, and was presented in the American Opera Society's usual concert form, with the characters dressed in tailcoats and evening gowns, a proceeding that, to my mind, detracted almost nothing from its dramatic power. Arnold U. Gamson, who arranged its ancient score—quite tastefully, I thought—in a form suitable for modern instruments, conducted it with care and precision. The enunciation of the various singers was gratifyingly clear, and their singing generally very eloquent indeed. The sultry-looking Gloria Lane made a perfect Poppea, and the majestic Mariquita Moll was admirably cast as Nero's outraged wife. Donald Gramm gave the role of the brooding and frustrated Ottone just the right touch of pathos, Paul Franke did a wonderful job as the vacillating and impulsive Nero, and Chester Watson performed with great nobility as Seneca.

April 9, 1955

THE SECOND APPEARANCE here of the Berlin Philharmonic provided another opportunity to estimate the talents of its conductor, Mr. Herbert von Karajan, and I must say that I was very much impressed. In a previous review, I discussed the orchestra itself, which is a remarkably well-drilled ensemble, not quite as brilliant as some of our own when it comes to individual instrumentalists but with the admirable quality of solid and methodical craftsmanship.

For this sort of orchestra, Mr. von Karajan is, to my mind, the ideal conductor—of the scintillating, inspirational type, capable of rousing his men to white-hot bursts of enthusiasm. The weakness one expects in this kind of conductor is a tendency toward flashiness and excessive melodrama, but Mr. von Karajan seemed everywhere to be holding his gifts as a musical dynamo under the most exquisite control, and the music issued from the orchestra with great taste and refinement, as well as passion. This was, I think, particularly true of his interpretation of Tchaikovsky's Fifth Symphony, a work that has been so done to death that before I heard this performance of it, I didn't think any conductor could freshen my rather jaded attitude toward it. I was mistaken. Mr. von Karajan conducted it with a combination of virtuosity and stylistic authority that gave me an entirely new respect for its qualities as music. I have no hesitation in saying that, considered as a job of conducting, this was one of the most magnificent presentations of the symphony I have ever experienced, and I am not forgetting a number of extraordinarily fine interpretations of the same work by Arturo Toscanini.

Mr. von Karajan's conception of the score is a bit different from Mr. Toscanini's. It is lusher, a little slower in some of the tempos, less icy and glittering, and generally more elastic. The handling of Tchaikovsky's singing melodies was extremely dashing, and at the same time had not a trace of vulgarity, and the inner lacework of the orchestration was crystal clear and balanced with the utmost discretion. I could have asked for a slightly more elegant performance of some of the wind solos—notably that of the first horn in the second movement—but such a lapse from absolute perfection was the fault of the orchestra, not of Mr. von Karajan.

The remainder of the program was done with the same care and spirit. It consisted of Beethoven's "Leonore" Overture No. 3, in which I especially admired the orchestra's dry, understated pianissimos, providing wonderful contrasts to the moments of climax, and two compositions by contemporary composers. Of these, I thoroughly enjoyed Samuel Barber's now fairly familiar

Adagio for Strings, one of the very few works by a modern American that I think can be regarded as masterpieces of their kind. The Concertante Music for Orchestra, by the Baltic-German composer Boris Blacher, struck me rather differently. It seemed an amusing showpiece, full of deft tricks of rhythm and somewhat Stravinskian in style. But despite a dazzling rendition, I could discover almost nothing in it except clever artifice.

April 16, 1955

It was inevitable, I suppose, that somebody should eventually write a book like Henry Pleasants' "The Agony of Modern Music." The situation it describes is a crucial one, and though I cannot bring myself to agree with all its conclusions, I think that a good deal of what it has to say badly needed saying. It is an exuberantly violent book, and has already caused considerable controversy in the daily press and on the radio, some of it apparently over the rather drastic question of whether the "modern" composer or Mr. Pleasants should drop dead. In my opinion, the heat of this controversy has tended to obscure a somewhat gentler issue; namely, that it might be a good idea for contemporary composers to reëxamine the nature and purpose of their art, and to pay a little more attention to the needs and tastes of the audience for which they are presumably writing.

Mr. Pleasants himself is, I think, responsible for the bitterness of the controversy, since he has stated his case as if it were an inexorable historical truth. His premise can be simply outlined: The phenomenon known as "modern music" is neither modern nor musically significant. The contemporary composer, being out of touch with the musical appetites of the contemporary audience, is in a hopeless position, and is merely seeking to perpetuate for his own glorification a musical tradition whose technical resources have been exhausted and which no longer has any cultural validity. He is, in fact, obsolete, and his place in modern society has long since been appropriated by the jazz band and the popular tunesmith. Important music, as Mr. Pleasants demonstrates at some length, and quite convincingly, has always been immensely popular in its own time. The "modern" composer is not popular; therefore his music is not important.

I cannot quite accept Mr. Pleasants' notion that immediate popularity is today the sole criterion of artistic importance, since by that criterion one could obviously arrive at the conclusion that, say, the *News* is more important literature than the work of our more thoughtful novelists. I cannot agree, either, that the cultivated listener who has developed a taste for symphonic or operatic music is likely to find a modern substitute for it in the arts of Dizzy Gillespie and Irving Berlin—two entirely different arts, by the way, each of which I find ingratiating enough, but both of which seem to me to lack the emotional vocabulary and intellectual ingenuity that the experienced concertgoer looks for in serious music.

Nevertheless, it *is* true, I believe, that popular music today shows a freshness and inspiration that are conspicuously lacking in the product of our high-brow composers, that items like Jerome Kern's "Show Boat" and George Gershwin's "Porgy and Bess" are far more significant works of art than most of the serious operas that are being turned out nowadays, and that the art of musical composition as practiced by its more "advanced" exponents has shown certain alarming symptoms of illness for more than a generation. As Mr. Pleasants says, the "modern" composer has lost the cordial contact with his audience that the great composers of the past had. He has often forgotten the communicative purpose of his art in the pursuit of obscure technical games played largely for his own benefit or that of his professional colleagues. He has expressed himself mainly in two idioms that are now pretty threadbare—neoclassicism, which is merely a process of arranging fanciful mosaics out of bits and pieces borrowed from older and more vigorous styles, and atonality, a technique that is surrounded with no end of cryptic theoretical jargon but in practice is about as complicated and artistically rewarding as dominoes. The trouble with atonality, by the way, is not, as even Mr. Pleasants seems to think, that it is mysterious or difficult to understand but simply that it is boring.

Arriving in the midst of this rather depressing spectacle, "The Agony of Modern Music" may, I think, serve as a valuable corrective. But I detect in Mr. Pleasants' reasoning a good deal of that blind, deterministic thought, derived originally from Georg Wilhelm Friedrich Hegel, that has been the curse of the very music Mr. Pleasants is attacking. He continually expresses himself in such phrases as "the historical course of music," "the exhaustion of resources," "evolutionary factors," "an art in progress," all of which make me suspect that he, like the atonalists, thinks of music not as the product of free, individual composers but as a sort of uniform substance emerging from some historical sausage grinder entirely in accordance with the laws of sociological

Zeitgeist. It is this attitude, it seems to me, that leads him to the fairly absurd conclusion that the contemporary composer is done for.

In my opinion, the prevalent notion that the musical art is the result of social forces and is under some pressing necessity to progress or evolve is precisely what is wrong with "modern" music, for it has deprived the contemporary composer of his individuality as an artist. The great fallacy in these Hegelian theories is that they assume that music is composed by society, or by processes of technical evolution, when the simple and obvious fact is that it is composed by composers. Thus, I am afraid I cannot give any more credence to Mr. Pleasants' idea that the contemporary composer is doomed to become obsolete than I can to the atonalist's idea that he is doomed to write atonality.

When one is told that music as an intellectual art form is going to pot, one has a right to ask "What music?," for there is, in reality, no single evolving organism called music. I can distinguish, for example, two quite independent traditions in the history of music over the past century or so, and there are doubtless others. The first is the symphonic tradition, a Germanic invention, which started with Haydn, and did for a time seem to show certain evolutionary tendencies—or at least certain tendencies toward increasing complexity—and appears at the moment to have stopped developing technically. The second is the hardy Italian opera tradition, which has never exhibited any evolutionary tendencies whatever, has expressed itself in masterpieces ever since the time of Monteverdi, and is still alive and kicking in the work of composers like Gian-Carlo Menotti, who writes in an idiom that hasn't changed much in three hundred years.

I can't help feeling that the solution to the contemporay composer's problem lies simply in ceasing to be the slave of dubious evolutionary theories and writing what he wants to write instead of what he imagines history expects of him. By this elementary expedient, he might well succeed in outfoxing Mr. Pleasants and his gloomy predictions.

April 30, 1955

SINCE, as the saying goes, the world is shrinking these days, I suppose it is natural that we should be getting better acquainted with the musical arts of cultures other than our own—arts that seem to differ from each other much as languages do. Unlike some of the others, the one practiced by the inhabitants of India evidently possesses those characteristics of intellectual complexity and emotional richness that we associate with art, as distinct from folk music.

I have, from time to time, heard and admired the playing of Indian musicians, both here and in India, but I have never before encountered quite the degree of virtuosity in this idiom that was displayed at the Museum of Modern Art last week by two superb Indian artists, Mr. Ali Akbar Khan and Mr. Chatur Lal, who had come to this country, at the invitation of Yehudi Menuhin—apparently something of an expert on these matters—to

participate in the Museum's current series of events entitled
"The Living Arts of India." Mr. Khan is a performer on the
sarod, a stringed instrument of beautiful design that is plucked
according to a highly intricate technique, and Mr. Lal is a drum-
mer who plays on remarkably expressive instruments known as
tabla. Mr. Khan's art, since his instrument is a melodic one,
draws upon that rich vocabulary of different scales that the
Hindus know as *ragas,* while Mr. Lal is concerned mainly with
the infinite complexities of *tala,* or rhythm. I found their music
endlessly fascinating from a technical point of view and curiously hypnotic in its emotional effect.

In listening to music of this unfamiliar sort, one's first impression is apt to be that it is mere exoticism. One is struck by its
great differences from our own; one is lulled by its distinctive
"Oriental" flavor; and one conjures up all sorts of tropical and
picturesque associations, which, I am sure, never occur to those
who make it or who understand it thoroughly. With further
acquaintance, one passes on to a second stage—an interest in its
abstract form. Having heard some of it previously and read a
few books about it, I found myself able, in a modest way, to
enter this second stage, and to follow—by thumping my hand
against my knee, so that I shouldn't get lost—some of the chains
of astonishing syncopation that Mr. Khan and Mr. Lal produced.
These syncopations are not entirely unlike those used in jazz,
but they are related to those of jazz much as higher mathematics
is related to elementary arithmetic.

As I listened, I found myself drawn into an exhilarating rhythmic game, in which I could identify myself now with Mr. Khan
and now with Mr. Lal in their joyful efforts to unhorse each
other by the sheer power of rhythmic imagination and intelligence. In their second number, a very complicated item im-
provised in what seemed to me to be fourteen-quarter time, I got
unhorsed myself and had to give up thumping my hand against

my knee. But Mr. Khan and Mr. Lal went right on expressing themselves in mathematical subtleties, which by this time were entirely outside my comprehension.

I am sure that, beyond all this, there is a third stage in the appreciation of Indian music—one in which the listener is able to grasp the emotional suggestions and associations that it has for the Indians. But I am equally sure that this stage is attainable only by those who have been in contact with it for many years and have learned it much as one would learn a foreign language. I could, however, discern even from my limited knowledge of the subject that the art in which these two Indian musicians were expressing themselves follows elaborate laws of structural logic that are found only in music of a highly developed and civilized sort.

SEVERAL WEEKS AGO, in reviewing a concert by the Berlin Philharmonic, I felt impelled to compare, at some length, Mr. Herbert von Karajan's conception of Tchaikovsky's Fifth Symphony with that of Arturo Toscanini. I made reference to "a number of extraordinarily fine interpretations" that Mr. Toscanini had given the work and noted several subtle distinctions between his reading and Mr. von Karajan's, pointing out that Mr. von Karajan's was "lusher, a little slower in some of the tempos, less icy and glittering, and generally more elastic."

Since this review appeared, I have received a number of letters respectfully requesting further information about these performances and expressing surprise that Mr. Toscanini had conducted the work. A little subsequent checking on my part revealed that he has never conducted it in his life. This fact, as you can imagine, was considerably disconcerting to me, especially in view of the fine adjectives and the ring of authority that my review contained.

Well, all I can say is that if Toscanini ever *had* conducted Tchaikovsky's Fifth, the characteristics of his performances and their points of differences from Mr. von Karajan's would have been precisely as I described them. Moreover, on reading what I wrote I find that, aside from the fact that these performances by Mr. Toscanini never took place, my description of them was quite perceptive.

SEASON OF 1955-1956

October 15, 1955

THE RUSSIAN PIANIST Emil Gilels created considerable excitement when the Philadelphia Orchestra, under Eugene Ormandy, brought him to town as the soloist of its first local concert this season. Much of this excitement was unquestionably owing to Mr. Gilels' reputation as the leading pianist of the Soviet Union and to the obvious fact that many members of his audience were anxious to welcome the breach in the cultural Iron Curtain that had permitted a Soviet artist to visit us for the first time in more than three decades. I found myself sharing in the excitement, for I, too, felt a degree of satisfaction in the breaking down of long-standing cultural barriers, and I was much interested in finding out something about the quality and character of musical performance as it now exists in Russia.

Mr. Gilels, a short, stocky, boyish-looking man with a thick mop of reddish hair, sat down at the piano and hurled himself into Tchaikovsky's B-Flat-Minor Piano Concerto with businesslike solemnity. From the very first notes, it was evident that he is a pianist of extraordinary muscularity, with the temperament of a robust and dashing virtuoso and with technical resources that, from the purely mechanical point of view, seem inexhausti- ble. His tone is large and powerful when power is called for, his octave passages are remarkably smooth, and his rapid fingerwork is steely and brilliant. If vigor were the sole measure of artistry, Mr. Gilels would, I think, rank very high among contemporary pianists.

Having noted these virtues, however, I was conscious of cer- tain defects that leave Mr. Gilels somewhat short of what I ex- pect a really great performer to be. His thundering fortissimos, though impressively loud, occasionally involved mere pounding; his indiscriminate use of the pedal often obscured the clarity of the dazzling cascades of sound that he drew from his instrument; and his breakneck approach, though exhilarating, tended to dis- tort some of the concerto's just proportions. Moreover, when Mr. Gilels reached the lyric melodies of the slow movement, his playing seemed to me simply rhetorical, rather than tender and poetic.

Mr. Gilels is, to my mind, a virtuoso of sensational physical gifts, and there was something quite pleasant about the hearty exuberance and the absence of preciousness with which he tackled his task. I do not, however, find him a particularly pol- ished artist or a musical interpreter of any notable subtley. These impressions were confirmed when he played a Bach-Siloti Choral Prelude as an encore. Here, deprived of the opportuni- ties for heroic display that the Tchaikovsky work had provided, and facing music of a restrained, classical sort, he seemed, for the moment, a fairly ordinary pianist. Mr. Ormandy and the orchestra gave him superb accompaniment in the concerto, and preceded his appearance with excellent performances of Bee- thoven's "Fidelio" Overture and Brahms' First Symphony.

October 29, 1955

WILLIAM WALTON'S opera "Troilus and Cressida," which recently was given its first local performance by the New York City Opera, is a fairly monumental work by a man who is, of course, one of the most respected of contemporary British composers. Its music is intricate and of considerable technical interest. Its story, which, I am told, derives, with certain modifications, from Geoffrey Chaucer's poem of the same title, is a dignified mythological tale of two hapless lovers separated by the Trojan War, and reunited under conditions that make the consummation of their love impossible and their deaths a tragic foregone conclusion. Throughout the narrative of their troubles, various lesser characters contribute to the events that inevitably lead to this conclusion, and the drama, despite its Greek and medieval origins, has an air of the Elizabethan about it.

The production was, on the whole, an excellent one. The scenery, by John Boyt, was extraordinarily tasteful and handsome, especially in the second act; the staging, by Margaret Webster, was always effective and sometimes quite gripping; and the complex choral and instrumental ingredients were admirably handled by Joseph Rosenstock, who presided in the orchestra pit. All in all, the performance should have added up

to an occasion of some historic importance, and the large audience, containing a substantial sprinkling of people who might be
called celebrities for one reason or another, that was on hand to
greet it was in an obviously anticipatory mood. To my mind,
however, "Troilus and Cressida" somehow failed to convey the
passion that would have fused its sterling components into a
really moving work of art, and I think that this failure can be
attributed mainly to the nature of Walton's music, though the
interminable wordiness of the libretto may have had something
to do with it, too.

The music, during long, long stretches, is written in the somewhat barbaric and exotic style that first came to my attention a
decade or so ago in the same composer's rather arresting cantata
"Belshazzar's Feast," and, although it is music that expresses
energy and tension well enough, I find it lacking in lyricism.
Here and there, on the other hand, Walton does introduce a
lyric note in a style strongly reminiscent of Wagner and Strauss,
and the points at which he does so are to me the most moving
and vocally rewarding ones in the entire opera. These points,
however, are rather few and far between, and the rest of the
score seems to me fairly blunt and noisy.

I could discern only a few passages in which "Troilus and
Cressida" really got off the ground into the realm of poetic magic,
and they all had touches of Wagnerian and Straussian style.
One of them was Cressida's aria in the second act, as she pre-
pares to retire for the night and thinks longingly of her absent
lover. Another was the farewell duet between Troilus and Cressida, at the close of the same act. Still another was the quite
touching moment of Troilus's death, shortly before the final curtain. In these passages, Walton seemed to have succeeded in
getting inside his characters and making their emotions those of
real and believable human beings.

Elsewhere, such emotion as the work contained appeared to

be in the nature of a detached commentary, only indirectly related to what was going on in the minds of the protagonists. To
sum up these rather scattered impressions, I came to the conclusion that "Troilus and Cressida" is an interesting composition
and, in fact, one of the most distinguished ventures into opera
that have recently been attempted. But its power over an audience seems intermittent, and I am afraid that I cannot foresee for
it a long, successful career.

In the work of the individual members of the cast, I found
some things to admire and others to cavil at. Phyllis Curtin, as
Cressida, was a handsome and affecting figure, but her enunciation occasionally left me baffled as to what she was singing about.
Jon Crain was a loud, energetic, and generally acceptable Troilus. Norman Kelley sang the role of Pandarus—a peculiar affair,
whose endless excursions into falsetto coloratura are apparently
intended as comic relief but in the long run take on the quality
of an irritating mannerism—about as well as anyone could. The
best singing of the evening, to my mind, was provided by Lawrence Winters, as Diomede, Prince of Argos. At least, I could
understand Mr. Winters' lines, and his vocal and dramatic tasks
were performed with dignity and vigor.

November 5, 1955

DURING THE PAST couple of seasons, New York concertgoers have been privileged to hear a number of fine European symphony orchestras, including the Amsterdam Concertgebouw and the Berlin Philharmonic, whose admirable qualities have suggested interesting comparisons with our own orchestras. None of them, however, has made an impression on me quite comparable to that created by the Philharmonia Orchestra of London, which came to town for the first of three concerts under the baton of Herbert von Karajan.

From the very first notes of Mozart's Divertimento No. 15 in B Flat (K. 287), which opened the program, it was obvious that the Philharmonia is an ensemble of the utmost brilliance, beautifully balanced in all its components and capable of a degree of virtuosity equal to, and at times surpassing, that attained by the finest symphonic organizations we have heard hereabouts in the past. Unlike most of our own foremost orchestras, which are more or less international aggregations of players, with sprinklings of artists from many parts of Continental Europe, it consists almost entirely of born and bred Britishers, and this surprised me somewhat, for I had never thought of virtuoso orchestra playing as a typically English pursuit, although, to be sure, I have heard some very remarkable English symphonic musicians from time to time.

The most impressive thing about the Philharmonia is the scrupulous clarity of its performances—a clarity so transparent and revealing that in the Mozart Divertimento and the reading of Debussy's "La Mer" that followed it I managed to hear a considerable amount of microscopic detail that often eludes me. The orchestra's strings perhaps lack the plushy, glamorous tone characteristic of these sections in some of our own most admired ensembles, but they have a sensitivity that our high-powered string choirs only rarely attain, and their palette of tone color is extremely varied, ranging from lucid fortissimos to a sort of dry, understated pianissimo that seems to be a specialty of European, as opposed to American, orchestras. The wind instruments in the Philharmonia are played with exceptional precision and elegance of style, and here the work of certain individual artists attracts special attention.

The most arresting of these is unquestionably the first horn player, Mr. Dennis Brain. An incomparable master of his difficult instrument, he plays his notes not only with faultless accuracy but with an aristocratic sense of musical phraseology that might be the envy of many a concert violinist or pianist. And there are other very distinguished craftsmen among the wind players, too. Mr. Gareth Morris, the first flutist, achieves a tone of altogether unusual richness, owing partly, I think, to the fact that he plays a wooden flute, instead of the more glittering but less expressive metal one we are accustomed to. Mr. Sidney Sutcliffe, the first oboist, can produce some of the most spectacular pianissimos I have ever heard from this instrument, and the sound he attains in the louder passages is gratifyingly reedy. Mr. Bernard Walton, the first clarinettist, is also a superb performer, and, indeed, so are the rest of the first-chair men, all the way down the line to the trumpets and trombones. The Philharmonia is evidently the product of a highly fastidious process of selection, and whoever put it together—whether Mr. von Karajan or Mr. Walter Legge, the prominent British record manufacturer who is the orchestra's backer and artistic director, or, very likely, both, in collaboration—has, I think, matched his players as deftly as a jeweller might match the diamonds in a royal tiara.

In conducting this extraordinary group of musicians, Mr. von Karajan disclosed a painstaking and rather objective approach that seemed to me to be quite a contrast to his fiery and impassioned work at the head of the Berlin Philharmonic when it visited us last season. Perhaps the difference in approach is attributable to the character of the music he chose to present, which on this occasion, apart from the Mozart item, was intellectual, sensuously complicated, and otherwise typically French, rather than exuberantly German or Russian, like the works he selected for his most memorable performances last year.

In any event, the conductor demonstrated a different aspect of his artistic personality, and showed that he is a consummate master of classical grace and restraint as well as a thundering pyrotechnician. His readings of Debussy's "La Mer" and Berlioz's "Fantastic Symphony" have perhaps been surpassed in fluency and dynamism here by such conductors as Toscanini and Koussevitsky, but Mr. von Karajan's nevertheless had qualities of poise and insight that bespoke a musical mind of the highest type. Indeed, Mr. von Karajan is, I think, one of the very few really exciting figures in the present generation of symphonic maestros, and I shall look forward to his future visits with more than ordinary interest.

November 19, 1955

THERE IS AN atmosphere of dedication about the performances of the American Opera Society in Town Hall that, to my mind, makes nearly every one of them an exciting and highly rewarding musical occasion. Mr. Arnold U. Gamson, who presides over them, is perhaps not the most brilliant conductor hereabouts, but he obviously rehearses his singers and the members of his orchestra within an inch of their lives, and he has a very pleasant faculty for subordinating his own personality to the task of conveying the meaning and style of the music he interprets. His singers and his orchestra, although they, too, occasionally disclose limitations of one sort or another, do not seem to be merely carrying out a job. They bring to each of the Society's productions the utmost they are capable of in technique and artistry, and sometimes this is a great deal.

Every season, the operatic works the group presents are chosen with notable intelligence, each one being well adapted to the method of concert performance the Society specializes in, and each one constituting a new and very unusual adventure in a field quite separate from that traversed year in and year out by the routine undertakings of our larger opera companies. Moreover, the audience that attends these productions is among the

most responsive and musically sophisticated audiences to be
found in Manhattan at the moment. It arrives at the hall braced
for something out of the ordinary, and, thanks to the unremitting zeal of Mr. Gamson and his associates, it nearly always
gets it.

Last week, this admirable organization presented what was, as
far as is known, the first American performance of "Medea," an
opera by Maria Luigi Carlo Zenobio Cherubini, and it turned
out to be of considerably more interest than might have been
assumed by those people (among them me) to whom its composer is chiefly known as a name in the books of musical history.
Cherubini, in case you have forgotten, was a contemporary and
friend of Beethoven; he was an academician of some stature (he
headed the Paris Conservatoire for many years, during which he
taught counterpoint to Hector Berlioz, among others), and a
formidable composer of operas, which brought him international
renown, at least in their time. His "Medea" lacks the easy
melodic fluency of some operas of its period, but in its treatment
of classical mythology it has a consistent nobility of style and a
sort of formal grandeur that suggest a comparison with the paintings of Jacques Louis David, who was active at the time it was
written. It tells the story of its vengeful and wildly passionate
heroine with a dignity and reserve that the Greeks themselves
might have admired, and in doing so it provides its central character with one of the most monumental and taxing roles ever
written for the soprano voice.

In negotiating this role, Eileen Farrell, an artist whose work
with various orchestras here I have admired in the past, sang
with a combination of dramatic sincerity, limitless physical resourcefulness, vocal agility, and controlled classical phrasing that
I have rarely heard equalled anywhere, and I shall remember
her performance as one of the most stunning vocal feats that
have come to my attention in many seasons. I hope that some

provision was made to record it, since singing of this sort—involving power and communicative warmth tempered by exquisite workmanship—is becoming a very unusual thing nowadays. The remainder of the cast was not quite up to the sensational standard set by Miss Farrell, but it nevertheless sang with scrupulousness and spirit.

December 3, 1955

AFTER HEARING two recitals by the Russian violinist David Oistrakh, I have arrived at the conclusion that he is the finest performer on the violin to come to light in the generation or so during which I have been listening to it. This conclusion is not the result of unrestrained enthusiasm—an emotion that violin recitals have long ceased to arouse in me. It is the result of a detached and sober analysis of the way Mr. Oistrakh plays the fiddle, and from a comparison of his artistry with that of other violinists who have recently appeared hereabouts. Roughly, Mr. Oistrakh's preëminence can be said to arise from a combination of two qualities that, in my experience, are seldom found in the same performer. One of these is limitless mechanical virtuosity—

something that, taken by itself, is almost a commonplace in the present-day concert hall. The other is the ability to make a violin the servant of a discerning musical intelligence—something that I find very rare indeed.

The two programs in which Mr. Oistrakh exhibited these admirable qualities consisted, for the most part, of some of the less frequently played and less showy items in the violin repertory, and I regret that we have not yet had the privilege of hearing him in one of the major violin concertos. The works he performed included several—like Beethoven's First Sonata for Violin and Piano, and Brahms' Third Sonata—that are at once totally devoid of opportunities for technical display and full of artistic pitfalls for any but the most musically sensitive performers. Only in the Tartini "Devil's Trill" Sonata, Prokofieff's brilliant Second Sonata, and a few shorter pieces did Mr. Oistrakh permit himself the luxury of unleashing his pyrotechnical powers, which turned out to be astonishing enough. The rest of the time, he occupied himself, in a remarkably self-effacing manner, with conveying the intricate musical substance of what he was playing. Nowhere did he seem, as most violinists do, to lose his bearings and wallow in mere tone or mere facility. He was at every moment in complete command of his instrument and of every phraseological subtlety of the music, and each composition emerged from beneath his fingers and his bow with a distinct style appropriate to its nature.

In mentioning tone in connection with Mr. Oistrakh's playing, one needs a different conception of the quality from the one ordinarily connoted by the word. To say that a violinist has a beautiful tone is very much like saying that an athlete has wonderful muscles. One's interest is not in his possession of the gift but what he does with it. Mr. Oistrakh's tone is as lush and sensuous as that of any living violinist when he wishes to make it so. On the other hand, when lushness is not called for, he has a whole palette of other acoustical colorings, ranging from absolute dryness to soft, poetic limpidity, and he uses it with extraordinary fastidiousness to express every degree of emphasis called for by the melodic contour of what he is performing. It is very unusual nowadays for a violinist to neglect the use of vibrato deliberately, for the sake of a point of musical good taste, and when this occurs—as it did in Mr. Oistrakh's playing—one is aware that the performer's mind is at work, as well as his fingers. There were other things about Mr. Oistrakh's playing that impressed me, too. He has a solid robustness in his approach to the violin that agreeably supplements his sensitivity. His left hand is amazingly swift and accurate. He has a noble intellectual comprehension of the elements of proportion and climax that make up the dramatic continuity of a composition. Altogether, as you may have gathered, I think Mr. Oistrakh is a great artist.

December 10, 1955

EVER SINCE 1913, when the Italian futurist Luigi Russolo propounded what might be called the theory of absolute musical materialism—a theory which holds, among other things, that mu-

sic consists of sound, that sound is scientifically indistinguishable
from noise, and that the future of the art of composition therefore lies in the invention of more, bigger, and better noises—a
small but valiant band of composers has been doggedly following his line of reasoning. The theory was somewhat more popular with the avant-garde musical public in the twenties and the
early thirties than it is today, and in its time it produced such
astounding musical curiosities as "The Iron Foundry," by Alexander Mossolov, a Soviet composer presumably liquidated later
on in accordance with the Kremlin's subsequently conservative
aesthetic line; using the rather imperfect resources of a symphony
orchestra, he managed to imitate with considerable exactitude
the sounds emitted by heavy industry in action.

Popular or not, Russolo's notion, in its various ramifications,
still claims adherents, and by far the most prominent and uncom-
promising of them is the Franco-American composer Edgar
Varèse. That Mr. Varèse has gone way beyond anything
dreamed of by such primitives as Mossolov was demonstrated
last week, in the first New York performance of his "Deserts,"
which, according to the program, is scored for "woodwind, brass,
and percussion ensemble with interpolations of organized sound
on tape stereophonically transmitted on two channels. Ampex
Model 350-2."

Mr. Varèse's composition, which lasts about half an hour,
sounded—and in describing it I am striving for precision, not
humor—like what might be heard in the switching area of a vast
railroad yard during an incessant wartime bombardment. I was
much impressed by the composer's ingenuity, but I couldn't help
noting that, for his purposes—which involved the creation of an
extraordinary variety of screeching, tooting, clanging, explosive,
and other nerve-shattering acoustical effects—the two stereo-
phonic transmitters that he employed in solo roles were far more
efficient than the human instrumentalists who accompanied

them. This clearly indicated to me that Mr. Varèse's next logical step is the total elimination of human performers, a step that would remove his activities from the concert hall, thus finally freeing him from music and music from him—on second thought, not a bad idea for everybody concerned.

The occasion on which this composition of Mr. Varèse's was performed—something sponsored by an organization called Camera Concerts—had, on the whole, a rather quaint period atmosphere that reminded me very much of countless concerts of "advanced" music I attended immediately following the First World War. There was the same eager gathering of vociferous aesthetes, and there was the same mingling of fervent applause and angry boos. Mr. Varèse's effort was preceded by an item entitled "In Memoriam Dylan Thomas," by Igor Stravinsky, written for four trombones, string quartet, and tenor voice. It, too, recalled the twenties, and I must say that I have never heard a more fumbling and wheezing bit of musical artifice dedicated to a worthy commemorative purpose.

The concert ended with Arnold Schoenberg's "Pierrot Lunaire," a composition that actually dates from just before the First World War and is, of course, commonly regarded as one of the great pioneering triumphs of the atonal school. I stayed to listen to it because it is a composition that I once got excited over, and I was anxious to see how it would strike me after all these years. I am afraid I now find the hysterical declamation involved in its solo rule—recited in this case by a soprano named Bethany Beardslee—to be in pretty bad taste, and the work as a whole extremely boring.

December 17, 1955

THE PART OF Tosca exists in the minds of most confirmed opera-goers as a composite of the vocal gifts, dramatic mannerisms, and personalities of many singers who have, with a greater or lesser degree of success, approached the archetype that it embodies. The role itself—that of a proud, jealous, petulant, strong-willed, but essentially tenderhearted and upright woman whose outraged instincts lead her to commit murder—has a way of transcending the melodrama and the music that surround it. As you know, it is the joint creation of Victorien Sardou, a playwright whose deftly contrived and rather overemotional plots have long since ceased to attract the attention of the legitimate theatre, and Puccini, whose music for this opera is at times somewhat coarse but whose dramatic craftsmanship and intuition in feminine portraiture always amounted to genius. Thus, while "Tosca," the opera, is mostly blood and thunder, Tosca, the character, has a certain authentic grandeur, and in some ways constitutes more than what is ordinarily thought of as an operatic role. One can say that it is sung or acted well or badly and still miss the real point, because singing and acting are only part of what a great diva brings to a great Tosca.

Above all, Tosca is a personality—an extremely dominating and affecting one—and the finest interpreters of the role have always had the peculiar faculty of convincing you, at the mo-

ment, that they *are* the passionate woman they depict, a faculty
that may or may not be directly related to such things as vocal
beauty and histrionic elegance. The special requirements of the
role account for the fact that there are so few great Toscas, and
explain why many an otherwise magnificent artist (I remember
Lotte Lehmann in particular) has fallen flat in tackling this
opera.

In listening to Renata Tebaldi's Tosca I was reminded, as
many others in the audience were, too, of several of her great
predecessors, some of whom, like Geraldine Farrar and Maria
Jeritza, were admirable singers, and all of whom were extraordinary theatrical personalities. The comparisons I made at the outset were unfavorable to Miss Tebaldi. Her first act, in fact,
struck me as rather tepid and cursory. I must say, however, that
by the end of the second act, I was in a mood to shout approval,
as those about me were doing. Miss Tebaldi had succeeded in
seizing the stage with the flamboyant and uninhibited fervor
that a fine Tosca must have; she looked very handsome, and she
sang with enormous conviction. It was obvious to me at this
point that the ups and down of operatic history had again presented us with a major figure capable of giving the role its due.

The remainder of the cast was in every way up to the standard
set by Miss Tebaldi, and the performance as a whole was as
stunning a one as you are likely to encounter nowadays at the
Metropolitan—or, indeed, anywhere else. Richard Tucker was a
superb Cavaradossi, and Leonard Warren sang beautifully as
Scarpia, a role whose calculated sadism is not exactly native to
his rather benign temperament but which he managed to make
quite persuasive. On the dramatic side, my only serious criticism
relates to the scenery, designed by Frederick Fox; the first-act set
was so cluttered and cramping that it deprived the proceedings
of the air of spectacular pageantry with which this act should
close.

Musically, the performance was a particularly fortunate one, and a great deal of the credit for its unusual bounce and vitality was due to the frenzied enthusiasm with which Dimitri Mitropoulos conducted it. I have already had my say, earlier this season, about some of his shortcomings as an interpreter of symphonic classics. Restraint, serenity, and lyricism are not among his virutes, and in the one lighthearted moment that "Tosca" contains, the humorous interlude involving the sacristan and the choirboys in the first act, his pacing was so furious and hard-driving that one of the opera's great contrasts—the sudden appearance of Scarpia's sinister figure—was completely lost. However, Mr. Mitropoulos is a conductor of notable energy, and "Tosca" is a notably energetic opera. The orchestra played for him as if its life was at stake, and, apart from a few lapses like the one I have described, the result was nothing short of brilliant.

January 14, 1956

DURING THE PAST WEEK, no new work by a contemporary American composer appeared on the program of any of Manhattan's principal concert halls. This fact does not make the week unusual, but I am afraid it does reflect a trend in public taste that has been noticeable thus far this season and that strikes me as distinctly unhealthy. Two aspects of this situation seem to me alarming: first, that the number of performances given over to compositions by young Americans is dwindling, and, second, that such new American works as we have lately been privileged to hear have tended to be restricted to two somewhat limited schools of composing. One is the atonal school and the other is what might be called the *Société des Elèves de Nadia Boulanger,* a group whose musical thinking derives, for better or for worse, from that eminent and influential Parisian pedagogue, and includes Aaron Copland, Walter Piston, Roy Harris, and their numerous imitators and pupils, among them William Schuman, president of the Juilliard School of Music, our most noted institution for musical education.

Both these groups—or schools of composition—have been around for a long time, and their members have now achieved the status of hoary academicians. Considered as individual artists, some of them have their points, but considered as exponents of musical doctrine they represent traditions that have become extremely repetitious and have not progressed in matters of technique for thirty or forty years. It is a pity, I think, that on the rare occasions when American music is performed at all, our concert programs should be so heavily weighted in favor of these groups. Somewhere there must be a younger generation ready to revolt against them as they themselves revolted against the traditions of such old-time American composers as Henry Hadley and Daniel Gregory Mason, just after the First World War. The tragedy is that we are not at present likely to recognize the works of any such younger generation, for the simple reason that we are not likely to hear them.

I cannot bring myself to place the entire blame for this situation on the apathy of concert audiences. Our concert audiences are, in general, remarkably patient, and during the past twenty years or so have listened dutifully to a colossal amount of American creative endeavor that is of no conceivable interest to any intelligent music lover. Now they appear to be tired of performing this duty, having found it so frequently unrewarding, and are in a mood to content themselves with listening to endless repetitions of well-worn classics. I can't believe, however, that they have completely lost their appetite for new music with emotional content and vitality. And I am sure that such music exists. The problem is to find it, and the solution of the problem rests, of course, with the conductors and other performing artists who put our programs together.

Since I am being rather pontifical about this business, I may as well explain what kind of new music I should like to hear. The requirements I have in mind are not really very difficult to meet, or very different from those often met in other arts. I should like to hear music that conveys some sort of genuine emotional experience, and does so simply and unabashedly— music that is free of self-conscious formulas and tricks of stylistic sleight of hand. It should, above all, communicate something, even if what it has to communicate is not strikingly original. I have long since given up looking for the fulfillment of these requirements either in the work of the atonalists, which to my mind consists entirely of formulas (awfully old ones at that), or in the work of Mme. Boulanger's ubiquitous disciples, who seem always to have subordinated emotional content to tricks of style and, in their anxiety to avoid the clichés of Romantic music, only to have replaced them with a set of modernistic clichés of their own.

Occasionally, in my rounds as a critic, I come across what I am looking for. I find it in the operas of Gian-Carlo Menotti, a craftsman whose deep understanding of the technique of a great art has been given expression in works that, though not staggeringly original, are undoubtedly communicative. I find it in Samuel Barber's Adagio for Strings, a composition that, because of its simplicity and avoidance of mere cleverness, has already become an American classic. I find it in Paul Creston's Second Symphony. Last spring, while attending an out-of-town music festival, I was rather surprised to find it in a work called "Prelude and Quadruple Fugue," by Alan Hovhaness, a composer whose eclectic mannerisms frequently bore me to death but who in this particular composition seems to have created something of really arresting freshness. I am sure that there is a great deal of music of this sort lying unperformed in the studios of today's composers, and I believe that young composers should be encouraged to write more of it, thus asserting themselves against the powers that seem to be dictating musical fashion. They have nothing to lose but their twelve-tone scales and their *Boulangerie.*

January 28, 1956

IN THE THIRTY YEARS or so during which I have been listening to symphony concerts, the virtuoso conductor has occupied an unrivalled position as the most glamorous figure in the musical world. A glance at the history books will show that this was not always the case; in fact, it was not until the late nineteenth century, when celebrated maestros like Hans von Bülow came along, that anyone paid much attention to conductors or thought of their métier as having the dignity of a specialized art. Today, however, the symphonic conductor outranks even the operatic prima donna in his hold over the romantic emotions of the public, and many people go to symphony concerts not only to hear the music but to watch the great man on the podium while he performs his more or less mysterious rites.

I am not, at the moment, in a mood to object to this curious development in musical mores. Great conductors have occasionally thrilled me, too. But I should like to point out that since the conductor does occupy this resplendent position and is, as a rule, the focus of the concertgoers' eyes, the purely visual impression he makes has become one of the inescapable ingredients of a symphonic program. I should also like to point out that the preoccupation of present-day audiences with such purely visual impressions occasionally gets out of hand, and encourages our maestros to feats of heroic choreography that really haven't much to do with the music they conduct.

It is very difficult to draw the line between the musically useful and the irrelevantly theatrical in this matter. I have found myself spellbound by the precise and eminently functional gestures of Arturo Toscanini. I have, at times, been slightly irritated by what seemed to me the overtheatrical visual spectacles provided by such dramatic wielders of the baton as Leopold Stokowski and Leonard Bernstein, though I must admit that both these men are very talented practitioners of their craft. I have watched with mild interest the energetic shrugging and rowing movements of Dimitri Mitropoulos and the incredibly ebullient lunging and fist-shaking of Sir Thomas Beecham, a maestro who has been known to fall off the podium in his enthusiasm, to hurl his baton inadvertently into the wings, and to break his suspenders, holding up his trousers for the remainder of the concert with one hand while conducting with the other. I have taken, and will continue to take, these things in my stride, but I have, of late, been rather disturbed by what appears to me to be an undue and disproportionate interest in them on the part of concertgoers, admen, and magazine photographers.

The trouble seems to have started with Toscanini, at the time when candid snapshots of his glowering face and whipping baton flooded the press. It now seems to have reached something of an apogee in a number of melodramatic photographs of conductors, part of a series of advertisements, entitled "The Sound of Genius," that are appearing in the Carnegie Hall programs and elsewhere. One of these photographs suggests an ecstatic hairdresser gesticulating with satisfaction over a completed coiffure, and another recalls certain impressions of Boris Karloff in a movie that, if I remember rightly, was called "The Mummy." The idea, I suppose, is to convey the agony or elation incident to the birth pains of a great symphonic performance, but the general effect strikes me as one of total mental derangement, and is, I think, rather unfair to the subjects of the photographs.

The prevailing notion of what a conductor should look like seems to conform, roughly, to the familiar concept of Jove hurling thunderbolts, and when a maestro makes an imperious gesture toward the bass, for example—the gesture is known, of course, as a cue—his movements are apt to be interpreted by the listener as an inspiring and indispensable call to action. Actually, however, the members of any well-trained symphony orchestra are quite capable of making their entrances without this sort of prodding. The gesture means very little to the orchestra, which needs only a precise and unostentatious beat to help it perform its duties. What it says is said to the audience, and this really boils down to something like "Behold! The brass has come in on time. Is not this impressive?" I have no doubt that this type of gesture is of some interest to auditors who otherwise would not realize that the brass had come in at all. But its bearing on the music that emerges from the orchestra is negligible.

These thoughts occurred to me in connection with the recent appearance of two eminent French conductors who undertook their tasks with businesslike practicality and a minimum of theatrical display. One was Pierre Monteux, who presided over the Philharmonic with efficient economy of motion. The other was Paul Paray, who appeared with the Philadelphia Orchestra. It is true that M. Paray fell off the podium at one point, but this mishap was so patently the result of sincere exuberance that I could not bring myself to hold it against him. Elsewhere, he showed a remarkably adult comprehension of the fact that thunderbolt-type cues are totally unnecessary in dealing with an orchestra whose members are as well drilled as the Philadelphians, and he managed to produce several very perceptive performances, including one of Tchaikovsky's Fourth Symphony that was about as dynamic and scintillating as any I have heard.

I was gratified to find that each of these conductors had included an American work in his program, and had chosen it with an unusual regard for solid and serious musical value. M. Monteux played Paul Creston's Second Symphony, and M. Paray played Samuel Barber's Symphony in One Movement, Opus 9. Both these compositions are of great intellectual interest; both are truly symphonic, in the sense that their structure involves the manipulation of themes in a context securely related to tonality; and both have a great deal of personal charm and evocative poetic feeling. It is the occasional appearance of works of this sort on symphonic programs that, to my mind, justifies the hope that American orchestral music may have a distinguished future.

February 11, 1956

OF ALL THE NUMEROUS tributes to Mozart that I have attended so far this season, in which, as nearly everyone knows by now, the two-hundredth anniversary of his birth is being observed, the most satisfying occurred last week, when Sir Thomas Beecham, after a long absence, conducted the Philadelphia Orchestra in a program of the celebrated composer's music. Sir Thomas has, of course, been famous as a Mozart interpreter for more than a generation, and to my mind he is one of the last survivors of a period noted for its magnificent Mozart performances—a period to which the fastidiousness and vigor of Arturo Toscanini, the elegance of Serge Koussevitsky, and the tenderness of Bruno Walter, as well as the special characteristics of various other maestros, have contributed a great deal.

Sir Thomas's particular way with Mozart has always held its own in competition with the Mozart style of all such admirable artists. For as long as I can remember, its individual qualities have included an engaging robustness, a wonderful pliancy, a pervading sunniness, and an eminently intelligent feeling for the proper emphasis in dealing with the subtle melodic contours of late-eighteenth-century music. The other night, these qualities were brought to bear on the playing of what, in my opinion, is unquestionably our finest orchestra, and the result, far from being just another Mozart evening, was an occasion for unusual rejoicing.

In watching the unself-conscious and graphic gestures with which this veteran maestro emphasized the points of the scores he conducted, I was reminded again that it takes more than mere energy to conduct Mozart—that the transparent delicacy of his musical language provides the ultimate test of any artist's gifts of taste and poise. Sir Thomas succeeded in imposing his personal style on the orchestra, which played quite differently for him from the way it plays for other conductors. The sound he drew from it had more variety and sensitivity than its usual uniform lushness and brilliance might lead one to expect, and there was everywhere an atmosphere of relaxation and leeway that permitted the orchestra's soloists—among them such estimable performers as the flutist W. M. Kincaid, the oboist John de Lancie, and the members of the Philadelphians' superb horn section—to exhibit their artistry as individuals. The effect was what one imagines would have been considered ideal in Mozart's own era —an era in which voluntary coöperation contributed a lot to music, and in which the driving virtuoso conductor was as yet undreamed of.

The compositions on the program were the "Prague" and the "Jupiter" Symphonies, the Divertimento No. 2 in D Major (K. 131), and the, to me, unfamiliar incidental music to "King Thamos" (K. 345). I shall not comment on the performances separately, except to state that the symphonies were set forth very authoritatively and occasionally in tempos more deliberate than some I have heard, and that the two other items were projected with a spirit of ingenuousness that I thought quite enchanting.

March 3, 1956

THE WEAKNESSES of the libretto Emanuel Schikaneder wrote for Mozart's opera "The Magic Flute" have been discussed at length for a hundred and fifty years or so, and there would be no particular point in bringing the matter up again except that it has a bearing on two recent performances of this opera here: the N.B.C. Opera Theatre's color television broadcast, and a current revival of the work at the Metropolitan Opera House.

The former production has been the subject of considerable controversy in the daily press, mainly because, having been cut by about a fourth and somewhat rearranged, for broadcasting purposes, it violated certain subtleties of continuity that are integral to the musical form of the work as Mozart conceived it. To be sure, from the purely musical point of view these violations—most of them made in the interests of tighter and more effective drama—were regrettable. Even so, I must say that although I would deplore the permanent editing of the work along these lines, I found the broadcast a rather charming affair, worthy of more than the single performance it got. It had the advantages of a superb English translation, by W. H. Auden and Chester Kallman, of remarkable taste in the use of color, and of what seemed to me a welcome adroitness in the manipulation of the opera's *mise en scène*.

However much one may regret what temporarily happened to some details of Mozart's music in the process, one can have no regrets at all about what happened to Schikaneder's libretto. This libretto is, of course, about as clumsy and childish a hodgepodge as has ever appeared on the operatic stage. It has been defended by heavyweight Germanic thinkers on the ground that it contains profundities of a symbolic nature, but just what these profundities are, aside from crude personifications of concepts like good and evil (which, after all, occur in cowboy films, too), has never been made clear. It has also been defended on the ground that it is a "magic opera"—that is, a fantasy—to which the obvious reply is that it is simply not a very good one, and on the ground that it is engagingly representative of suburban theatrical taste in eighteenth-century Vienna, to which the obvious reply is that suburban theatrical taste in eighteenth-century Vienna must have been extraordinarily bad. "The Magic Flute," unlike "Don Giovanni" and "The Marriage of Figaro," is not a supreme operatic masterpiece. It survives only because it contains some of Mozart's most beautiful music, along with a few rather quaint little tableaux, which have a sort of sentimental charm for the seasoned listener, comparable to that which might be evoked by a Punch-and-Judy show.

The Metropolitan Opera, unlike the National Broadcasting Company, is an institution dedicated to the highest and most traditional artistic standards, and it would be unthinkable for it to tamper with Mozart's score. The other night, it gave "The Magic Flute" a new production, in English, that was lavish and elaborate, and placed its musical direction in the hands of no less an artist than Bruno Walter, with results that were very gratifying. All the same, I couldn't help getting a little restless around the middle of the long second act, when Tamino was at last on the point of attaining the Eagle Scout status that would entitle him to marry the heroine.

Most of my restlessness was due to the familiar juvenility of the libretto, but there were also things about the production itself that I didn't like. Harry Horner's sets and costumes, for example, often clashed unpleasantly in color, and seemed to reflect no consistent style—suggesting at one time or another everything from Stonehenge to the ruins of postwar Berlin, with occasional digressions into the sort of ironwork that ornaments the lobbies of Bronx apartment houses. Then, too, the translation, by Ruth and Thomas Martin, is not as graceful as the one by Auden and Kallman. Curiously, the all-American cast seemed —with the notable exception of Theodor Uppman who did the role of Papageno—incapable of singing English with any kind of clarity or elegance.

March 17, 1956

IN THE CONFUSING AREA of contemporary musical aesthetics, it is useful, I think, to distinguish between two entirely different types of music, one of which might be termed the communicative and the other, for want of a better word, the decorative. In the first type, the various ingredients of musical structure—notes, phrases, chords, instrumental coloring, and so on—form part of an extensively understood and fairly traditional language, and are used to evoke ideas and emotions in a way somewhat analogous to that by which words evoke them in the art of writing. In the second type, these ingredients are used as objects in themselves, and make their appeal not through any commonly understood meaning but purely through their sensual effect on the ear.

So great is the disparity between the composer's approach to these two types of music that they seem to constitute two quite distinct arts—the former seeking to convey to the listener the emotional content that lies behind the actual sound, and the latter seeking to fascinate or startle him through the more or less ingenious manipulation of the sound itself. The communicative approach is the more widely accepted, being found in virtually all the religious, symphonic, operatic, and other masterpieces of the past, as well as in all folk music and all contemporary popular music. The decorative approach, though discernible in the work of such earlier composers as Berlioz and Debussy, is largely a phenomenon of the present day, and has been used by countless modern composers, often with results that have been at least momentarily arresting.

Of all today's decorative composers, Igor Stravinsky has proved the most resourceful and the most consistently interesting. He is, like other composers of the type, primarily a creator of sound effects. But his sound effects have been produced with such wizardry and such an unfailing flow of invention that they have continued to astound audiences for more than a generation. One finds him at his best as a composer of ballet scores, and this is hardly surprising, for the ballet, with its frequent emphasis on light, bizarre, and exotic theatrical effects, offers great scope to the writer of decorative music. Here Stravinsky is an unequalled master of artifice and a musical scenic designer of wit and originality. In the concert hall, he is, I feel, less satisfying, mainly because the decorative approach is extremely limited in its capacity to move an audience.

I was reminded of these things in Carnegie Hall last week when Leonard Bernstein, the Symphony of the Air, and various soloists undertook the performance of three of Stravinsky's finest scores. The first of them was the opera-oratorio "Oedipus Rex," written in 1927 for a libretto by Jean Cocteau and first performed here under Leopold Stokowski in 1931; the second was the "Capriccio" for piano and orchestra; and the third was the now very familiar "Firebird" suite, an unquestioned masterpiece of its genre.

I had not heard "Oedipus" since the American première by Stokowski, and I remembered it as an imposing composition, somewhat dour and ascetic in character but full of theatrical thunder and loud declamation. When I reheard it, I must confess that it struck me as slightly dated. The Stravinskian fireworks were still there, but they were not sufficient to sustain any real grip on my emotions, and the whole hour-long production had something of the atmosphere of a prosy essay on archeology, suggesting the parched grandeur, and the bloodlessness, of an ancient sarcophagus. Here and there, as in the narration by Jocasta at the beginning of the second act, there was an inhibited approach to a kind of lyricism that recalled the style of Gustav Mahler, but even such moments were rare, and as a whole the work seemed noisy, pompous, and devoid of life. The soloists in "Oedipus" coped bravely with their declamatory roles, and though I should hesitate to refer to their activities as singing, they did manage to squeeze a certain amount of grim melodrama out of the lines allotted to them.

I much preferred the "Capriccio," which is unpretentious,

brilliant, and frankly superficial in its aims, and which offered the pianist Jesús María Sanromá an opportunity for an impressive pyrotechnical display. Mr. Bernstein conducted throughout the evening with vigor and dramatic fire, proving himself as eloquent a Stravinsky interpreter as I have ever heard.

April 21, 1956

I HAVE ALWAYS regarded Gustav Mahler as a composer of considerable stature, if only because of his talent for communicating a certain very poignant kind of emotion, which seems peculiar to his own curious, and perhaps fairly restricted, musical personality. The emotion I am referring to is highly neurotic, extremely introspective, despairing rather than affirmative, and occasionally downright hysterical. But it is genuine for all that, and the intimacy with which Mahler conveys the gloomy fantasies that evidently afflicted his mind makes many of his works both poetic and deeply moving.

Mahler is the nearest thing in music to what in the field of painting is called an Expressionist. He has not only the violence of feeling but the intense subjectivity that this term implies, and his gigantic and often somewhat apocalyptic symphonies are all autobiographical, in the sense that they are descriptions of Mahler's soul—a soul that was at odds with the world, and even at odds with itself. Despite their size, these symphonies are not primarily interesting as architectural monuments; their form is often diffuse and discursive, and dictated by impulse and passion, instead of by abstract structural considerations. The appeal they make is essentially an appeal for sympathy with Mahler's own multifarious woes, and to listeners who are not in tune with his morbid outlook they are apt to seem grotesque.

After listening to a lot of Mahler's music, however, I have discovered that I can discern a great deal of beauty in the shifting detail that it contains. I find him at his most coherent as a composer of songs, and even in his more extended compositions, where the overall effect is likely to be baffling, I am continually fascinated by little songlike snatches that rise to the surface of his complex and highly original scoring, providing a note of nostalgia in a context of what is sometimes no more than bombastic self-pity. These moments of lyricism, to my mind, make Mahler's symphonic music worth listening to, and I try never to miss such infrequent performances of it as are given nowadays.

Therefore, last week I went to Carnegie Hall, where Dimitri Mitropoulos and the Philharmonic undertook to perform Mahler's massive Third Symphony. I cannot say that I had really heard the work before. According to the program notes, it had received but one previous performance by the Philharmonic—under Willem Mengelberg, some thirty-five years ago— and my only acquaintance with it had been based on a very much shortened, and otherwise unsatisfactory, reading given it in the early forties at the Radio City Music Hall, of all places, under the baton of Erno Rapee. Mr. Mitropoulos, unlike Mr. Rapee, allowed the composition to unwind its full length—about an hour and a quarter—and he conducted it with the affectionate care he has often shown in dealing with Mahler's scores and, I am sure, set it forth in the best possible light.

Perhaps because my sympathy with Mahler's dour outlook had not yet been fully ignited, I found the lengthy first movement, which abounds in wild trumpet calls and interminable death marches, slightly tedious. But with the onset of the second movement things began to brighten, and again I was able to discern and enjoy the lyric moments and the iridescent play of orchestral effects that seem to me to justify his music.

I wish that Miss Beatrice Krebs had sung the mezzo-contralto solo (the words are an excerpt from Friedrich Nietzsche's "Also Sprach Zarathustra") in the original German, instead of in English, because in German they have a kind of Gothic eloquence that does not survive translation into a more civilized tongue. "O Mensch! Gib Acht!" has a certain primitive dignity, but when it comes out "O Man! Give heed!" it sounds pretty flat.

THE NATIONAL SYMPHONY ORCHESTRA, of Washington, D.C., recently came to town and presented a concert under the direction of its American-born conductor Howard Mitchell. Except for Berlioz's "Roman Carnival" Overture, the program consisted entirely of contemporary compositions, and it proved, on the whole, to be of great interest. The Howard University Choir, a remarkably well-drilled and spirited Negro chorus, helped out in the performances of William Schuman's "A Free Song," which seemed to me an intermittently imposing work, and Heitor Villa-Lobos's familiar "Chôros No. 10," the second half of which is beginning to sound to my ears like an unrestrained cooch dance. Aaron Copland's "Appalachian Spring" was also performed—

quite well, I thought—and again it struck me as essentially ballet music.

By far the most engrossing composition of the evening was
Paul Creston's Fifth Symphony, which stood apart from the
others in that it had both emotional vitality and an intellectually
developed form. It was my first hearing of the work, and I did
not like it quite as well as Mr. Creston's now rather celebrated
Second Symphony, which is less austere and has more immediate punch. But I am sure that there is more in the Fifth
than first meets the ear, and I should like to have the opportunity
of hearing it again.

As for the National Symphony Orchestra itself, it impressed
me by the vigor and clarity of its playing, and in Mr. Mitchell
it has a virtuoso conductor of agreeably poised and unexhibition-
istic bearing, who can perform modern music, at least, with
great insight.

OF "SCHOOL FOR WIVES," a new opera by the Swiss composer
Rolf Liebermann, which was given its first New York performance by the New York City Opera Company, I can say very
little except that it constituted one of the most intolerably boring experiences that I have ever encountered. An extended
account of just why it was so boring would probably bore
you, too, so I shall content myself with noting that it was based
on a mildly entertaining seventeenth-century play by Molière,
which it proceeded methodically to crush with arrogantly cacophonous music and a combination of archness and theatrical clumsiness that almost caused me to walk out in the middle of it.

In wondering how it might possibly be improved, I thought
first of the desirability of eliminating Mr. Liebermann's music,
then of the desirability of eliminating the artless libretto it was

set to, and, finally, of the desirability of eliminating the embarrassing efforts of the singers to cope with their awkward assignments. That would leave the set, which was designed by Wolfgang Roth and was actually quite charming.

SUMMER MUSIC FESTIVALS OF 1956

FLORENCE

THE FIRST TIME I visited Florence, some thirty years ago, I thought it must be one of the world's noisiest cities. But that was before the invention of the Vespa motor scooter, an instrument that has given Florentine noise such technological efficiency that I am now convinced it is unmatched anywhere. The Vespa scooter's aural effect is roughly that of a mobile buzz saw, and its approaching and receding racket echoes through the streets and piazzas of the old town with an insistence that makes conversation difficult and contemplation all but impossible. The racket seems to be increased by the narrowness of the city's medieval streets, through which thousands of motorized Florentines propel themselves like projectiles through gun barrels, their heads bent forward in the style of bicycle racers and their trajectories scattering pedestrians to the comparative safety of the miniature sidewalks.

My first thought on seeing and hearing all this was that the

Florentines were universally bent on going somewhere in a hurry, but the fact that the whole city can be traversed on foot in about half an hour, coupled with some subsequent observations, showed me that I did not have the true explanation. Most of these subsequent observations concerned a man with a pneumatic drill below my hotel window, who has been engaged for some time in a resonant but plainly hopeless task—demolishing one of the huge pylons of Renaissance masonry that supported the Ponte Santa Trinità before the Germans blew it up to cover their retreat during the war.

This man doesn't seem to be getting anywhere at all. The masonry is a veritable mountain of stone and, as far as I can see, is not decreasing perceptibly in size. But he clearly enjoys his work. He starts promptly at eight o'clock in the morning and continues until half past five in the afternoon, filling the whole basin of the Arno with a bedlam that even dims the sound of the Vespas. Between his bouts with the masonry, he spits on his hands, bows with an engaging grin to the throngs of Florentines who have gathered on the riverbank to applaud him, and gestures with pride at the formidable implement of which he is the master. Everybody but me seems deeply gratified by his performance, and it isn't difficult to deduce from this that the Florentines make noise not because they have to but simply because they love it.

These remarks may seem a rather indirect way of approaching my main task, which is to report, as an itinerant critic, on some of the events of the Maggio Musicale, Florence's traditional spring festival of music, but I think they have some bearing on it. Music is, after all, an art that is cultivated most successfully in noisy nations. The sedate and reserved Anglo-Saxons and Scandinavians have never been very good at creating it. Its starting point is the conveyance of emotion by means of sound, and, obviously, people who love sound—any kind of sound—are more susceptible to a love of music than people who love silence. This is, at any rate, a serviceable theory for me at the moment, since it certainly applies to the Florentines and also makes me a bit more tolerant of what they are doing to my ears.

Before getting on with the doings at the Maggio Musicale, I think I might properly mention another sort of approach to the festival. That is the approach of Count Guido Chigi-Saracini, an enormously wealthy Tuscan nobleman who lives in the nearby city of Siena and is widely regarded as Italy's greatest patron of music. Count Chigi's approach to the Maggio Musicale consists of not approaching it at all. This is a cause of considerable regret to the Florentines, since Count Chigi is the outstanding musical monument of Tuscany, and a visit from him would confer on their festival a dignity nearly comparable to that attendant upon a visit from the Pope.

But Count Chigi has rarely travelled the forty miles of winding highway that connects his city with Florence, and he has never in his life deigned to spend the night here. The suggestion that he might sometime do so induces in him an air of utter outrage. "What? In Florence?" he asks rhetorically, as if the reason for his refusal were self-evident. The reason, actually, is rather complex, and has nothing whatever to do with the circumstance that the Count himself runs a rival festival in Siena, which takes place in September and is somewhat shorter, but by no means less distinguished, than the Maggio Musicale. The Count is above such petty rivalry. Indeed, he is such a great man that rivalry of any sort is practically unthinkable in connection with him. His distaste for Florence and the Florentines springs from far deeper sources. Through a slight acquaintance with him over a period of years, I had become aware of this distaste, and on paying a call on him at his vast palazzo in Siena I found it quite undiminished.

Count Chigi is the last remnant of an ancient Sienese family that has produced at least one Pope and whose genealogy reaches back uninterruptedly to the thirteenth century. The family's money, like that of the Medicis of Florence, was amassed in the Renaissance banking business, and today the Count is occupied in dispensing it on a scale reminiscent of the lavishness of that famous Florentine clan. In addition to his music festival and numerous charitable and civic undertakings, he supports a summer music school in Siena, at which some four hundred graduate students from all over the world gather annually to receive the final polishing that he hopes will turn them into artists. Their instruction, at the hands of internationally famous musicians whom he collects in Siena for the purpose, costs them nothing. Though the students live in various hotels and palaces scattered about the city, most of the classes are held in the Count's own palace, a tremendous, rambling medieval structure, whose cavernous rooms, decorated with sombre damask and plush hangings and an unbelievable accumulation of Renaissance art, have remained unchanged—in atmosphere, at least—since the seventeenth century.

The Count frankly describes his summers at the palace as "a sort of musical Hell," and he often retires from the din to a simple upstairs bedroom, where he sleeps on a thoroughly modern cot. Nevertheless, he is a firm believer in the civilizing effect that his aura of Renaissance tradition has on the minds of his protégés, and he is something of a stickler for old-fashioned propriety, strictly forbidding his female students to wear slacks and preferring that they do not wear their hair short. The Count also disapproves of women's riding horses astride. "The sidesaddle is infinitely safer," he maintains. "A woman's knee, thank God, is shaped differently from a man's."

Apart from setting forth a few such taboos and prejudices, Chigi treats his musical wards with fatherly solicitude and truly stunning patrician gallantry, and the alumni of his school look back on their experiences there as an enriching communion with the aristocratic atmosphere that characterized the Golden Age of their art. Above all, the Count seeks to instill in the students a respect for the gentler and more gradually flowering aspects of both art and life. "I pity young people who have finished with everything by the time they are twenty," he says. "They moan that life is unsatisfactory and empty. Naturally! That which you have immediately on asking for it is immediately exhausted. It is the lovely slow transitions of life that give it its quality—the first time one realizes that another person finds one not wholly unsympathetic, the first time a gift of flowers would not be considered presumptuous, the first time (sometimes after years of acquaintance) one is permitted to use a Christian name. Intimacy should dawn, not erupt."

Chigi is now seventy-six years old. He is a very tall, spare, white-haired man with a craggy, aquiline face and a presence as imposing as that of a Gothic cathedral. He carries the weight of his role as a great gentleman and a living anachronism with unaffected grace and pride, laughing good-naturedly at the incongruities it sometimes leads him into in a progressive world, but firm in his faith in the eternal survival of the values he represents. Though he made a short, early, and disastrous venture into marriage many years ago, he is, in effect, a lifelong bachelor. He loves the company of beautiful women and enjoys the opportunity for social contact with them that his academy provides. His attitude toward them, as toward everything feminine, is that of a confirmed romantic—wildly enthusiastic, worshipful, gallant, and slightly aloof.

He is pleased but somewhat taken aback by the occasional demonstrations of affection that come his way from his female students, particularly the Americans. "When I have known them but a short time," he remarked to me, wonderingly, "they come up and throw their arms around me. But they mean nothing by it," he added hastily. "They are so simple and honest, and they have such vitality. I love vitality."

The Count, whose observations I have been translating from a combination of French and Italian, is reputed to know no English except the word "Dammit." A friend of his reports that once, when captivated by an American lady who knew neither of his languages, he gazed at her helplessly for a few moments, then plucked a rose from a nearby vase and, bowing, offered it to her with a reverent "Dammit!"

Count Chigi is devoted to the Madonna, with whom, in the words of his American secretary, Olga Rudge, "he has a very special relation." During the recent war, when the Allied armies were approaching Siena, the Count made a vow to the Madonna that if the city was spared destruction he would present a pair of bronze doors to Siena's cathedral. His prayer was granted, and today the magnificent doors—elaborately sculptured, like those Ghiberti made for the Baptistery in Florence—are in place, one panel depicting the gaunt, patrician figure of Chigi himself, standing in meditation before the Madonna's image while the Archbishop of Siena looks on.

Count Chigi's enmity for the Florentines, like everything else about him, is a matter of tradition, but it is not on that account less deeply felt. As many Sienese are, he is a descendant of a long line of Ghibellines, whereas the old Florentine families are descendants of the Guelphs. The persistence of this distinction, involving the historic feud between the Pope and the head of the Holy Roman Empire, may strike the modern visitor as slightly quixotic, but to the Sienese it is still a burning issue. The Count himself feels so strongly on the subject that he becomes quite irritated if a guest at his palace remarks that the weather happens to be better in Guelph Florence than in Ghibelline Siena. Though Sienese have been known to marry Americans, Germans, and even Indo-Chinese, a Sienese who married a Florentine would be summarily ostracized by his fellow-citizens. In the minds of the Sienese, the great symbol of this age-old feud is the famous Battle of Montaperti, in which, in the year 1260, their forces defeated the Florentine Guelphs just outside the walls of Siena, massacring some ten thousand of them and dragging the Florentine flag, with its emblem of red lilies, through the city in dishonor. A glance at the history books shows that the Florentines subsequently clobbered the Sienese pretty thoroughly and that, later on, King Philip II of Spain made a present of the whole city of Siena to the Florentine Medicis. These depressing facts, however, do not dim the glory of Montaperti one whit in the view of the Sienese. Other wars have come and gone, but when a Sienese speaks of *the* war, he means the one that culminated in the Battle of Montaperti.

Count Chigi, from the towers of whose palace the news of the Sienese victory was proclaimed, can describe the battle in detail and with the passion of an eyewitness, gloating with flushed pride over the humiliation of the Florentine forces. On the ceiling of the vast music hall that is the central architectural feature of his palace he has caused an enormous mural to be painted. In tribute to the art of music, it contains likenesses of the great musicians Guido d'Arezzo, Frescobaldi, Palestrina, and Monteverdi, but its main subject is a huge depiction of the Battle of Montaperti, with the victorious Sienese warriors trampling the defeated Florentines into the dust.

Though united on the subject of Montaperti, the Sienese have their political divisions. For many years, the city has had a Communist mayor, who thoroughly disapproves of Chigi's status as Siena's largest landowner, and who talks vaguely about a coming revolution in which Chigi will be dispossessed, though he agrees that the revolution should be so timed that it will not interfere with either the Count's September music festival or the famous Palio, the semiannual medieval horse race in the

town square, over which Chigi also presides. In the opinion of
the average Sienese, however, Chigi, as Siena's leading citizen,
holds a position of civic and anti-Florentine grandeur that puts
him above politics, and during a recent election campaign the
walls of the city were chalked with the somewhat incongruous
but resplendent slogan

VIVA IL COMUNISMO!

VIVA CHIGI!

VIVA MONTAPERTI!

The Florentines—who, after all, inhabit a considerably larger
city than Siena—regard this intensely embattled attitude with a
combination of sadness and humor. They refer to it as *campanilismo,* a word that may be roughly translated as "belfryism" and
that connotes something by no means uncommon among the res-
idents of Italian towns. A *campanilista* is a man who believes
that the people surrounding his own campanile are the truly
civilized élite of the earth, while those surrounding other campaniles are apt to be thieves and assassins. *Campanilismo* is
nationalism reduced to parochial dimensions, and it is a real political force in Italy, even though enlightened Italians are inclined to smile at it. And even though the Florentines smile at
the *campanilismo* of the Sienese, they are not without traces of
the same complaint.

I came across a rather fine example of *campanilismo* some
years ago, when a Florentine pianist and composer—a Maestro
Brugnoli—fixed me with a sober stare and said, "Of course, everybody knows that all good music is Italian, and that it was the
Florentines who invented it."

This arresting statement struck me at the time as utterly outrageous, and I collected myself sufficiently to ask, "What about
Bach and Mozart?"

"Typically Italian composers," he replied blandly.

"And Wagner?"

"Well, when Wagner is good, he is typically Italian. Unfortunately, his work is somewhat uneven in quality."

I have since become more indulgent toward Maestro Brugnoli's views. It is, of course, true that the style of Bach and Mozart, like that of nearly all eighteenth-century music, owes much to Italian influence, and it is also true that the Italians, throughout musical history, have hewed firmly in their music to certain basic aesthetic principles, from which the peoples of the north have sometimes deviated, at their peril. The Italians have never lost sight of two important facts—that the essential ingredient of the art is melody, and that all good melody originates in the glorious traditions of song. The intellectual divergences from these principles that show up in the foggy chromaticism of Wagner, in the impressionism of Debussy, and in the arid cerebral idiom of the modern twelve-tone composers have all been evolved outside Italy, and anyone who agrees that singable melody is the essence of music is justified in the view that these divergences are responsible for a good deal that is extra-musical.

Thus, the Italians, in their firm addiction to melody, do have some claim to consideration as the musical nation par excellence, and their simple, direct approach to music may well survive all the mental complexities that have been heaped upon the art in other environments. Moreover, the second part of Maestro Brugnoli's statement, while oversimplified, also contains an element of truth. It is not true that the Florentines invented music, but it is an undeniable fact that they invented the art of opera. In the latter part of the sixteenth century, under the rather curious impression that they were re-creating the Greek drama, a group of Florentines, including Jacopo Peri, the great musical innovator, and Vincenzio Galilei, father of the astronomer Galileo, gathered at the palace of Count Giovanni Bardi, in Florence, to work out a new theatrical art form, in which song was to be substituted for speech. This new form caught on with tremendous speed, and although its major developments took place outside Florence, the credit for its origin rests securely with the Florentines. The presence of a chorus as a standard feature of most operas today is a remnant of the supposedly Greek tradition these Florentines sought to revive—a survival into modern times of the chorus of Sophocles and Euripides.

Having invented opera, the Florentines apparently soon lost interest in it. The important music of Italy has mostly been composed in other cities, and the only widely celebrated musical figures Florence has since contributed to the world are Jean Baptiste Lully and Luigi Cherubini (both composers whose careers were associated with France, rather than with Italy), the pianist, composer, and musical theoretician Ferruccio Busoni (although even he was actually from a town a few miles away), and the singer Luisa Tetrazzini. Count Bardi's palace, where the historic invention was made, still stands on the Via de' Benci, near the Arno, and bears a marble plaque that proclaims Bardi's prowess as a military man but makes only a casual reference to the group of musicians (known as the Florentine Camerata) who gathered there in the fifteen-hundreds. The old palace has a rather run-down and neglected appearance and has been divided into several private apartments. After locating it, with some difficulty, I approached the concierge with the idea of visiting the rooms in which Peri, Galilei, and their companions had thought out the principles of Italy's greatest musical art form. But she told me such a visit was impossible. In fact, she seemed slightly mystified that anyone should display an interest in the ancient edifice whose keys were entrusted to her.

THE MAGGIO MUSICALE, on the strength of which Florence makes its present claim to being one of Italy's leading musical centers, owes more to the city's status as a tourist attraction than to any outstanding musicality on the part of today's Florentines. It is supported by a grant from the Italian government. The opera house in which its most important productions take place— an old theatre that was once known as the Politeama Fiorentina and is now called the Teatro Comunale—is, of course, Florentine, and so are the permanent and quite serviceable orchestra and chorus. The operatic casts, conductors, and artists who participate in the festival, however, are drawn largely from other parts of Italy and from the rest of the world, so the affair has an international character, and, thanks to the brisk tourist trade, it has an international audience as well.

The Maggio Musicale's distinguished history began in 1933, but was temporarily interrupted in 1945 and 1946, because the theatre's stage had been destroyed by American bombardment. ("It was not the Americans' fault," one of the theatre's directors assured me courteously. "The Teatro Comunale was, regrettably, located close to a strategic railway yard. Fortunately, no one was hurt.") Since 1946, the Maggio Musicale has taken place annually, presenting many important premières and revivals and a very impressive array of world-famous musicians. It has been particularly noteworthy for its revivals of operas by the great Giuseppe Verdi, having put on no fewer than fifteen of his stage works, including such rarely performed items as "Nabucco," "I Lombardi," "Macbeth," "Luisa Miller," "I Vespri Siciliani," and "Aroldo," in addition to the usual "Aïda"s, "Trovatore"s, "Traviata"s and "Rigoletto"s. From the very beginning, it has shown a tendency to spread beyond the month of May, from which its title derives, and now it extends from the last weeks of April well into July, encompassing such varied activities as chamber-music concerts in various palazzos and outdoor ballet performances in the beautiful Boboli Gardens, adjoining the Pitti Palace.

The schedule of the current Maggio Musicale includes appearances by the pianists Claudio Arrau and Mieczyslaw Horszowski, the violinists Jascha Heifetz and Nathan Milstein, an institution known as the Orchestra da Camera Olandese, and the "Coro Maschile dello Harvard Glee Club." It also includes productions of Verdi's "La Traviata," "La Forza del Destino," and "Don Carlo," and, in the Boboli Gardens, some lavish ballets, among them Beethoven's "Le Creature di Prometeo," Verdi's "Le Quattro Stagioni," and Richard Strauss's "La Leggenda di Giuseppe."

So far, the festival's biggest event has been the first performance in Florence of Wagner's complete "Nibelung" cycle, sung by a visiting troupe of artists—mostly Germans, Austrians, and Scandinavians—in the original German, despite the program's adherence to the Italian habit of designating its component operas as "L'Oro del Reno," "La Walkiria," "Sigfrido," and "Il Crepuscolo degli Dei." By good fortune, I arrived in time to attend the entire cycle, and though I am not by any means a starry-eyed Wagnerite, I found it rather interesting to expose myself again to this mammoth agglomeration of preposterous drama and inspired music, which has been absent from the New York musical scene for several years.

THE TEATRO COMUNALE is certainly not one of Europe's handsomer opera houses. Its interior is as drab as the inside of a hatbox, and its gallery seats are no more than bare concrete benches, on which the holders of the cheaper tickets perch uncomfortably, with nothing to lean against but the knees of the people behind them. The people on the parterre floor, however, dispose themselves in luxurious plush-upholstered armchairs that make listening to practically anything a pleasure. Happily, my position as a visiting critic entitled me to one of them, and I sank into it with satisfaction before "L'Oro del Reno" began. The lobby outside was magnificently decorated with potted azaleas in full flower, and the presence at the main door of two carabinieri—in splendid uniforms, with swords in their hands and tricorne hats on their heads—had given my entrance a gratifying air of pomp.

The performance, like all opera performances in Italy, was late in starting, but since "L'Oro del Reno" is comparatively short, it had run its course before midnight. "Sigfrido" and "Il Crepuscolo" turned out to be marathons, the latter commencing shortly after eight and, what with the long, social Florentine intermissions, continuing until well after one in the morning. The theatre was packed for every performance, and though some tourists were in evidence, they were nothing like as numerous as the Florentines on hand to greet this unprecedented artistic invasion from across the Alps.

In the matter of scenery and staging, I found the Wagnerian productions slightly disappointing. The sets, designed by Cajo Kuhnly, of the Stuttgart Opera, were so modernistic and stylized as to be somewhat monotonous, and they did not do justice to the tricks of supernatural stagecraft that Wagnerian opera demands. Personally, if I am to be subjected to the mythical rigmarole of the "Ring" at all, I like to see my Rhine Maidens swimming in midair, my Erda rising mysteriously out of the stage floor, and my Alberich changing himself by miraculous theatrical prestidigitation from a gnome into a serpent. These points were completely neglected by Herr Kuhnly, perhaps on the ground that they are too old-fashioned and childlike to be bothered with, and the result—Rhine Maidens merely wandering about with perfunctory swimming motions of the arms, Erda merely walking onto the stage, and Alberich merely stepping behind a flat, as if to tie a shoelace, while an unconvincing serpent was flashed on the backdrop beside him by means of a projector—had none of the atmosphere of infantile magic that, to me, is part and parcel of the Wagnerian wonderland.

The orchestra of the Maggio Musicale, moreover, seemed to lack the smoothness and incisiveness of German and American ensembles, its brass, in particular, sounding both rather thin and rather coarse in the opening "L'Oro del Reno" performance. Its work picked up substantially in quality in the more familiar "La Walkiria," but it never quite attained the organlike richness these Wagnerian scores call for. On the other hand, it had an excellent conductor in Herbert Charlier, of the Bremen Opera, and the singers in the various casts—several of whom were from the Festspielhaus, in Bayreuth—had the authoritative manner and the scrupulous craftsmanship so often found among members of German and Austrian opera companies.

Chief among these singers was the Bayreuth *Heldentenor* Wolfgang Windgassen, whose somewhat vaporous name was completely belied by his admirable voice in the roles of Siegmund, Siegfried, and Loge (in "L'Oro del Reno"). While lacking the brilliance our Lauritz Melchior had in his prime and the lithe stage appearance that Set Svanholm brought to his Metropolitan Siegfrieds, Herr Windgassen nevertheless turned out to be an actor of considerable presence, and he sang with agreeable tone quality and without the forcing that is unfortunately somewhat characteristic of German tenors. The male side of the roster also contained some other first-rate performers —notably a Yugoslav bass named Tomislav Neralic, who sang the role of Wotan with insight and refinement; Gustav Neidlinger, who was a superb Alberich; and a gigantic bass named Otto von Rohr, who handled the villainous parts of Fafner, Hunding, and Hagen with dignity and with a voice that, if sometimes a bit rough, was about as powerful and as deep in range as any I have recently heard.

On the female side, the star of the performances was Birgit

Nilsson, of the Stockholm Opera, a sturdy-looking soprano who undertook the various Brünnhilde roles. Miss Nilsson's "Ho-yo-to-ho"'s were accurate and full of the requisite vitality, and the upper part of her voice, at least, was ringing, clear, and always meticulously in tune. I have heard more eloquent Brünnhildes, but hers was, on the whole, an unusually precise, workmanlike one. Herta Wilfert, a soprano from Bayreuth, was the prettiest Sieglinde I have ever seen, and though her singing was not always as secure as I could have wished, she showed qualities of temperament and vigor that, I think, may in time make her an important personality of the Wagnerian stage. One other female artist who impressed me was Ruth Siewert, who cames from Karlsruhe and is shortly to be connected with the Düsseldorf Opera. Miss Siewert appeared as Erda and, later on, as the Valkyrie Waltraute, and in both roles she displayed a voice of very distinguished calibre and a sense of musical style that was impeccable.

Thus, in spite of some shortcomings here and there, Florence's first taste of the complete Wagnerian "Ring" cycle—or "L'Anello del Nibelungo di Riccardo Wagner"—was quite a success. And though the productions of the operas were in most ways firmly Germanic, I think that even my one-time friend Maestro Brugnoli would have conceded that they had enough of the "Italian," or melodic, side of Wagner to qualify as music. Certainly the Florentines seemed to think so. They applauded and bravoed the visiting northerners like a football crowd, and I couldn't help reflecting that Count Chigi, proudly immured in his palace in Siena, was missing a pretty good thing.

FOLLOWING THIS production of the "Ring," I attended a performance of "La Traviata" in which Renata Tebaldi sang the part of Violetta. Since Miss Tebaldi has not yet sung the role at the Metropolitan and is scheduled to do so next season, I was glad to avail myself of this opportunity for a preview. The production as a whole proved to be spirited and visually pleasing, with particularly lovely, if completely traditional, sets and costumes, designed by an Italian named Attilio Colonnello. The conductor was the respected veteran Tullio Serafin, whose artistry in the Italian repertoire is remembered by Metropolitan audiences of a couple of decades ago, and the two principal male roles, those of Alfredo and his father, were taken by singers of some distinction—a tenor named Nicola Filacuridi, who had a fair-sized voice that was a little on the robust and throaty side, and a baritone named Ugo Savarese, who turned out to be an experienced performer with a pleasantly reserved and tasteful musical style.

The orchestra of the Maggio Musicale, obviously more at home in Verdi than in Wagner, played eloquently, and the chorus sang with exemplary precision. The tempos adopted by Mr. Serafin had an elasticity that, as is likely to happen in Italian performances, occasionally got out of bounds by American standards, and both the music and the action were more uninhibited emotionally than what we are accustomed to.

Encores were not only permitted but encouraged, and in the second act Miss Tebaldi, whose "Amami, Alfredo" had brought down the house, made her saddened exit from the stage and then returned to do the whole aria over again, much to the delight of the audience—and I must say to mine, too. Before I heard her as Violetta, I had had some doubts about the agility and sparkle she would bring to this brilliant and difficult part, since her voice has always seemed to me a bit heavy for the role's coloratura requirements. But in this I found myself somewhat mistaken. Mr. Serafin assisted her in "Sempre libera" by taking it at a slightly reduced speed, and at this speed her negotiation of its trills and roulades was remarkably clean and accurate.

I have never been one of Miss Tebaldi's completely unreserved admirers. To me, her voice, though certainly of the first rank in opulence, has not so far shown itself to be particularly expressive, and I have pointed out in reviews of her New York performances that she has a rather bad habit of using melodramatic tricks—sudden pianissimos and explosive swells—that are not always in accordance with the canons of refined *bel canto*. On this occasion, she again used these tricks now and then. Her "Dite alla giovine," in the second act, for example, began in an almost inaudible pianissimo and progressed to some very loud lamentations, which tended to distort the niceties of the aria's musical phraseology, although the result was sensational enough, I am sure, to be good box-office. On the whole, however, her interpretation was a lusty one, and I look forward to hearing it repeated—with, I hope, a few emendations in the direction of discipline—at the Metropolitan this winter.

VIENNA

ON THIS VISIT to Vienna, as on most of my previous visits, I approached the city from the south, by way of the railroad that runs across the Carinthian Alps and through the mountain towns of Villach and Klagenfurt. Near the village of St. Veit, a bit farther downhill, the train passes a striking medieval castle known as the Hoch-Osterwitz, which sits atop a tremendous crag and dominates as beautiful a sweep of countryside as one is likely to encounter anywhere.

I daresay that for the connoisseur of castles there may be better castles than the Hoch-Osterwitz, but it is conveniently located for viewing from a train window, and it has always had a special significance for me. It looks very much like the castles that appear in old fairy-tale illustrations by Howard Pyle or Maxfield Parrish, and it serves notice that one has left behind the sunny realism of Italy and entered an entirely different world. I know nothing whatever about its history, but I have no doubt that it was once inhabited by a robber baron. Red Ridinghood unquestionably met the wolf in a forest under the ramparts of some such fortress. The landscape of adjacent woodlands and fields is so like the archetypal fairyland one remembers from childhood that one half expects to see it populated by witches, gnomes, wise old men with long white beards, and all the other characters of Germanic folk mythology.

What especially distinguishes this scene from the tile roofs, campaniles, and neatly planted cypresses on the other side of the Alps is the element of fantasy that it suddenly evokes. One has passed from the realm of Mediterranean clarity and objectivity into a region where people have always thought, to a certain extent, in terms of myths, symbols, abstractions, and dream images. The simple supernatural folk tales collected by the Brothers Grimm represent only one facet of this thinking, which also includes the complicated symbolism of Goethe's "Faust," and has produced fantasies ranging from the stories of E.T.A. Hoffmann to the twentieth-century movie "The Cabinet of Dr. Caligari." Everywhere appears that curious fascination with and reverence for the irrational and mysterious that are peculiar features of the Teutonic mind.

The earliest record of this reverence for irrationality that I have come across is a passage in Tacitus' essay on the Germans, in which that great historian and observer, writing in the first century, A.D., noted that it was the Germans' custom in tribal councils to get very drunk before making a new set of laws, and then to amend the laws the next day, in the grim light of their hangovers. This odd process, however unsound it may seem to people accustomed to more objective methods, made a typically Teutonic allowance for the contribution of the irrational side of the human psyche. Centuries later, German philosophy, in its continuing preoccupation with the opposition between the irrational will and the rational intellect, was dredging the lower depths of the Teutonic psyche, and finally Sigmund Freud seems to have brought the problem into fairly scientific focus by distinguishing between the conscious mind and that impulsive part of the mental mechanism that he termed the unconscious. Freud, as has doubtless been pointed out before, could never have existed except as a product of Germanic thought. Only Germans and Austrians take irrationality so seriously, and are on such intimate terms with it.

This intimacy, I am convinced, has a great deal to do with the character of German and Austrian music and with the fact that music, of all the arts, has been the most congenial to the Central European mind. Where the Italian thinks of music mainly as simple song, expressive of concrete ideas, the Teuton has converted it into a quasi-religious ritual, involving feelings, moods, and intimations that defy expression in words. His rather dour sense of poetic fantasy finds in music a language ideally adapted to its needs. He is able to communicate through music a whole world of sensations, associations, and subliminal thoughts that lie outside, or can be no more than remotely suggested by, the processes of conscious reasoning. What the music-appreciation books call "absolute music"—that is, music divorced from all literary concepts—is largely a Teutonic invention. One need only attempt to describe a Beethoven symphony in words to realize how profoundly its message is embedded in mental areas that are beyond the scope of verbal logic.

I CAME TO VIENNA to report on the city's current music festival, and if you are wondering why I have chosen to start my report with this fairly sweeping lecture on the dimmer aspects of the Teutonic mentality, all I can say is that the subjects are somewhat related, and that the Hoch-Osterwitz, brooding on top of its crag, jolted me into this line of thought by reminding me that I had again entered a part of Europe where mysticism, fantasy, and emotion have often taken precedence overe logic, and sometimes even over common sense. After a great deal of winding through mountainous scenery, my train reached the eastern Austrian plain, and I was deposited in the city whose past artistic achievements have reflected this odd Teutonic genius more eloquently than the artistic achievements of any other city in Central Europe.

In visiting Vienna, I have always found it desirable to make a firm distinction at the outset between the real city and what might be called the Viennese myth. The myth is a glamorous concoction derived from "Rosenkavalier," "Fledermaus," and "Mayerling," garnished with nostalgic waltzes and operetta tunes, and dripping with the cultural magnificence of the old Hapsburg Empire. It conjures up a magically gay city, full of beautiful women, easily aroused affections, elegant living, urbanity, warmheartedness, and superb artistic taste. The Viennese themselves often seem to believe in the mythical Vienna, and the visitor who is fortified by enough *Heuriger* wine and Johann Strauss music can deceive himself, momentarily, into thinking that it actually exists. When he returns, like the ancient Germans after their tribal councils, to the plane of rationality, however, he is struck by a number of disconcerting flaws in his dream.

Vienna is not really a particularly gay city, nor are its inhabitants particularly notable for urbanity or for any very cultivated artistic taste except in the field of music. I cannot offhand think of a single Viennese painter of historic renown, and only a handful of names come to mind—Schnitzler, von Hofmannsthal, Grillparzer—that might lend the old city any dignity whatever as a literary capital. In the minor but omnipresent art of interior decoration, Viennese taste, in its progress since the Biedermeier era, has arrived at a sort of neo-Flatbush romanticism littered with doodads that practically simper. Vienna is the only city, for example, where I have encountered light bulbs with knitted slipcovers. The old Hapsburg magnificence has long since departed, leaving only a few props and backdrops—the Hofburg, the Schönbrunn and Belvedere palaces, the Ringstrasse, and various fine baroque churches—to remind one of its passing. The women, while often pretty, are anything but smart in their dress; indeed, the curious, slightly dowdy effect that is known as *die Mode* on the Kärntnerstrasse would cause a French or Italian couturier to moan in distress.

Viennese cooking is undoubtedly the worst to be found west of the Iron Curtain. I hasten to add that this is the result not of postwar austerity but of simple culinary incompetence. I have eaten in Vienna, off and on, since the early twenties, and I can assure you that the dispiriting repertoire of sauerkraut, goulash, dumplings, pickles, and watered-down salad dressing that passes for food here represents a long-cherished tradition, and is not the desperate alternative to starvation that one might suppose.

The service in Vienna's hotels and restaurants, moreover, is so boot-headedly and stolidly inefficient as to be unique in Europe. The average Viennese waiter seems to regard his customers as wayward children whose demands for attention must never be allowed to interfere with the progress of certain cryptic ceremonies that occupy his thoughts—ceremonies that, as far as I can see, involve dusting the furniture, conferring with the *Oberkellner*, dropping odd bits of silverware on the floor, and doing nearly everything but wait on table. He brings you marmalade with toast but not with rolls, because everybody knows that marmalade goes only with toast. In general, a request for any specific service automatically causes him to embark with fervor on some task that is quite unconnected with it. Ultimately, in the interests of sanity, you are forced to submit to his whims and gratefully receive not what you want but what he thinks you ought to have for your own good.

Minor frustrations of this sort, added to the fact that the Fifth World Power Conference has just crammed some three thousand delegates into an already overcrowded city and sent many music-festival patrons scurrying into lofts and rooming houses in search of lodging, have made Vienna during my stay an exceedingly uncomfortable place. Just why the authorities in charge of such things chose to hold the music festival and this mammoth gathering at the same time is beyond me. Apparently, they, too, have been preoccupied with arcane rituals, and have forgotten that tourists need some place to live, and that Vienna, still somewhat battered after her wartime bombardment, is capable of housing only a limited number of visitors.

THE FESTIVAL has certainly been the occasion for a colossal amount of music-making, and the throngs of eager and rapt listeners that have packed the recently rebuilt Staatsoper, the Grosser Musikvereinsaal, the Volksoper, and lesser auditoriums have shown that Vienna's sober enthusiasm for the art is as strong as

ever. I arrived in the middle of the festival, and I have been
present for its final ten days. On practically every one of these
days, there has been a choice among at least three opera productions (in the Staatsoper, the Volksoper, and the Redoutensaal of
the old Hofburg, where the smaller Mozart operas are given)
and at least a couple of major symphonic or choral concerts.

The Vienna Philharmonic, which has been reorganized since
the war and is again a notably refined and well-drilled, if not
overwhelmingly vigorous, ensemble, has been very much in evidence, not only in the orchestra pit of the Staatsoper but in
numerous symphonic undertakings. The Berlin Philharmonic,
the Amsterdam Concertgebouw, the Prague Philharmonic, and
the Leningrad Philharmonic have all paid extended visits,
though only the last has appeared during my stay. Mozart concerts, operas by Gluck, Verdi, and Richard Strauss, and operettas
ranging from "Zigeunerbaron" to "Kiss Me, Kate" have succeeded each other in bewildering profusion.

Prices for tickets to nearly all these events have been remarkably low (the best seats at the Staatsoper can be had for a little
more than three dollars), and from the billboards on the kiosks
of the Ringstrasse one gets the impression that nowhere could
one find a comparable amount of fine music heaped into a few
festival weeks. A closer look at things, however, reveals some
weaknesses in this tremendous schedule. There has been a
rather jarring absence of first-rate conductors, except for such
briefly visiting dignitaries as Bruno Walter, Herbert von Karajan, and Eduard van Beinum. There have been very few performances of important contemporary music. Above all, there
has been almost no music by contemporary Veinnese composers.
The schedule at the Staatsoper has included only two recent
works—something called "Penelope," by Rolf Liebermann, the
atonalist whose "School for Wives" was such a disastrous flop in

New York last spring, and an opera called "Der Sturm," by Frank Martin. Both Mr. Liebermann and Mr. Martin are Swiss.

Somewhat surprised by the lack of any evidence of native creative talent in the city that produced, or played host to, half the greatest composers in history, I made some inquiries. I was told, sadly, that from the point of view of musical creation Vienna is now a dead city. Even the most optimistic of my informants could recall the names of only two or three Austrian composers of any standing whatever, the most prominent among them being Gottfried von Einem, and he has apparently not turned out a major operatic work since "The Trial"—an item I heard, and commented upon unfavorably, in New York a couple of years ago. Musically, Vienna seems to be living almost entirely on the prestige of its past.

The most talked-about operatic event of the festival—since it represented the world première of a large-scale work—was Mr. Martin's "Der Sturm," and I was lucky enough to get here in time to attend it, in the company of a particularly dressy and critical audience. A famous guest conductor—Ernest Ansermet—had been imported to whip it into shape, and the production had scenery and costumes designed with an imaginative eye by Georges Wakhevitch, a Russo-Parisian whose past achievements have included décors for French movies and the Paris Opéra.

On the whole, the occasion had the atmosphere of a gala affair. The reconstructed Staatsoper shone with spanking-new gilt and crystal, the audience munched ham sandwiches and drank beer and cognac in the buffet before the show and during the intermissions, and all the intelligentsia of Vienna seemed to be focussing their peculiarly serious and bespectacled faculties on what was in progress. I noted with some gratification that the Staatsoper is still the same wonderfully intimate theatre (much smaller than the Metropolitan or La Scala, for example), giving

its audience of two thousand-odd a rare sense of participation in
what is going on.

It was from the program notes that I learned Mr. Martin is a
Swiss, despite his strikingly Anglo-Saxon name—which, by the
way, is pronounced around here with a French accent. I also
learned that he is sixty-five years old and a veteran of nearly all
the adventures in musical style that have disturbed the past half
century, and that most of his earlier efforts were cast in the form
of choral works, chamber music, or orchestral compositions of
one sort and another. Although I had never heard any of these
works, I gathered that Mr. Martin was a highly respected figure
in contemporary European music, so when I took my place in a
quite comfortable parterre seat, I was in a mood of pleasant
anticipation.

"Der Sturm" is, of course, German for "The Tempest," and
Mr. Martin's opera turned out to a be a reasonably faithful musical adaptation of Shakespeare's play, as translated by Friedrich
Schlegel. In staging it the Staatsoper had obviously made use
of its finest resources of craftsmanship. A full-rigged ship, wal-
lowing on canvas waves, filled the entire stage during the first
act, and pitched and rolled so realistically that the singers
clutched ropes and masts to steady themselves. In the later acts,
a series of Surrealist forest scenes gave things an appropriately
magical air, and at one point a gigantic globe resembling an egg
or a puffball mushroom accommodatingly split apart to reveal
the lovers, Ferdinand and Miranda, playing chess inside. The
role of Ariel was performed not by a singer but by a mime, who
danced his part in tights and in one of those catcher's masks
associated with characters in Surrealist paintings while the lines
he was supposed to be speaking were chanted offstage by a small
chorus.

All this was quite tricky and engaging, and might have fur-
nished an engrossing evening's entertainment had Mr. Martin's

music equalled it in charm. But the score he provided seemed neither to have any particular coherence nor to be very well suited to vocal purposes. During the first act, it consisted mostly of tame echoes of Debussyan impressionism; during the second act, it bristled with rhythmic ideas derived from jazz; and during the third and final act, it was cluttered with archaisms reminiscent of the seventeenth century. The musical backgrounds for Ariel's scenes relied heavily on weird sounds for voices, harps, and glockenspiel—a scoring device that has become a cliché for supernatural effects in Hollywood and that in this case had the further disadvantage of rendering Shakespeare's lines unintelligible. The sounds accompanying Caliban included some pretty obvious roaring and bellowing on the part of the trombones. In one place, the members of the orchestra laid their instruments aside and clapped their hands rhythmically. I could find nothing very original or very enchanting about this, and I must confess that toward the middle of the evening things began to seem distinctly dull. The most absorbing moments of the performance, I regret to say, were a few stretches of comedy in which Mr. Martin stopped his music entirely, permitting one the great relief of hearing pure, unadulterated Shakespeare, even though in German.

In the work of the performers I noticed some admirable points. The mime who took the part of Ariel—a ballet dancer named Willy Dirtl—is a superb artist, and his light-footed evanescent interpretation of the role was the hit of the evening. Caliban, a powerful bass named Endre Koreh, was extremely effective; a young American singer named Frederik Guthrie disclosed a distinguished manner of singing as the King of Naples; and, as Miranda, a very pretty soprano named Christa Ludwig revealed vocal abilities that deserved better opportunities than they got. Mr. Ansermet conducted the opera with great expertness, but I cannot say that I foresee any substantial prospect of success for it.

THIS WORLD PREMIÈRE having been duly celebrated, the Staatsoper got down to its more conventional repertoire, and I was able to hear Richard Strauss's "Rosenkavalier" and "Elektra" and Puccini's "Turandot."

The first of these, of course, has always been considered something of a Viennese specialty, and I looked forward with interest to hearing it here. There were several nice elements in the production—notably, some lavish, heavily gilded scenery and some spots of comedy on the part of the minor characters that attested to more careful rehearsal than we get at the Metropolitan Opera House. Lisa Della Casa, familiar in the role of the Marschallin at the Metropolitan, sang it here quite beautifully and acted with perhaps a shade more maturity than I have found in her New York performances. Hilde Gueden, also familiar at the Metropolitan, was as acceptable as usual in the role of Sophie. On the other hand, the Baron Ochs and the Octavian, sung by Ludwig Weber and a guest artist from the Munich Staatsoper named Hertha Töpper, respectively, were humorless and otherwise disappointing, and the Vienna Philharmonic, under a more or less routine conductor named Rudolf Moralt, seemed nowhere to rise to the degree of brilliance the score calls for.

I liked "Elektra" a good deal better. Christel Goltz, the fiery German dramatic soprano who appeared the year before last in New York as a rather overemotional Salome, seemed ideally cast in "Elektra's" more boisterous and uninhibited title role, and her interpretation of it was about as hair-raising as any I have seen since the great Rose Pauly did it in Manhattan. Miss Goltz was very well seconded in her gloomy duties by the American contralto Jean Madeira, who gave a redoubtable portrayal of Klytemnestra, and by Leonie Rysanek, a soprano of considerable power and temperament, who appeared as the peace-loving and well-intentioned Chrysothemis. Here again, however, I found the playing of the orchestra merely suave and polished, and a score that should have boiled and steamed did not manage, under the direction of a conductor named Heinrich Hollreiser, to reach any noteworthy temperature.

Of "Turandot" I can find very little to say in approval. It is a weak opera to begin with, and its production was purely conventional. Miss Rysanek hit some agreeably ringing high notes in the main female role, and would probably have hit them even better if the work had been sung in Italian, instead of in German. Altogether, the performance was ordinary and uninspired —neither better nor worse, perhaps, than the general run of opera is almost anywhere, provided it is halfway decently produced.

These performances, I fear, did not compare in any way with the splendid ones I used to hear in Vienna in the twenties, when conductors like Franz Schalk and Richard Strauss and singers like Maria Jeritza, Lotte Lehmann, Elisabeth Schumann, Richard Mayr, and Maria Olczewska made the city unique as a center of operatic craft. The wonderful workmanship that used to be lavished on creations by Strauss and Mozart in those days —a workmanship that gave every performance the subtlety and perfection of chamber music—seems to have disappeared. I am somewhat at a loss to explain this, since the quality of the voices at the Staatsoper is actually still quite high. I can attribute it only to a lack of gifted conductors, and perhaps to the political intrigues that, I am informed, have dominated the local opera for some time.

According to my fellow-critics here, the resignation a few months ago of Karl Böhm, a reasonably impressive artist, as general director and chief conductor of the Staatsoper has left

Viennese opera without any authoritative chief. The glamorous Herbert von Karajan has taken over the job for this coming winter, and he will undoubtedly do as much conducting as his other engagements—in Berlin, in Salzburg, in London, and at La Scala—permit. But the outlook is distinctly discouraging, and —for the moment, at any rate—opera in Vienna is emphatically not what it used to be.

To ME, the most rewarding event of the festival was the visit of the Leningrad Philharmonic. My only previous acquaintance with this orchestra had been through some rather rough recordings I'd heard in New York, and I now realize that these recordings entirely fail to do it justice. It is a dazzling ensemble, with magnificent strings and with brass of thundering power, and though its woodwinds are perhaps slightly heavy and thickly articulated, it plays with a vitality that I have heard equalled only in the very finest American orchestras. It practically set Vienna's audiences on fire, and the demand for tickets to its concerts was so huge that I had some difficulty in getting to hear it. I missed its first concert, at which, I understand, its principal conductor, Eugene Mravinsky, held his listeners on the edge of their seats with a sensational performance of Tchaikovsky's Fifth Symphony. I managed to attend its second appearance, which was presided over by a lesser maestro named Kurt Sanderling, and this concert—which not only had David Oistrakh as soloist in a Mozart violin concerto but also gave a quite stunning reading of Rachmaninoff's Second Symphony—was impressive enough.

Being thwarted in my attempts to hear Mr. Mravinsky conduct, however, I complained to some of my colleagues among the local critics, and was informed that the orchestra was making recordings for a German firm in the Konzerthaus and that I might be able to sneak into one of the recording sessions. This proved to be a hazardous undertaking. My guide was a fellow-critic, Count André Razoumovsky—a lanky young man equipped with a goatee, a practiced knowledge of the hallways and fire escapes of Vienna's concert halls, and a family tree that includes the well-known nobleman for whom Beethoven wrote some of his greatest quartets.

Count Razoumovsky took me in hand with implacable calm. The Konzerthaus was surrounded by guards, but we managed to elude them and get into a box. From this we were promptly ejected by indignant Russians. But the Count was by no means at the end of his resources. There are always venal guards, and he found one. After a whispered conference, the guard assumed a blank air and said, "I do not see you. To me, you are obviously not here—but hurry, and be quiet!" We entered a side door and tiptoed up three flights of stairs to the back of the highest balcony, where, crouching behind a row of seats, we were able to see and hear what was going on.

This adventure in aesthetic espionage proved to be well worth the trouble. It was interesting to note that the Leningrad orchestra spent a lot of time in meticulous sectional rehearsals, going over details of the score under an assistant conductor, who carefully drilled each section in turn. Then Mr. Mravinsky took over. He is a tall, gray-haired, partly bald man, with a sharp, prominent nose and a look of immense authority; from the moment he started to conduct, it was evident that the orchestra was responding to him with the instinctive submission and rapt attention that only conductors of unusual gifts are able to command.

While the Count and I held our breath and strove to ease the cramps in our legs, Mr. Mravinsky conducted most of Tchaikovsky's "Pathétique" Symphony. His gestures were precise and quite untheatrical, and the reading itself was conservative and devoid of sensationalism. It was also about as eloquent a reading of the "Pathétique" as I have ever heard anywhere. When it was over, the Count and I made our way furtively downstairs, and again managed to elude the guards. We were both convinced that Mr. Mravinsky is a virtuoso of the top rank, and—in Russian music, at least—a formidable artist.

SALZBURG

THE GREAT Wolfgang Amadeus Mozart, having been born in this pleasant little Austrian city, spent a large portion of his youth scheming to escape from it, and in his later years he succeeded, apparently without much remorse, in abandoning it for the more metropolitan life of Vienna, where most of his maturer compositions were written. This circumstance has not prevented Salzburg from celebrating its distinction as his birthplace with enormous fervor, and the Salzburg Summer Festival, which was first held almost forty years ago and is devoted largely to his music, has become the most famous affair of its kind in the world.

The peak of the Festival's glory, as nearly everybody knows, occurred in the years just preceding Hitler's Anschluss, when Max Reinhardt's annual production of "Jedermann" was one of the Festival's main features, and the participation of such formidable conductors as Wilhelm Furtwängler, Arturo Toscanini, Bruno Walter, and Felix von Weingartner and an assemblage of gifted artists drawn from Vienna and from the rest of the world gave its performances, especially its operatic performances, a truly gala character, well worth a pilgrimage from almost anywhere.

To my regret, I didn't visit Salzburg during that period, and up to this year my only acquaintance with its great summer event had derived from a short stay during the twenties and another stay, equally short, just after the Second World War, when general disorganization and the confusion attending the American occupation of the city made the holding of any kind of festival whatever a considerable triumph. Nevertheless, these two visits, plus a certain familiarity with the work of most of the artists who appeared here in the golden era and with the particular form of operatic art practiced in Austria over the past generation, had given me some idea of the Festival's onetime magnificence. And though I was aware, from various reports, that Salzburg today is not quite what it used to be, I entered the city a couple of weeks ago hoping that enough of the fine tradition of its past had survived and enough new and important talent had been added to make the occasion still one of the outstanding summer festivals of Europe.

Certainly, to judge by the advance notices, things were to be on a fairly high artistic plane this year. The year itself, marking the two-hundredth anniversary of the composer's birth and locally dubbed *der Mozartjahr,* is, of course, being solemnized nearly everywhere by special attention to his music. "Don Giovanni," "Le Nozze di Figaro," "Il Seraglio," "Idomeneo," "Così Fan Tutte," and "The Magic Flute" were all to be performed in

Salzburg. The Vienna Philharmonic, several well-known artists from the Vienna Staatsoper, a few distinguished foreign singers, and some able conductors, including George Szell, Dimitri Mitropoulos, Karl Böhm, and Fritz Reiner, had been assembled. There were to be lieder recitals by Cesare Siepi, Irmgard Seefried, Elisabeth Schwarzkopf, and Dietrich Fischer-Dieskau, and no end of chamber-music concerts, by groups from Italy, Yugoslavia, and Czechoslovakia as well as Austrian and German groups. "Jedermann" was to be presented in the Cathedral Square in the postwar production by Ernst Lothar, and Goethe's "Egmont," a drama seldom seen anywhere, even hereabouts, was scheduled for a performance with Beethoven's well-known overture and incidental music. Finally, the New York City Ballet was to pay a visit, enlivening the last week of the Festival with works by George Balanchine and Jerome Robbins.

I missed in all this the attention I should have liked to see given to contemporary music and contemporary drama. Still, the Salzburg Festival is a rather specialized occasion. I suppose that one attends it mainly to hear Mozart, after all, and in this respect, at least, there would be plenty going on.

The crowds of tourists swarming in the narrow streets when I arrived testified to the fact that the Salzburg Festival, whatever its current artistic merits, is still a thriving business proposition. Greeks and Spaniards by the busload, Hindu women in saris, chattering French visitors, and colossal numbers of Americans gave the place a cosmopolitan air that had been notably absent from the Vienna festival of a few weeks earlier. The town, especially at night, had a slightly garish appearance, which contrasted strangely with its solemn medieval and baroque architecture. Neon lights shone from hillside cafés, and gigantic searchlights played on all the principal points of interest, including the castles on the surrounding mountains and the fine old churches in the town itself.

The center of Salzburg had been equipped with a system of traffic lights that would do credit to Times Square, and the quantity of traffic the system was called upon to control showed that it was indispensable. Everywhere, visitors were trudging purposefully about in raincoats and galoshes (Salzburg is one of the rainiest places in Europe), examining the Mozart *Geburtshaus* (whose ground floor now houses Salzburg's finest liquor store) and the vestiges of the bombed-out Mozart *Wohnhaus*, where the family lived later on, as well as the house where Franz Schubert once stayed and various special exhibitions of manuscripts, mementos, and pictures dating from Mozart's time. There were some mementos of Harry Truman's recent visit, too, including a full-length photograph of him in Tyrolian costume proudly displayed in the window of one of the smarter men's-clothing stores.

Indoors, in crowded restaurants, the visitors were coping as best they could with the hazards of Salzburg cooking, which, if such a thing is conceivable, is even worse than Vienna's. In one place I noticed the leading hero of the Festival, the Italian basso Cesare Siepi, staring in helpless gloom at a plate of *Kalbsnierenbraten mit Kartoffelsalat* while people asked him for autographs. I am sure he would have been willing, as I was, to trade all the glamour of Salzburg for a dish of spaghetti and a few decently cooked vegetables.

On every hand, guidebooks, histories of Salzburg, and scholarly philosophical tracts on Mozart's works, his *Zeitgeist*, the *Entwicklungsgeschichte der Mozart-Kultur*, and related profundities were being studied with truly Hegelian solemnity; I have never witnessed a more thoroughly documented festival. Tickets to the operas, which were given in the outdoor Felsenreitschule and in two theatres, the Festspielhaus and the Landestheater, were outrageously expensive by Austrian standards, running to as much as ten dollars for the better seats, but every performance had apparently been sold out well in advance, and was given before a packed house. Escape from Mozart's music was impossible, even outside the scheduled events of the Festival. The sounds of rehearsal issued from auditoriums and studios in the daytime, and radios and phonographs leaked Mozart symphonies and string quartets from windows all over town and far out into the suburbs. Clearly, if one wanted to listen to Mozart in quantity, this was the place to come.

WHAT ONE LOOKS FOR in Salzburg—what has, in the past, given the best Austrian performances of Mozart operas a special quality, seldom found elsewhere in the world—is a peculiar tradition of interpretation, which has always been known in these parts as "*der echte Mozartstil,*" or "the genuine Mozart style." Austrians are justifiably proud of it, and if you ask the average Salzburger or Viennese exactly what the secret of this tradition is, he will reply blandly that Mozart is performed here with more "heart" than in other countries. To my mind, this explanation is wholly incorrect, granted that it means anything at all. Austrians are only too apt to attribute such virtues as they have to the workings of a mystic entity known as "*das schöne österreiche Herz,*" and ignore the quite obvious truth that it is superior workmanship, not indefinable emotional factors, that gives their musical performances the finish and subtlety they often possess.

Der echte Mozartstil is, actually, a triumph of musical and dramatic intelligence and ingenuity. Whether it is really the only *echt* way of doing Mozart's music may be open to some doubt, and whether Mozart himself would have approved of it may also be questioned, since Mozart, as his letters show, was a great admirer of the uninhibited vocal style of Italian opera—

something that is at the opposite pole from the carefully knit and very deliberate Austrian tradition I am speaking of. But, *echt* or not, *der echte Mozartstil* is an admirable and often delightful thing, painstakingly nurtured by generations of Austrian singers, orchestra players, conductors, and stage directors, and when it is at its best, it produces a crystallization of musical and theatrical elements that can make a Mozart opera a remarkably unified and polished affair.

What one admires in *der echte Mozartstil* is often effort, rather than genius. It requires vast amounts of rehearsal. Every musical phrase, every gesture and facial expression, every dramatic nuance is studied and worked on until it fits perfectly into its proper place in the total production. Nothing is left to chance, or even to momentary inspiration, and the teamwork of the orchestra and the various soloists is so intricately balanced that the effect takes on something of the character of chamber music. The quality of the production as a whole has a way of exceeding that of the sum of its parts. Singers of very moderate talents sound like great artists, because of the discipline and exactitude that are demanded of them, and this fact, incidentally, goes a long way toward explaining why leading Austrian operatic artists imported into the less disciplined and more individualistic environment of the Metropolitan sometimes fail to make a corresponding success there.

In Salzburg and Vienna, when Mozart opera is being well done, the entire performance is under the thumb of the conductor, and things move forward with the planned precision that we expect from our symphony orchestras. Musical and dramatic climaxes are always in the appropriate place and in just proportion. If gifted singers are present to infuse extra touches of individual artistry into this well-organized collective endeavor, the result can be unforgettable. If they are not present, the re-

sult can verge on mere pedantry, but even then one is con
strained to approve the technical efficiency.

IN THE FIRST PERFORMANCE I heard in Salzburg, that of "Don
Giovanni," *der echte Mozartstil* had a rather difficult time mani-
festing itself. The performance took place in the Felsenreitschule, an open-air, canvas-roofed arena that originally served
the Archbishops of Salzburg as a riding academy and still has
an appearance slightly suggestive of a bull ring.

It was a cold, wet night, and the audience, clad in evening
clothes, wore overcoats while the opera was in progress, remov-
ing them only during the intermission, when it was possible to
seek shelter in a hall that is used as a common lobby by the Felsenreitschule and the adjoining Festspielhaus. Through some
whim of an Archbishop who lived before Mozart's time, the ceiling of this hall is decorated, in late-Renaissance style, with a
huge fresco depicting several handsome, armored horsewomen
gaily chopping the heads from a couple of helpless prisoners of
war. I have always found this bit of Teutonic merriment somewhat depressing, particularly when eating ham sandwiches and
sausages directly underneath it between the acts, but I am sure
I succeeded in keeping it from souring my attitude toward what
went on in the auditorium.

Unfortunately, the performance was plagued not only by cold
but also by rain, which intermittently fell in torrents on the
canvas roof, producing a sound like a drum roll and making large
parts of the opera all but inaudible. The Vienna Philharmonic,
which occupied a stone-lined orchestra pit that strikingly resembled an open grave, was suffering from the dampness. Its
tone was pardonably soggy and its intonation pardonably vague.
The conductor was Mr. Mitropoulos, an artist who, far from
exemplifying *der echte Mozartstil* at its best, seems to have a

special gift for conducting Mozart's music as if he thoroughly detested it. In fact, that evening Mr. Mitropoulos seemed happy only toward the end of the opera, when, in the scene portraying Don Giovanni's death, he was able to whip things into a thundering and not altogether Mozartean climax.

Despite these tribulations, however, the production had some good things about it. The set, by Clemens Holzmeister, a built-in affair in which the façades of various buildings served as backgrounds for the successive scenes, reminded me a little of the single "Don Giovanni" set that is currently used at the Metropolitan. Like all arrangements that enable this opera to be produced without any scene-shifting, it had the effect of rendering the two great interior scenes—those that close the first and second acts—a trifle unconvincing, since they are necessarily played against the same façades that represent exteriors in the rest of the work. Except for this limitation, though, the set was an effective one, and its spaciousness gave the stage director, Herbert Graf, no end of opportunities for handling the crowds of peasants, courtiers, monks, and Furies from Hell that are part of the opera as currently produced here. The costumes, by Rolf Gérard, were as lavish and elegant as any I have seen.

The singing of the principal roles was, with few exceptions, of a very high order. Mr. Siepi's Don Giovanni, though somewhat boyish, and intuitive rather than intellectual, is one of the most dashing and vocally pleasing interpretations of this role to be witnessed anywhere today, as those who have seen it at the Metropolitan are aware. Lisa Della Casa, though she does not possess the temperament of the ideal Donna Elvira, is nevertheless a scrupulous artist, and on this occasion she sang quite beautifully. Elisabeth Grümmer, a soprano hitherto unfamiliar to me, took the part of Donna Anna with admirable authority, while Leopold Simoneau succeeded in making Don Ottavio much more than the cardboard figure he usually is, and lacked the utmost brilliance only in the aria "Il mio tesoro," where he seemed slightly in danger of running out of breath. The other roles, including the Leporello of Fernando Corena and the Commendatore of Gottlob Frick, were, on the whole, excellently done. From the standpoint of singing, at least, this was a reasonably distinguished "Don Giovanni," and what faults it had are attributable mainly to Mr. Mitropoulos and the acts of God I have mentioned.

Der echte Mozartstil came through somewhat more successfully in the next performance I saw, that of "Le Nozze di Figaro," which was held indoors, in the Festspielhaus. This is an intimate theatre, with an engagingly simple décor and a very small stage, on which it is possible to observe details of acting that are often missed in large opera houses. The cast was a fine one—nearly all of it from the Vienna Staatsoper—and the intensity and smoothness with which it tackled the subtleties of the score bespoke the absolute security that comes from unassailable tradition and diligent rehearsal. The conductor was Karl Böhm, who, I understand, is something of a Mozart specialist, and this time, under his baton, the Vienna Philharmonic played with notable expertness and grace.

On the male side of the cast, neither Herr Fischer-Dieskau, as Count Almaviva, nor Erich Kunz, as Figaro, produced any overwhelming beauty of tone, but both performed with great technical skill. On the female side, Miss Schwarzkopf, as the Countess, and Miss Seefried, as Susanna, sang very beautifully indeed, though Miss Schwarzkopf's interpretation seemed to me refined almost to the point of mannerism. I was particularly struck with the Cherubino of Christa Ludwig, a very young singer, whom I had previously heard in the Vienna production of "Der Sturm." Miss Ludwig has an exceptionally pretty, slightly kittenish stage appearance and an agreeably handled

mezzo-soprano voice. I shouldn't be surprised if operatic audiences on both sides of the Alantic were to hear more from her.

THE TWO REMAINING performances that I attended were, I am
afraid, rather disappointing. The first of them was a production
of Mozart's opera "Idomeneo," which I found interesting only
because I had never heard it before. Its drama is one of those
numerous classical operatic affairs dealing with what happened
to various Greeks and Trojans after their historic war, and its
music is, for Mozart, somewhat academic and stilted, being more
in the earlier styles of Gluck and Handel than in what we think
of as the typical Mozart idiom. The action is extremely formal,
requiring little more of the singers than that they stand around
and declaim long recitatives and arias. The vocal score, on the
other hand, is very Italian in conception, and very exacting, piti-
lessly revealing any flaws in poise or elegance on the part of the
principals. The flaws revealed on this occasion were, I fear,
pretty damaging. Not one singer in the cast—and it included
Christel Goltz, who had been imported from Vienna to sing the
role of Electra—showed any acquaintance with those niceties of
bel canto that could have made the evening rewarding. Such
virtues as the performance had were confined to the neat playing of the orchestra, under Mr. Böhm, and to an amusing series
of period stage sets, by Caspar Neher.

The second of these disappointments was an exceedingly dull
performance, in the Felsenreitschule, of "The Magic Flute"—
such a dull one that I left before the last act, and was glad to
get away. Some of the individual singers—notably Herr Frick,
as Sarastro—performed with vocal distinction, but it takes more
than a few well-sung phrases to bring this fairly silly (though
musically beautiful) old operatic fantasy to life. Herbert Graf's
staging on this occasion was conventional, and the endless pa-

rades of priests that seem to be an inevitable part of the spectacle looked as though they had been transferred, with a mere change of costume, from some routine production of "Aïda." The outdoor sets, provided by Oskar Kokoschka, an artist whose work off the stage I admire, were rather tricky in their use of projected light but on the whole struck me as drab and unimaginative.

Adding these impressions to my impressions of the previous works, I can conclude only that the Salzburg Festival has become a highly uneven affair, badly in need of fresh, and perhaps foreign, contributions. Plans to this end may very well be in the making. For one thing, a brand-new and much larger Festspielhaus is about to be constructed, at considerable expense, and the Festival's management is at present occupied with projects for overhauling both the schedule of works performed and the methods used in performing them. I hope that these plans and projects result in something livelier than what I have seen this year. The Salzburg Festival is too great an institution to be permitted to languish indefinitely.

BAYREUTH

It is impossible to attend the productions of the Bayreuth Festival without experiencing a curious sense of domination by the shade of Richard Wagner. This sense of domination comes not only from his music but also from the atmosphere of the place, the customs of its inhabitants and guests, and the spirit of reverence and ritual that pervades the performances of his music dramas. According to one's temperament, one feels either exalted or intolerably oppressed—or perhaps one feels both at different times. One is never neutral.

The power of Wagner's personality—arrogant, inspired, commanding, pompous, and whatever else it may be—extends to every detail. One does not merely "attend" the productions of his works; one is subjected to them. One finds oneself not in an opera house but in the sprawling Festspielhaus, a temple built by the Master himself as a memorial to his own genius. The seats—cane-bottomed affairs arranged in close-packed rows and resembling pews—are exceedingly uncomfortable, but one's discomfort is a tribute exacted by the colossus of Bayreuth. Who, after all, has a right to consider comfort when his mind should be on higher things? One finds the doors of the auditorium locked while the operas are in progress, lest the slightest dis-

turbance interfere with the ceremony. One is permitted to applaud only at the end of each act, and at "Parsifal," of course,
one does not applaud at all. One is expected to have studied the
intricate ramifications of Wagner's plots beforehand, and to have
come prepared with a knowledge of the musical motives that at-
tach to various characters and points in the action, so one does
considerable homework, no matter how many times one may
have gone through it all before.

Even one's gastric processes are subject to the whims of the
great man. The shorter operas begin at seven, giving one time
only for a hastily swallowed dinner, and the longer operas begin
at four in the afternoon, allow an hour's intermission for an inadequate snack at the Festspielhaus restaurant, and continue until well after ten, leaving one with the feeling of having put in a
heavy and undernourished day's work.

One's fellow-worshippers (in Bayreuth the Teutonic instinct
for religiosity is so pronounced that the word fits them precisely)
sit through each act holding their breath. Between the acts,
they parade solemnly about the grounds of the Festspielhaus
with hypnotized expressions. By some mysterious process of selection and adaptation, perhaps similar to that through which
dogs come to resemble their masters, they seem to have grown
to look like the characters in the spectacle. Massive Brünnhildes
with ground-gripper shoes under their flowing evening gowns
walk majestically by. Wotans with craggy faces scarred by student duels have put on their white ties and tails in the middle
of the afternoon to honor the occasion. A formidable-looking
woman leads an enormous Saint Bernard soberly through the
throng. He, too, is imposing, dignified, and Wotanlike. One
wonders, momentarily, whether the dog also has a seat in the
auditorium, but then one realizes that he has been released from
a parked car for an intermission walk.

The crowd bears no resemblance whatever to any other oper-

atic audience one has ever seen. There are some foreigners—
quite a few French and a sprinkling of English and Americans—
but they are in the minority. The bulk of the gathering consists
of middle-aged Germans, exuding the air of gravity and ponder-
ousness that often arises from being middle-aged and being German. But these people are of a special type, even among
Germans. They are Wagnerian Germans. For them, the Festival is obviously the crowning moment of a year of anticipation
and preparation. They have come to it in a spirit of religious
dedication, and though I observed one man riding up the street
to the Festspielhaus on a motorcycle with the tails of his evening
coat flapping in the wind, most of them give the impression of
having arrived on their knees. With only a little exaggeration,
Bayreuth might be termed the Lourdes of the musical world. Art
there is not the gracious adjunct to life that it is in England,
France, or Italy. It is an obsession, involving a sacred duty and
an act of submission.

THE FIGURE that continues to inspire this remarkable devotion
was undoubtedly a fascinating one, and he remains fascinating
today—among other reasons, for the curious ambivalence of feeling with which intelligent people must, I think, regard him.
There is much about Wagner's personality that evokes admira-
tion and very little that evokes affection. He was, of course, a
thundering self-propelled egotist, a windy thinker, and a man of
little subtlety in his relations with others. He was also, of course,
an authentic genius, a tremendously inspired musician, and
something of an intellectual octopus. In addition to the technical
influence of his music, which dominated the styles of lesser composers for at least two generations and is still felt in some quar-
ters today, there is the influence of his ideas about art and life—
something that, as far as I know, has never been completely

assessed. He fired such diverse imaginations as those of Friedrich Nietzsche, George Bernard Shaw, Charles Baudelaire, Auguste Renoir, and Adolf Hitler, and his thinking has spread so widely that one will find it echoed in the writings and attitudes of extraordinarily varied minds—for example, those of D. H. Lawrence, Frank Lloyd Wright, and Isadora Duncan.

Wagner was probably the greatest revolutionary in the history of art, and he was also, in a psychological sense, the first modern composer. It is in his collected prose works—a vast accretion of polemical writing, running to many volumes and containing an amazing flow of ideas that are by turns brilliant and sophomoric —that one finds the first references to "the art of the future." He is continuously preoccupied with breaking through frontiers, and impatient with the limitations of performing artists whose traditional craftsmanship he feels to be inadequate for the expression of his personal visions. In this respect, the contrast between him and, say, Mozart is striking indeed. Where Mozart, out of profound respect for the art of performance, frequently altered his melodies to fit the virtues or weaknesses of some singer or other, one finds Wagner insisting that ordinary singers are incompetent to convey his towering musical thoughts, and one finds him satisfied only when an entirely new type of performer is created, tailored expressly to his requirements.

Wagner demanded not only a new kind of singer but a new kind of theatre, properly equipped for his own, highly individual style of drama, and even a new kind of audience, willing to approach his works with reverence and spend no end of effort studiously trying to penetrate the complexities of his thought. He was the first composer, probably, to assume that he owed no responsibility to anything but his own genius, and that it was up to his audience to puzzle out his lofty inspirations as best it could. He was obsessed with progress, and was a prodigious inventor of new technical ideas, pushing the resources of his art to undreamed-of excesses, evolving iridescent harmonies and cascades of tone that must have struck his contemporaries as opening up an entirely new world.

Fortunately for Wagner, he lived during the peak of the Romantic era, when the artist had come to occupy a lordly position in society and when the breaking up of conventional attitudes had caused many people to adopt the rather confused idea that art was somehow a substitute for religion. In this curious intellectual environment, he appeared to his contemporaries as not only a composer but a prophet and spiritual leader, and his notions about life and morals—even when they were half-baked—were taken as seriously as his notions about art. Here, too, the contrast between Wagner and Mozart is instructive. Where Mozart, dominated by the aristocratic taste of his time, strove to fulfill or to outwit the artistic regulations laid down for him by connoisseurs like the Archbishop of Salzburg, one finds King Ludwig II of Bavaria practically crawling to Wagner, overwhelmed by the honor of assisting so great a genius in the pursuit of his headstrong aims.

Much of the pomp and aesthetic piety associated with this grandiose period and its great man still survive at Bayreuth. But the Wagnerian dream, for such visitors as are not quite willing to submit themselves to it without reservation, has a way of coming apart at the seams. The weaknesses of Wagner—his total lack of the charms of graciousness and modesty, his lack of subtlety in dealing with human fallibility, his magnificent but slightly irritating arrogance, and his lack of humor except in its cruder forms—stand out starkly.

The Ring cycle, impressive though it may be from the purely musical standpoint, looks like what it is—the overblown apotheosis of a national folklore reflecting tribal doings not very different from those recounted in the legends of such moderately developed hunting-and-fishing peoples as the Ojibway Indians.

Siegfried, the hero who knows no fear (just how one who knows no fear can possibly be considered a hero is a psychological point outside the scope of Wagnerian thought), seems beefy, youthful, somewhat unpleasant, and distinctly uninteresting from an intellectual point of view. Though well-intentioned, he is unquestionably an egregious bonehead, and is thwarted and cheated by the more intelligent villains of the piece with the greatest of ease. One is supposed to feel sorry about this, but somehow one cannot entirely accept the Wagnerian hypothesis that such virtues as youth, vigor, and brute strength are more admirable than brains. Jean-Jacques Rousseau's Noble Savage is exaggerated here into a monstrosity, and the morals of the drama are those of a barbaric society—the sort of society that we might thank our stars we've escaped from. All this makes it extremely difficult for the auditor to identify himself with the main characters, and he finds his sympathies wandering to such lesser figures as seem to possess traces of human frailty—Siegmund and Sieglinde, who are involved in an understandable domestic tragedy, and even the villains Mime and Alberich, who at least seem to know what they are about.

What saves the proceedings from becoming a dreadful bore is, of course, the intoxicating power of the music. This power is such that one is cajoled, in spite of oneself, into a temporary acceptance of Wagner's faulty morals and his insensitiveness to human values. When this music talks about love, courage, or the poetry of nature—and it *does* talk all the time about something specific (the point Thomas Mann was making when he observed that Wagner's librettos may not be literature, but his music is)—it is eloquent to a degree that is probably unsurpassed anywhere in art.

Nevertheless, the whole spectacle is assuming a noticeably dated aspect. It is becoming clear that the great artistic revolutionist got himself out on a limb, where his work now stands—

not as part of an advancement of musical tradition but as a sort of dramatic curiosity, unrelated to the main developments of civilized culture. The colossal theatrical machinery he created, with its mammoth singers and its stupendous scenic effects, has had no imitators. The works of his more modest contemporaries —Bellini and Verdi, for example—and of his forerunner Mozart seem more immediate today than his world of fantastic heroics and splendid barbarism.

Wagner's revolution was so drastic and his prestige so great that for a time he succeeded in dislocating the aims of the art of music. The world has not since produced a composer of comparable gifts. But the gifts now seem to have been destructive as well as awesomely arresting, and subsequent composers have, to a large extent, been occupied in picking up the pieces he left behind and getting their art back on a sane basis.

IN AN EFFORT to minimize the dated and romantically excessive qualities of the Wagnerian cosmos, and bring its worth-while components into line with modern thought, the present directors of the Bayreuth Festival—Wagner's grandsons Wolfgang and Wieland—have, as is well known, done a considerable job of housecleaning. Their efforts have brought about a sort of urbanization of the theatrical side of Wagner's music dramas, and—a good deal of sacrosanct Wagnerian furniture having been thrown out the window in the process—the net outcome, in most respects, is more convincing to today's audiences than the more or less realistic stage conceptions of the past.

The first thing that strikes one about these new productions is the total absence of beards, flowing hair, breastplates, and those unsightly horned and eagle-winged helmets. The heroes and villains are now as clean-shaven and clipped as the characters in any drawing-room comedy, almost nobody wears a hat of any sort, and the heroines are dressed in simple tunics that resemble up-to-date evening gowns and give their wearers some legitimate pretensions to glamour. The stage on which they move—in the Ring, at least—is swept bare of everything but indispensable properties. There is practically no scenery in the old-fashioned sense, the grandiose atmosphere of the Wagnerian wonderland being merely suggested, by extremely ingenious uses of projected light. The stage floor, in every scene, is a tilted disc, somewhat resembling the top of a gigantic drum and reminiscent of the circular area frequently used for acts in night clubs, and the action that takes place on it is simplified and formalized, leaving all detail to the imagination. The method entails some disappointments for the old-time Wagnerite. There is, for example, no dragon in "Siegfried," and the hero is reduced to some rather vague shadowboxing in his efforts to convince the onlookers that he is actually engaged in slaying one.

The system of projected lighting has the apparently inevitable effect of suffusing the entire production in murky shadow, even when things are supposed to be happening in broad daylight. The first act of "Die Walküre," traditionally an interior, is played on a dim, bare stage before a single, gigantic tree trunk. The second act looks as if it were taking place at the bottom of a coal mine, and the final scene—the one in which Brünnhilde is put to rest on her flame-encircled mountaintop—leaves that heroine looking no more impressive than a dead fly on a stove lid.

Elsewhere, however, these simplified sets turn out to be more imposing. The opening scene of "Das Rheingold," with three very nearly naked Rhine maidens disporting themselves high up on a proscenium that seems to be bathed in foam—appearing, disappearing, and reappearing as if actually diving and swimming in a torrent—is the most effective staging of this episode that I have ever seen. The rushing horde of Nibelungs that bring the Rhine treasure aboveground later in the opera swirl around the stage very dramatically, and the treasure itself looks less like a pile of old suitcases than it usually does. Everybody is fairly handsome or striking—or at least handsomer and more striking than is customary—and all details of the drama have been studied and coördinated with meticulous efficiency. True, there are points in the text where references are made to objects —trees, animals, helmets, weapons, and so on—that do not exist before the eye. But these discrepancies don't seem to matter much, in view of the consistency and coherence of the spectacle as a whole.

On the purely musical side, there has, of course, been no tampering with Wagner's original conception, and here, I must say, the Bayreuth Festival is truly a festival, in that it is an occasion for a unique experience. The acoustics of the old Festspielhaus are perfect, and the hidden orchestra pit has the virtue of slightly diminishing the orchestral sound, so that one does not feel that the singers are continually engaged in an unequal battle with the trombones. The orchestra, an all-star gathering assembled from various orchestras throughout Germany, is by far the finest I have encountered in Europe. Its woodwinds and brasses are almost incredibly smooth, its strings are very rich in tone, and things like the exceedingly difficult Siegfried horn calls emerge with a degree of polished virtuosity that I have never heard equalled.

The singers are so well coached and rehearsed that one tends to become absorbed in the illusion they are creating and to forget their individual peculiarities as artists. I have heard quite a few of the roles more brilliantly sung at the Metropolitan, during the great days of Flagstad, Melchoir, Lawrence, Schorr, and Rethberg, but I have never heard Wagnerian singers perform with such coördination as a group. Some of them also turn out, on closer analysis, to be rather remarkable artists. Gustav Neidlinger and Paul Kuen, as Alberich and Mime, respectively, pro-

duce the most eloquent interpretations of these sinister roles
that I have ever encountered. Hans Hotter makes a noble and
physically imposing Wotan, and Jean Madeira a superb Erda.
In "Götterdämmerung," Wolfgang Windgassen and Astrid Varnay, as Siegfried and Brünnhilde, cut loose with some really
inspired singing. In fact, as the awakened Brünnhilde, Miss
Varnay creates some of the finest moments of the entire Ring
cycle, singing like an angel, hitting her high notes with magnificent ease, and acting with such freshness and warmth that
one's critical faculties are, for the time being, completely dis-
armed.

AFTER WITNESSING the Ring, I stayed on in Bayreuth to see two
additional items—a "Parsifal" and the controversial and now
somewhat notorious new production of "Die Meistersinger." I
am not much of a "Parsifal" enthusiast. The long, slow-motion
duel between sex and piety that is its central theme has always
struck me as both tedious and slightly fatuous, though the opera,
of course, is full of beautiful music. I can only report that it
was presented with the same simple décor and modernized stagecraft that characterized the Ring; that Hans Knappertsbusch
(who had also presided over the Ring dramas) conducted the
score in a masterly fashion; that the singers—especially Martha
Mödl, as Kundry—sang with great authority; and that the whole
performance, to those who like "Parsifal," must have seemed
reverent and impressive.

The new "Meistersinger" was, I am afraid, an altogether different matter. In witnessing this, one finds it difficult to avoid
the suspicion that Wolfgang and Wieland, having suffered since
earliest childhood under the overpowering weight of their grandfather's solemnity, had long nourished a suppressed desire to

have some fun by producing a revue, and that this desire had finally broken loose. The trouble is that "Die Meistersinger," though a comedy, is still a pretty dignified and ponderous affair, and that Wieland's scenic ideas, which might have proved effective enough in some such surroundings as Billy Rose's Diamond Horseshoe, don't fit it at all. Most of Wieland's jazzing-up takes place in the second act and the final scene of the last act. In the former, which is supposed to take place on a quaint street in old Nuremberg, the curtain rose on something that looked more like a chic window display at Lord & Taylor's. There wasn't a house in sight. Two park benches constituted the only properties. A gigantic globe—evidently a stylized hydrangea bush—hung at one side of the stage, like an exhibit in a planetarium. Hans Sachs, beardless, looked curiously like certain early photographs of Wagner himself—a not inappropriate note—and Pogner, also beardless, strikingly resembled the late Warren G. Harding. Of the picturesque medieval atmosphere that should make this scene one of the most enchanting Wagner ever wrote, not a trace remained.

The opera's final scene was even more drastically remodelled. The singing contest between Walther and Beckmesser took place in an arena that looked like the operating theatre of an overpopulated school for surgeons. Choristers stood in tiers in the background, the women dressed in what appeared to be nineteenth-century housemaids' uniforms and the men wearing oilskins complete with sou'westers. There was no parade of Nuremberg guildsmen and apprentices. Instead, there was a queer and badly choreographed ballet, in which the ballerinas looked like candidates for a fourth-rate production of "Swan Lake." The thing lacked only a naked woman on a platter to become a splendid travesty. As I looked at it, I could not restrain a certain sympathy for the long-frustrated psyches of Wolfgang and Wieland. But this sort of huggermugger obviously can't go on. Grandpa's ghost is sure to get them in the end.

MUNICH

In Munich, the musical atmosphere is more normal than Bayreuth's, and though the city is having an opera festival, too, people seem to be attending its performances with no aim other than that of having a good time, which, for a change, I find rather refreshing. Appropriately, this festival has been devoted largely to the comedy operas of Mozart, who liked Munich and spent a good deal of time here, and to the works of Richard Strauss, who was, of course, Munich's own great home-town composer. Among the latter, there have been performances of Strauss's less frequently given operas, including "Capriccio," "Arabella," "Die Frau Ohne Schatten," "Die Aegyptische Helena," and "Ariadne auf Naxos," and I have been glad to avail myself of the opportunity of hearing some of them—"Die Frau Ohne Schatten" and "Die Aegyptische Helena," in particular, since as far as I am aware, the former has never, and the latter very seldom, been performed in America.

Operatic production in Munich is still being carried on under handicaps. The old Nationaltheater, which for more than a hundred years housed the city's finest operatic spectacles, remains a bombed-out hulk, and today's performances are held in the smaller auditoriums known as the Prinzregententheater and the Residenztheater. But there is an air of freshness, vitality, and theatrical ingenuity about these performances that matches Munich's extraordinary vigor in other fields—a vigor that one notices in its teeming shops and in the zeal with which its incredible wartime damage is being repaired. The stages of these auditoriums may be small, the orchestra of the Munich State Opera, which plays in their pits, may not be quite as smooth and brilliant as those of Vienna and Bayreuth, and the singers may not always be up to the most exacting vocal standard, but the doings behind the proscenium seem both adventurous and enthusiastic, the teamwork is excellent, and the visual side of things shows resourcefulness and originality.

I was especially taken with two Mozart performances that I heard—of "The Marriage of Figaro" and "Così fan Tutte"—since I found in them a fulfillment of the close-knit German-Austrian Mozart tradition (what is sometimes called *der echte Mozart-stil*), which I had missed in most of the performances at the Salzburg Festival earlier this summer. Indeed, the production of "The Marriage of Figaro" was a masterpiece of its kind, though I am thankful that the method used is not universal, since it somewhat minimizes the purely sensuous features of the Mozart vocal style.

In Munich, "The Marriage of Figaro" becomes a tightly directed and fast-moving play in which the singing is subordinated to the dramatic action and the general fabric of the score. The recitatives are done according to the rules of *recitativo secco* (a German and Austrian specialty), which means that the lines are rapidly declaimed in what amounts to a whisper and take on the character of all-but-spoken dialogue. The arias, too, are sung with very moderate volume and with no pretensions to vocal display. The result is a sort of miniature performance, suited only to small and intimate opera houses like the Residenztheater, where this one took place, but the drama has been accentuated and speeded up, and the outcome, within its frame, is wonderfully satisfying. I cannot say whether the singers involved in all this were artists of major vocal calibre, since their singing was so subdued as to utilize only a small part of their physical equipment. The conductor, Eugen Jochum, kept things going at a crisp, rapid pace. The tone he got from the orchestra was brilliant and at times slightly harsh, but in a production like this beauty of tone does not seem to be as much of an object as clockwork precision, and while, as I've said, I am glad that Mozart is performed in other ways elsewhere, the Munich way has its admirable points and is well worth hearing.

The productions of Richard Strauss's "Die Frau Ohne Schatten" and "Die Aegyptische Helena" turned out to be interesting for other reasons. They were given full-scale performances, with scenery that was at once charming and extremely elaborate, the former opera involving what must have been twenty or thirty changes of scene. Both operas are comparatively late Strauss works; "Die Frau Ohne Schatten" dates from 1919 and "Die Aegyptische Helena" from 1927. Both have enchanting musical moments, and their scores exhibit considerable lyric strength and the great respect for the human voice that made Strauss the last of the important composers who have written for it eloquently.

It is nevertheless easy to see why neither of the operas has become internationally successful. The reason lies in their librettos, which are so inept and unconvincing that they make no coherent dramatic impression whatever. The paucity of good librettos in German and Austrian opera is an arresting phenomenon, and while it is too complicated to discuss here at length, I might note in passing that aside perhaps from "Der Rosenkavalier," "Die Meistersinger," "Tristan," and most of the works of Mozart, there are very few decent librettos to be found in the operas of Central European composers, and that a vast amount of first-rate music by these composers—notably that of Carl Maria von Weber and Hans Pfitzner—is unperformed in the world's opera houses today simply because the dramas to which it is set are so childish or silly that nobody but Central Europeans can take them seriously. I might also point out that the greatest of Mozart's operas (which are also, of course, the greatest of Central European operas) all had librettos written by a foreigner, the Italianized Spanish Jew Lorenzo Da Ponte, and that when Mozart turned to a fellow-Austrian, Emanuel Schikaneder, for the libretto of "The Magic Flute," he was rewarded with the peculiar hodgepodge that blights an otherwise beautiful creation.

The inference that one might draw from these observations is that Germans and Austrians have always been somewhat lacking in the special kind of craftsmanship that produces serviceable plays to which operatic music can be set, and I am afraid that Hugo von Hofmannsthal, the librettist of both "Die Frau Ohne Schatten" and "Die Aegyptische Helena," has proved an exception to this rule only in his unique operatic comedy "Der Rosenkavalier." His libretto for "Elektra," while also successful, is by no means pure von Hofmannsthal, being a mere adaptation of Sophocles. When von Hofmannsthal was on his own, he appears to have fallen only too easily into the realm of supernatural hocus-pocus, badly carpentered situations, and ill-defined characters that is apt to engulf the lesser literary products of the Germanic mind.

"Die Frau Ohne Schatten," like de La Motte-Fouqué's "Undine," concerns the hazards of falling in love with a female creature who is not quite human—in this instance, a forest sprite who lacks a shadow and tries very hard to obtain one, because, for some reason, her shadowless state dooms her human husband to be turned to stone. To avert this calamity, she finally buys a shadow from the wife of a poor dyer, and this complicates the dyer's life no end, since his wife is now shadowless—a condition that in her case seems to induce a tendency toward marital infidelity. From here on, things get a bit incomprehensible, but it is clear that this shadow-bartering involves a crime of some sort, for which the principals must do penance, and after a series of trials and tests rather reminiscent of those in "The Magic Flute" the forest sprite magnanimously gives the shadow back to its original owner and finds, to her relief, that her husband doesn't have to be permanently petrified after all.

I daresay that, treated with a certain amount of humor, this outrageous plot might conceivably have served as the basis of a ballet or something of the sort. But "Die Frau Ohne Schatten" contains no humor. It is, on the contrary, quite earnest, and, to judge by the program notes, one is supposed to find in it a lot of profound symbolism about the nature of love. I am afraid that this symbolism escaped me, and that in spite of the Strauss music and the opera's lavish scenic wonders, designed (in the style of Persian miniatures) by Emil Preetorius, the whole thing seemed to me very turgid and a little adolescent in its point of view.

"Die Aegyptische Helena" is perhaps a trifle more coherent, but not much. Its action, which takes place in Egypt after the Trojan War, concerns the problems of Menelaus, who is, at this point, extremely jealous of Helen, because she was a pretty naughty girl in Troy and may, for all he knows, still be thinking some nice thoughts about Paris. In a rage, he kills her—or at least he thinks he does. As it turns out, a sorceress has replaced the real Helen with a phantom, and it is the phantom that he has killed. After that, with the real Helen still around, Menelaus—a very mixed-up fellow indeed—finds that he is not in love with her but with the phantom he has killed. This schizoid situation is finally assuaged by the unexpected appearance of a child Helen bore him before the war. I could extract no point from the whole thing except possibly the moral that when one is dealing with people like Menelaus it's always a good idea to have a well-trained sorceress handy.

The scenery and costumes in which the Munich State Opera clothed these doings were again extraordinarily charming, however, and the Strauss score sounded sparkling and subtle. The singer who took the part of Helen, a lusty, good-looking soprano named Leonie Rysanek, whom I had previously heard and admired in Vienna, seems to be one of the mainstays of Central European opera at the moment. I understand that she has recently been signed up by the San Francisco Opera, and in my opinion, she is likely to prove a considerable success there.

VENICE

THE ITALIANS, as I have pointed out—or, at any rate, hinted—previously, are, to my way of thinking, of all peoples the least confused about music. They have never tended to mistake mere ingenuity for substance, and they have never regarded the art with any great amount of religious awe.

If you suggest to Italians that the composer's primary purpose is to fulfill a historic destiny by pushing forward the frontiers of technique, and writing for future generations instead of his own, they will conclude that you are mad, which I am inclined to feel is not an altogether unreasonable inference. The composer's primary purpose, in their view, is simply to please and interest his audience—a purpose as fundamental as the shoemaker's purpose of making shoes that fit his customers' feet. They know that what pleases and interests an audience is the elusive quality referred to as heart, sentiment, humanity—whatever you like to call it—and that if this quality is lacking, the music is just no good, regardless of how much artifice has been expended upon it. This basic and, to me, eminently healthy attitude has been clashing with, and drawing sparks from, a great deal of contemporary music that has been played here over the past couple of weeks, in the course of Venice's Festival Internazionale di Musica Contemporanea.

The Festival, indeed, has been about as lively a musical occasion as I have recently experienced, for the Venetians not only appear to be vitally interested in modern music but are extremely vocal in expressing their opinions about it. At one concert, I sat through the performance of a long and exceedingly tedious atonal composition by a certain Riccardo Malipiero—something called a Concerto Breve for Ballerina and Orchestra—to which a young American dancer named Shirley Broughton contributed a rather unimaginative and awkward dance of her own devising. In Carnegie Hall, the presentation would probably have elicited a flurry of polite applause. But not in Venice. When it was over, Mr. Malipiero appeared on the stage to take a bow and was greeted with a tremendous chorus of boos. Undaunted, he went on bowing gravely, and, as the boos continued, came out for a second curtain call, perhaps with the aim of thoroughly savoring his martyrdom—or possibly he found the angry shouts of the rabble like music to his cultivated ears. I must say that all this struck me as highly refreshing. Mr. Malipiero was being taken very seriously, and his composition had called forth a genuine reaction.

The concert, which was the opening event of the Festival, was held in the old Teatro La Fenice, the famous Venetian opera house where "La Traviata" and "Rigoletto" received their world premières in the middle of the nineteenth century—a veritable jewel box of a theatre, dripping with peach-and-blue rococo ornament, and quite the most enchanting auditorium of its kind that I have ever seen. In it, one's mind could wander pleasantly from the music to the various nymphs and caryatids that ogled the audience in the orchestra seats from the tiers of old-fashioned boxes, and there was even a clock embedded in the ceiling, to remind one, realistically, of the passage of time. The ushers were dressed in eighteenth-century livery, with tails and knee breeches, and the whole scene had the atmosphere of nostalgic and elegant theatricality that is found in nearly everything typically Venetian. The crowd, too, was smartly dressed, and had arrived in a gala spirit to participate in a ceremony of some artistic importance, conscious that its role was as indispensable to events of this sort as that of the performers.

Although Mr. Malipiero's effort did not fall into the category of fine music, there were several items on the program that were not without merit. One of them was a composition for baritone and orchestra called "Symboli Chrestiani," by Nicolas Nabokov—a sort of religious cantata based on various early Christian texts. Mr. Nabokov's style of composition in this work proved to be identifiably Russo-Parisian, which, I suppose, might have been expected, since he cut his teeth as a composer in Paris during the Diaghilev era. But, for all its echoes of the ballet manner of that period, it was a sober and, in spots, poetically evocative piece, somewhat archaic in mood and very expertly written for the orchestra. Another pleasant item was a Suite Concertante for Violin and Orchestra, by the prominent Czech composer Bohuslav Martinu. This, like much of Mr. Martinu's other work, was rhapsodic in character and full of ideas distilled from gypsy folk music. Its idiom was very aptly suited to the violin, but I think the suite might have sounded more effective if the solo part had been entrusted to a more brilliant musician than Mr. Blaise Calame, the violinist for this performance.

The hit of the evening, however, was a composition of a completely different sort—one from which the stock mannerisms of modern musical fashion were entirely absent. When I saw this work coming up on the program, billed as a "Concerto for Mouth Organ and Orchestra," I expected a stunt of some kind, but its actual effect turned out to be quite seriously musical and as refreshing as a cold shower. The composer was Alexander Tcherepnin, a Russian now living in Chicago, and the soloist who played the mouth organ, or harmonica, was John Sebastian, an American virtuoso of whose existence I had been aware but whom I had not previously heard.

In undertaking to compose for this folk instrument, which, like the guitar and the accordion, is rather happily limited to clear and simple diatonic musical utterance, Mr. Tcherepnin had chosen to accept its limitations and make the most of its strong capacity for lyric expression of a purely elementary sort. His approach was interesting precisely because he permitted himself no self-conscious tricks of style but, instead, wrote music of forthright sincerity, well adapted to his medium. In listening to it, I could not restrain the fleeting thought that the technique of many other contemporary composers might be immeasurably benefited if they were to write music for instruments designed, like Mr. Sebastian's, for nothing but the most straightforward melodic expression. Within the frame imposed by the harmonica, no bluffing was possible and no refuge was to be found in elaborate technical mystification. Mr. Tcherepnin was obliged to write melody as clean and revealing as Giuseppe Verdi's, and resign himself to success or failure solely on the basis of his talent, with no cerebral machinery obscuring his heart from his audience.

In my opinion, his talent, thus set forth in all its nakedness, stood up very well. The Concerto for Mouth Organ and Orchestra established itself as that extremely unusual thing among present-day compositions—a work of indubitable infectiousness and charm. I am sure that its honesty and communicative power will make it thoroughly liked wherever it is performed in the future. As for Mr. Sebastian, he proved himself to be an artist of great accomplishments by any standards, able to draw from his little mouth organ music of an eloquence and refinement that might well be envied by virtuosos who play more conventional instruments. The orchestral accompaniment was very effectively conducted by Fabien Sevitzky, and the Venetian audience, sensing that the composer had beautifully fulfilled his primary purpose, applauded with vast enthusiasm.

AN EVENING OR so after this concert, I went to Saint Mark's Cathedral to attend what was generally regarded as the most momentous event of the entire Festival—the première of a work, for orchestra, chorus, and soloists, by the great Igor Stravinsky, portentously entitled "Canticum Sacrum ad Honorem Sancti Marci Nominis." Commissioned—at considerable expense, I understand—by the Municipality of Venice, it had been written specially for this occasion. The cathedral was made available

for its performance by a dispensation of Venice's Cardinal Ron-
calli, in recognition of the composer's genius and in honor of
the city's patron saint, to whom the work was dedicated, and Mr.
Stravinsky himself was on hand to conduct it.

An enormous crowd was present, including a large scattering
of fashionable tourists, as well as most of the city's music lovers.
The Cardinal made a ceremonial appearance prior to the performance, and the impressive old church, with its soaring golden
Byzantine interior, seemed like a vast stage set, ready for a religious drama of stunning grandeur, as rows of four-foot candles
illumined the cavernous scene with a flickering light. The
orchestra, chorus, and soloists sat on a raised dais directly under
the central dome, while press photographers, anxious not to miss
a moment of the proceedings, dangled from the upper galleries,
shooting off flash bulbs.

The place was obviously primed for one of those gaunt,
slightly barbaric, theatrical, and eminently Byzantine compositions that Stravinsky (himself a Russian Orthodox communi-
cant) had often turned out in the past. By way of prelude, the
young American conductor Robert Craft led the orchestra and
singers through some music by sixteenth- and seventeenth-century Venetian composers, among them Andrea and Giovanni
Gabrieli and Claudio Monteverdi. These preliminary items
proved to be gorgeous and resplendent, and it was a privilege to
hear their finely chiselled archaic counterpoint echoing in the
setting that had witnessed their birth more than three hundred
years ago. Then Mr. Stravinsky climbed briskly to the podium,
and the cantata in honor of St. Mark began.

It would be a pleasure to be able to report that Mr. Stravinsky's new work was a fitting compliment to these imposing
surroundings. But this, I am afraid, was not the case. The
cantata lasted about seventeen minutes, and those minutes were

filled with about as feeble and incoherent a hodgepodge of sound as I have ever encountered. Even listening with the utmost sympathy and trying to discover moments of originality, if not beauty, I was unable to find anything in it that was either striking or intellectually stimulating. It was simply a very silly and very boring affair. When it was over, there were neither plaudits nor boos, but this silence was imposed by the sacredness of the locale and had no reference to the feelings of the public. Next day, some of these feelings broke loose in the form of a unanimous roasting by the Venetian critics. I must say that I agreed with them. Whatever Mr. Stravinsky's claims to eminence may be, this particular work in no way sustained them.

BACK IN THE Teatro La Fenice a few nights later, I attended a concert of music by young Italian composers. The audience, this time, was small and clearly in a mood to encourage, rather than criticize, and most of the works performed were immature, and interesting only for occasional evidences of promise on the part of their creators. If the lot of them can be taken as a sample of what the more youthful Italian composers are up to, it would be fair to conclude that atonality is by no means the dominant fashion here, for aside from a single twelve-tone composition, by a man named Carlo Prosperi, all the works played hewed to relatively conventional schemes of tonality.

Only one of the compositions seemed to me to indicate a musical mind with really distinguished potentialities—a Divertimento for Strings, by a thirty-one-year-old Roman named Olivio di Domenico. Mr. di Domenico's style of writing was logical and emotionally expressive, and he had a neat and scrupulous way with counterpoint. Casting about for a comparison that might give an American reader some idea of its effect, I can only say that it sounded something like the work of our own Samuel Barber.

WITH THIS CONCERT, the strictly contemporary aspect of the festival came to an end. To be sure, the New York City Ballet, which has been extraordinarily busy in Europe this summer, opened a week's engagement here, and I attended its initial performance, but since its repertoire consisted entirely of items long familiar to New York audiences, I shall not trouble you with an account of what it presented. Its dancers and conductors seemed to be in excellent shape, and the Venetian public seemed to like them enormously.

There remains only one other event worthy of note—an appearance of the Vienna Philharmonic, under Dimitri Mitropoulos. Neither of the two large compositions it presented fitted into the category of modern music as we ordinarily use the term. One was Arnold Schoenberg's early tone poem "Pelléas and Mélisande," completed in 1903, years before his style had congealed into the dry atonal formula for which he subsequently became famous; the other was the "Alpensinfonie" of Richard Strauss, a descriptive composition of rather late vintage as Strauss's purely orchestral works go, having been completed in 1915.

Hearing these pieces was well worth while, since neither is performed very often nowadays, and the two of them made a moderately striking contrast, even though they were more or less similar in technique, both reflecting the lush chromatic manner of composition that has always characterized the followers of Richard Wagner. Of the two, I preferred the Schoenberg work by far. It is a brooding, neurotic affair, whose agonies seem deeply felt, and its total effect, in this performance, was one of tragic dignity. It brought home once again the fact that the early, pre-atonal Schoenberg, as revealed in this work and in the equally emotion-drugged "Gurrelieder" and "Verklärte Nacht," was a composer of considerable evocative power.

In comparison, Strauss's "Alpensinfonie" seemed merely exhibitionistic and facile. It is an essay in heroic musical landscape painting, having as its subject, of course, the moods induced by contemplating the awesome scenery of the Alps, and the orchestration calls for an immense array of instruments, including Bayreuth tubas and cowbells. The sort of nature painting that Strauss attempted here has been brought off successfully by other composers—notably Wagner and, later, Sibelius, a subtle and eloquent master of the art—but this hearing of the "Alpensinfonie" merely convinced me that Strauss was out of his element in the open air. His birdcalls, avalanches, and shepherds' pipes all have a corny ring that brings to mind the vulgarity of a picture-postcard scene, and his treatment of nature is so suffused with sentimental touches reminiscent of "Der Rosenkavalier" that his Alps seem to be viewed from the window of a Viennese boudoir.

Mr. Mitropoulos gave both the "Alpensinfonie" and the Schoenberg work magnificent performances, proving once more that, whatever his shortcomings as a conductor of serene classics, he is a superb interpreter of music that is flamboyant and highly charged with emotion. Mr. Mitropoulos, if I may borrow a favorite distinction of Friedrich Nietzsche's, is a Dionysian, rather than an Apollonian, maestro, and in this concert he was at his Dionysian best.

SEASON OF 1956-1957

October 27, 1956

THE ONLY COMPOSER of the past forty years to whom I would unhesitatingly apply the adjective "daring" is Mr. Carl Orff, of Munich. His particular daring lies in the unblushing use of certain rather refreshing musical devices—the C-major chord, the oom-pah accompaniment, and four-four time—which have been more or less tabooed by the "advanced" composers of his generation, and which, since they are in consequence rarely encountered at today's highbrow musical gatherings, are likely to produce the sort of shock that might attend the sudden appearance of gin fizzes at a meeting of the Woman's Christian Temperance Union.

It was this sort of shock, I think, that overcame the intellectually fashionable and modern-minded audience present at the American première of his opera "The Moon" last week, and resulted in what was perhaps the greatest demonstration of booing and catcalling I have ever heard in an American musical auditorium. I was all in favor of this demonstration, because I love to see any audience vent its feelings dynamically, and wish that more musical audiences would do so. But I am afraid that I also found Mr. Orff's opera a highly engaging affair, and that the momentum of its throbbing rhythms, the simple clarity of its harmonic style, and the deftness of its choral writing kept me agreeably stimulated and entertained during most of the evening.

"The Moon" is a slight, unpretentious, and completely unconventional work. Its subject is a Grimm fairy tale about four adventurers who steal the moon from an oak tree in a neighboring town, set it up in a tree in their own community, and later, on their deathbeds, demand that it be cut in four pieces and buried with them. This flagrant misuse of a public utility disturbs St. Peter, who descends to earth and, after delivering a somewhat long-winded sermon on the human propensity to err, pleases everybody by putting the moon where it belongs—up in the sky. As you can see, this is not the stuff that operas in the grand manner are made of, and perhaps "The Moon" is not really an opera at all. But, whatever it is, it has enough quaint fantasy and rollicking music to infect any but the most doctrinaire audience.

In this respect, it appeared to me to outdistance by far Igor Stravinsky's "L'Histoire du Soldat," which appeared as its companion piece on the program, and which was received with considerable reverence. For some reason, nobody ever mentions the librettist of "L'Histoire"—as I remember, he was a Swiss named Charles Ferdinand Ramuz—and to my way of thinking he deserves the lion's share of whatever credit is due this mild bit of vaudeville. Stravinsky's contribution to it is limited to five or six bits of incidental music, and I must say I thought their humor rather forced and their strictly musical content pretty stale. The New York City Opera gave both "L'Histoire" and "The Moon"

performances that were exuberant enough, if not always enchanting from the visual standpoint.

HAVING BEEN A BIT late for the opening of the New York musical season, I missed the première of "Susannah," the much-
talked-about opera by the young South Carolina composer
Carlisle Floyd, and it was not until last week that I got around
to hearing it. I attended the performance at the City Center in
a mood of pleasant anticipation, but what I heard exceeded even
the hopes I had built up while reading the reviews that greeted
its first showing. I found myself caught up in something that
seemed to me a very important artistic experience.

To my mind, "Susannah" is probably the most moving and
impressive opera to have been written in America—or anywhere
else, as far as I am aware—since Gershwin's "Porgy and Bess,"
and in many ways it is a more genuine opera than that justly
celebrated but slightly uneven work. Lest you think that my
unaccustomed enthusiasm is running away with me, I hasten to
add that "Susannah" has its faults. Its orchestration is occasionally on the crude side, and Mr. Floyd has not yet mastered
all the skill required to set the vowels and consonants of the
English language to music with maximum effectiveness.

But these flaws are insignificant in view of "Susannah's" dramatic sweep and the heartening sincerity of its musical style.
This style owes a great deal to the homely idioms of rural American religious and folk music, but Mr. Floyd's work is by no
means the dreary essay in musical ethnology that American "folk
operas" have usually turned out to be. The language he employs
in telling a story that moves forward with enthralling intensity
is clearly his own, and he uses it with the intellectual control
and the theatrical flair that bespeak both the serious composer
and the born musical dramatist. Nowhere does he fiddle with

stylistic tricks for their own sake, as does Mr. Stravinsky, and even Mr. Orff. He is too busy writing music of robust creative power and underlining the grim drama that is the subject of his piece.

"Susannah," as I suppose everybody knows by now, is about a Tennessee hillbilly girl who, because of her good looks and her innocent habit of bathing naked in a secluded creek, becomes the victim of vicious gossip. Hounded to the point of distraction by her neighbors and by a hypocritical revivalist who claims to be interested in her soul, she wearily permits this gentleman to seduce her—something he has obviously had in mind all along. In a manner slightly reminiscent of Somerset Maugham's "Rain," this incident unhinges the revivalist's mind, and ultimately brings about his death at the hands of her rightous and muddleheaded brother. The opera includes a stunning revival-meeting scene, and Mr. Floyd has written a great many hauntingly beautiful arias, among them "The Jaybird Song," in the first act, and the wistful melody "Come Back, O Summer," which Susannah croons in the lonely moments preceding the seduction scene.

Altogether, "Susannah" is that rare thing, an American opera that invites no apologies or qualifications. The settings, by Leo Kerz, were extremely tasteful, the musical direction, by Erich Leinsdorf, was superb, and the work of several of the principals —notably Phyllis Curtin, as Susannah; Jon Crain, as her brother; Eb Thomas, as a dimwit; and that admirable artist Norman Treigle, as the distraught revivalist—had an air of authenticity that was quite stirring.

November 10, 1956

MARIA MENEGHINI CALLAS has, perhaps unfortunately, entered the New York operatic scene amid a blare of publicity, which gave her début on opening night at the Metropolitan Opera House, something of the atmosphere of the invasion of a local tennis tournament by a star outsider. A few of her listeners were evidently prepared to welcome what they expected would be the most spectacular diva to appear at the Met since the days of Maria Jeritza, but many others—partisans, I imagine, of such well-loved rivals of hers as Renata Tebaldi and Zinka Milanov—were quite defensive about the whole thing, and the result was that during the first part of the evening, at least, Miss Callas's reception was distinctly cool.

The majority of the critics also tended toward coolness, and their reviews next day betrayed a firm determination not to be stampeded by the eloquence of her advance billing. Now that the shouting, and the compensatory frigidity, has somewhat abated, I think it should be possible to arrive at a detached estimate of Miss Callas's gifts, which do not in any way resemble those of Miss Tebaldi or Miss Milanov, and which, to my mind, are by no means inconsiderable.

First of all, Miss Callas is a very striking theatrical personality.

Her slim, rather angular, and slightly Oriental appearance—which, though rather handsome, is sometimes reminiscent of those elongated female demons depicted in Balinese shadow plays—is supplemented by the intense temperament of a born tragedienne. When she appears on the stage, the eye as well as the ear tends to become fascinated by what she is doing, and her entrances, in particular, have that immediate magnetic quality that one associates with such opera singers as are also distinguished women of the theatre. Her talents as an actress, I suspect, are limited to the more fiery range of Latin operatic tragedy, but within that range they are extraordinarily elastic and have the power to draw an audience into the life and emotions of the character she is portraying—a power that is not very common among singers when one approaches them from the purely visual standpoint.

When it comes to the matter of Miss Callas's voice, one must distinguish between her physical equipment and the manner in which she handles it. The physical equipment is remarkable for its scope and agility, rather than for the quality of the tone it produces. Miss Callas's voice is not an especially large one, and its prevailing timbre is distinctly reedy—a characteristic that, while it tends to add a fillip of intensity and passion to her singing, becomes in the long run slightly monotonous. Her voice is, however, one of enormous compass, with brilliant—at times slightly shrill—high notes and a throaty, somewhat feline lower register. Moreover, it is capable of the utmost flexibility throughout this compass, and its flexibility, coupled with its range and not unrespectable power, give her the combined virtues of a dramatic and a coloratura soprano—a coincidence of vocal gifts that is at least rare, and therefore quite impressive.

As for what Miss Callas does with this unusual equipment, I shall content myself with reporting what she did with it on opening night. The opera was "Norma," and "Norma," as every confirmed operagoer knows, offers its leading soprano the most exacting challenge, both in point of technique and in point of style, to be found in the currently performed repertory. This challenge is so exacting, in fact, that in the course of several performances of the work that have taken place at the Metropolitan since the time of Rosa Ponselle (whose Norma I was unfortunately not privileged to hear) I have not witnessed an adequate, let alone an inspiring, interpretation of the role. Miss Callas's reading of it was certainly adequate, and at times something more than that. She spun out the long, extremely taxing phrases of "Casta Diva" reticently but with superb control and with admirable refinement where niceties of accent and emphasis were concerned. She went on to tackle the formidable coloratura hurdles of the role with practiced precision, singing nearly everything in tune (a feat noteworthy in itself) and giving each passage an appropriate elegance of style.

I can imagine more effortless Normas (Miss Callas seemed desperately anxious the other night to get everything just right, and I was sometimes constrained to admire her zeal, rather than to relax in simple enjoyment, as I should have preferred to do), but this was an astonishingly neat and well-handled one, and I can now look forward with pleasure to what Miss Callas will do with such roles as Tosca and Lucia, which, from the purely vocal point of view, are a great deal less demanding.

THE MET'S OPENING WEEK also included performances of "Die Meistersinger" and "Don Pasquale." Both entailed what may be regarded as standard Metropolitan productions, but a recent visit to many of Europe's leading opera houses has, I must say, given me a new appreciation of just how high this standard is at present. Certainly nowhere else, to my knowledge, is there an opera house capable of following an interesting "Norma" with an excellent "Die Meistersinger" and a superb "Don Pasquale"—all gratifyingly sung in their original languages and with generally fresh and brilliant, if not always absolutely perfect, vocal results.

November 17, 1956

THE GREAT ANTON BRUCKNER was a composer who, in his music, talked very simply and earnestly about very profound things—mostly about faith, love, the beauty of the world as he saw it, and the glory of God. His symphonies do not contain any trace of technical display for its own sake, or of the bitter, passionate critical faculty that lends spice and color to the work of more restless, revolutionary, and egocentric nineteenth-century composers. His musical language is everywhere notable for its vast sincerity. He says what he has to say in the most unabashed and direct terms, pushing his message home with long, leisurely phrases and punctuating these phrases with exclamation points that often strike the over-sophisticated listener as pretty obvious.

There is, nevertheless, a certain grandeur in nearly everything Bruckner ever wrote—a grandeur of a sort that, to my mind, is matched only in the religious compositions of Johann Sebastian Bach. No one, having once encountered this grandeur, is likely to forget the experience, or to regard Bruckner as anything less than a supreme master of deep musical communication. The trouble is that, in order to encounter it, the listener must have before him a performance as sober and dedicated as the music itself, and such performances, in this age of speed, polish, and superficial brilliance, are by no means frequent.

In its recent American début, the Vienna Philharmonic, under the baton of Carl Schuricht, offered New York concertgoers a performance of this kind. The symphony was Bruckner's Seventh, the most often performed of all his works (if one can use the word "often" in connection with any Bruckner composition), and one that has been done here in the past by various orchestras and maestros of considerable distinction. The fine Viennese ensemble and its courtly seventy-six-year-old conductor succeeded, however, in adding a new dimension to Bruckner interpretation as we know it, and the symphony emerged with a coherence, warmth, and eloquence that very rarely falls to its lot.

Perhaps this new dimension was, in part, a result of the painstaking traditions of the orchestra, which is obviously better acquainted with the work of its fellow-Austrian than is any other ensemble on earth. But much of it was also a result of the orchestra's great emotional absorption in its task, and of the contribution of Mr. Schuricht, who has a way of turning himself into the ideal tool of Bruckner's thought. Nowhere did one feel that Mr. Schuricht was hastening or brightening up things by way of apology for Bruckner's leisurely method of expression. As a matter of fact, the opening and closing measures of the first movement were played slower and more deliberately than I had ever heard them played before, and there was an expansive plasticity about the conductor's tempos in general that gave Bruckner's melodic pronouncements the air of unhurried and serene majesty properly belonging to them.

When it comes to the virtues of the Vienna Philharmonic as compared to those of the numerous other admirable ensembles that have visited us recently, I should say they lie in the direction of exquisite refinement of phraseology and extraordinary mellowness of tone. These virtues showed themselves not only in the Bruckner work but in an early Mozart symphony (K. 181) and in Beethoven's "Egmont" Overture—the items that preceded it on the program. The orchestra's strings, in particular, have a luminous sonority and suavity of articulation that are, as far as I am aware, unique, and the rapport among the various choirs—strings, woodwinds, and brasses—is remarkably well balanced and intimate.

Where sheer flash and energy are concerned, there are undoubtedly orchestras that surpass this one, but it was pleasant the other night not to be bowled over by mere exuberance, and to find, instead, the sort of mature artistry that makes its appeal through charm and elegance, rather than supercharged virtuosity. In Mr. Schuricht, moreover, the orchestra has a conductor of great sensibility and modest demeanor, whose gestures produce the maximum musical result while remaining visually as unpretentious as possible. Altogether, the evening that their collaboration provided was a continuous delight.

AT OTHER TIMES during the week, I attended various performances at the Metropolitan Opera House, for various reasons. I went to hear "Il Trovatore" because I like it, and I am afraid I was somewhat disappointed by a performance that found Kurt Baum, as Manrico, in bad voice, Fedora Barbieri out of control as Azucena, and Max Rudolf conducting things with the rigidity of a chief of police. I extracted some solace, however, from

Leonard Warren's singing as the Count di Luna and from a few luscious phrases provided here and there by Zinka Milanov. I went to hear "La Bohème," mainly to check up on the conducting of Thomas Schippers, who has now added this work to his Metropolitan repertory—a repertory that up to then had been limited hereabouts to "Don Pasquale," I found Mr. Schippers, as usual, a scintillating technician, but I wish that he would learn to relax a little and allow the native ebullience of his singers the sort of leeway it needs in frankly sentimental and romantic music like this.

Finally I went to "Rigoletto," primarily to witness the Metropolitan début of the American soprano Mattiwilda Dobbs, as Gilda, and I must say that on this occasion I experienced not the slightest bit of disappointment. Though betraying the normal nervousness associated with such ordeals, Miss Dobbs sang, on the whole, with amazing assurance, giving the role both the requisite coloratura brilliance and a very rare and engaging quality of emotional subtlety.

In recent years, most of the Met's Gildas, including those of such redoubtable artists as Lily Pons, Patrice Munsel, and Roberta Peters, have been noted for deft marksmanship and cool, flutelike tone, and in listening to them for so long I had almost forgotten that Gilda can also possess a heart. I was gratifyingly reminded of this by Miss Dobbs, who seems to possess not only superb marksmanship but innate musicality, a voice of glowing timbre, and the ability to project the feelings of the character with simplicity and conviction. She is, in addition, quite pretty, and her acting is pleasing and tasteful. The remainder of the production was exceptionally good, too, its principal attribute being the Rigoletto of Leonard Warren, which, as everybody should know by now, is one of the great monuments of current operatic history.

November 24, 1956

IN THE COURSE of countless hours spent in concert halls and
opera houses while devoting myself to the more or less exact
science of discriminating between good and bad performing artists, I have evolved a number of labor-saving tests that, to my
mind, are precise indicators of musical artistry and, in addition,
have the virtue of making it unnecessary for me to listen to an
entire evening of music before forming my conclusions.

One of these tests, which I use on violinists, is the first theme
of the first movement of the Beethoven Violin Concerto. This
theme, as you will probably remember, is played by the soloist
immediately after the quasi-recitative passage (beginning with
the octaves) with which he makes his initial entrance. I listen
carefully for the sixth and seventh notes of the theme, and if
the sixth is louder than the seventh, I know that I am in the
presence of a distinguished artist; if the seventh is louder than
the sixth, I know that the violinist is a mediocre one, no matter
how much luscious tone and scintillating technique he shows
himself capable of. The principle of the test is very simple, involving the superiority of mind over matter. These two notes
form the subsiding end of a phrase, and all the laws of cultivated
musicianship demand that the phrase subside properly. At this
juncture, however, the violinist finds his bow moving from point

to heel, and the natural tendency of the bow when moving in that direction is to produce a greater, rather than a lesser, volume of tone. A fine artist will thwart the tendency for the sake of the music; a mediocre one will allow the clumsiness of the bow to distort the contour of the phrase by producing a crescendo instead of a diminuendo. I have never known this test to fail.

Another of these tests, useful for gauging the artistry of Italian-type tenors, rests on exactly the same principle. A performance of "Aïda" is an essential part of this one, but listening to the entire opera is by no means necessary; the first two phrases of the aria "Celeste Aïda"—conveniently near the beginning of the first scene—tell the whole story. Nearly all tenors have high notes that are louder than their low notes. Therefore, a tenor in whom matter is dominant over mind (a not unusual condition) sings these very difficult rising phrases, "Celeste A-i-DAH! Forma di-vi-NAH!," bellowing the final note of each phrase at the top of his lungs. This, of course, proves that he has ringing high notes, but it also proves that his head is being used primarily as a resonator and that he belongs not in an opera house but in some less fastidious environment, like the bar of a Neapolitan restaurant. A great tenor, on the other hand, puts the musical accent where it belongs—on the "i" of "Aïda," and on the "vi" of "divina"—and gallantly lets his top notes subside, leaving perhaps some doubt as to whether he can holler as loud as the next man but proving himself an artist. I have never known this test to fail, either, and if you want to experience a fine example of a positive (or extremely artistic) reaction to it, I heartily recommend to you the recording of the aria made by Enrico Caruso.

During the performance of "Aïda" last week, I was gratified to find my "Aïda-divina" test running true to form. Mr. Carlo Bergonzi, a tenor new to the Met, was the Radames. His "Celeste Aïda" contaneed a final "da" and "na" that could be described neither as examples of unrestrained bellowing nor as the elegant, trailing sighs they become when sung by a master, but were somewhere in between. "Well," I said to myself after analyzing this data, "the reaction is neither markedly positive nor markedly negative. Mr. Bergonzi is, therefore, not a great artist, but he is also not a terribly bad one"—and, sure enough, in the remaining three and a half acts nothing was added to or subtracted from my original impression. Mr. Bergonzi sang with a tone that was often nice and golden and that consistently had sufficient power for the role, and he acted with stolid simplicity, but he had done all this in those two phrases.

Indeed, I might easily have left immediately after applying my test to Mr. Bergonzi, confident that I had completed my job, if it had not been for the fact that I had another singer to check up on—Miss Antonietta Stella, who was making her Metropolitan début as Aïda. Unfortunately, I have not yet been able to evolve an absolutely dependable two-note or two-phrase test for a soprano, and it took me the better part of the evening, with a few changes of mind, to arrive at an estimate of her talents. These, in the end, added up to something not so very different from the sum of Mr. Bergonzi's. Miss Stella, I concluded, is an unusually handsome singer with a dramatic-soprano voice of striking power and a vigorous, if not particularly subtle, manner of singing. What gifts she has as an actress are expressed in gestures, sobs, and other visually impressive phenomena but do not, regrettably, make themselves felt in the voice itself, which is, of course, where one expects the major part of a great singer's acting ability to be. I should describe her as a promising (she is in her twenties) but by no means overwhelming Aïda.

The rest of the cast was, I thought, highly uneven. Fedora Barbieri, as Amneris, had dressed herself in a costume that clashed rather unpleasantly with her surroundings and, in addition, looked as if it might have clothed a siren on the lid of a box of Egyptian cigarettes. She remains a singer of distinction, but the distinction was apparent only here and there, being interspersed with a good deal of vocal attitudinizing and some moments of badly focussed tone. The only principal who brought any notable intelligence and poise into the proceedings was George London, as Amonasro. The auditorium was crowded with people whose tests, I'll wager, are not as accurate as mine, and they roared their approval after every aria and obviously had a much better time than I did.

December 15, 1956

OPERA MAY BE a branch of the art of music and a variety of drama, but it is also—at least in its effect upon many of its devotees—a kind of sport, and those who regard it as such have been exceptionally conspicuous at the Metropolitan House over the past month or so. During this time, I have encountered more symptoms of combative emotion—cheers, boos, hisses, arguments, standees clutching their temples or wringing their hands in the lobby between the acts, even minor scuffles—than had previously come to my attention in many years.

On a recent evening, a group of Miss Zinka Milanov's partisans turned up wearing large buttons inscribed with the slogan "Viva Zinka!," and, as everybody knows by now, there has been one authentic case of the hurling of vegetables. The cause of it all, of course, has been the appearance among us of Maria Meneghini Callas, a rather remarkable singer with, I understand, a highly competitive approach to her work, and I bring up the matter not in order to call further attention to incidents that have already been quite thoroughly publicized but to examine such grains of justification as may lie behind this curious behavior.

As far as I can make out, the rumpus stems mainly from the fact that Miss Callas' admirers have claimed for her a unique rank as a sort of world's champion soprano, and her detractors don't think she deserves the title. I don't, either, but I must say that, to my knowledge, she has broken two records this season. On opening night, as I indicated at the time, she sang the only adequate Norma heard at the Metropolitan in thirty years, and by last week she had become the first soprano in the entire history of the Metropolitan to undertake both Tosca and Lucia.

These achievements, considered simply as athletic feats, clearly have nothing whatever to do with such elusive matters as taste and charm. Like any record in the field of sport, they involve precisely measurable factors. In "Norma," Miss Callas sang more notes in tune and in place than either of the two other sopranos who have attempted this difficult role at the Met since the time of Rosa Ponselle. In singing both Tosca and Lucia, she provided an almost incredible example of versatility—something that might be compared to successive demonstrations of prowess at weight-lifting and the hundred-yard dash.

Despite these accomplishments, though, one is not obliged to like Miss Callas' singing. I find the quality of her voice somewhat monotonous and at times disagreeably feline. I have heard better Lucias than hers, and, having heard Eileen Farrell sing the similarly exacting title role of Cherubini's "Medea" with the

American Opera Society last year, I suspect that the operatic world contains a greater Norma. But Miss Farrell, after all, works in another league, and the concluding point from which she has been momentarily distracting me is that Miss Callas is indeed a formidable, if not a unique, all-round vocal athlete, for while many singers can sing some roles of the Italian repertoire better than she does, I don't know of any who can sing as great a variety of roles as well.

From the technical point of view, Miss Callas' Lucia, was less impressive than her Norma. It was so because of one specific and rather damaging flaw—an athletic rather than an artistic one, in that she failed to negotiate her high notes with any ease whatever. Those in the first act emerged like desperate screams, while one in the first part of the Mad Scene was passed up in favor of the optional lower octave, and the final one in the scene ended in complete disaster. Except for these faulty notes, however, I found her interpretation of the role interesting, and occasionally even thrilling. Her coloratura was extraordinarily agile and accurate, the quality of her voice in *mezza voce* was warm and expressive, and her handling of accent and phrasing was always scrupulous, elegant, and authoritative. Miss Callas, in sum, again showed herself to be a remarkable singer, but she also showed that her striking physical resources have their limits.

LÁSZLO

December 29, 1956

THERE HAS BEEN, I think, a fair amount of confusion hereabouts lately on the subject of sopranos. They come, as every connoisseur of the subject should know, in a number of models, suited to more or less specific purposes, and the statement that "So-and-So is a better soprano than So-and-So" is without meaning unless it is made with reference to singers of pretty much the same type.

There are lyric sopranos—Lucine Amara is a good example—who make wonderful Mimis and Antonias but would be totally unsuitable as Toscas. There are dramatic sopranos, like Renata Tebaldi, who make fine Toscas, Desdemonas, and Aïdas, and even good Violettas, but lack the agility to undertake such roles as Norma and the Leonora of "Il Trovatore." There are coloratura sopranos of the bravura type, like Roberta Peters, whose gifts fit them exclusively for a very special repertoire that includes Lucia, Gilda, and the Queen of the Night. There are German- or Austrian-type coloraturas, like Hilde Gueden, who are noted more for refinement of style than for spectacularity, and who shine particularly in the lighter and subtler Mozart roles. There are Wagnerian sopranos—Kirsten Flagstad was a superb instance—who are splendid artists in their chosen field but are not extraordinarily good at anything but Wagner. Then, there are some singers who have the versatility to cross one or more of the lines demarcating these types.

Finally, there is a rare kind of super-soprano, who combines dramatic power and great emotional expressiveness with coloratura agility and is capable of tackling a role like Norma. Supersopranos usually attract a lot of attention. Their history is studded with big names; Lillian Nordica, Lilli Lehmann, Rosa Ponselle, and Elisabeth Rethberg come to mind, among others. On the Metropolitan Opera's roster at the moment, Maria Meneghini Callas and Zinka Milanov seem to be the most prominent representatives of the type.

Though there has been a terrific hullabaloo at the Met this season over the merits of these rival super-sopranos, the greatest artist in this category currently before the public—in my opinion, at least—is the American singer Eileen Farrell, who last week repeated her magnificent interpretation of the title role of Cherubini's "Medea" with the American Opera Society. Miss Farrell, like most singers of her kind, is a rather plump figure of a woman (I am not sure but that Miss Callas lost something besides weight by the rigid course of dieting that preceded her Metropolitan début), and since the performance was in concert form, I am in the dark as to just what sort of actress she would make from the visual standpoint.

But one goes to "Medea," as one goes to "Norma," primarily to hear fine singing and to enjoy the specialized art of acting with the voice, which is the unique dramatic province of the operatic artist. Miss Farrell possesses the powerful voice and the accurate coloratura technique that are the basic requisites of her type. She also has an authoritative style of singing, and can project the niceties of classical phrasing with faultless emphasis. Moreover, her voice is one of agreeable quality and is capable of an extraordinary range of emotional expression.

I noted all this last year, when Miss Farrell sang "Medea" for the first time, and I went to hear her again the other night not so much in the line of duty as to indulge myself in one of those rare occasions when even a hard-pressed music critic may relax and have a good time. Miss Farrell's performance will remain, I am sure, one of the high points of the current musical season.

January 5, 1957

NEARLY EVERY INTELLIGENT concertgoer knows that all music worthy of the name conveys a meaning lying behind the mere sound of the notes that go to make it up. But just what that meaning is is extraordinarily difficult to describe. Nobody is more keenly aware of this problem than that poor devil the music critic. He writes that a composition is "expressive," but he is baffled when he tries to explain what it is expressive *of*; he refers vaguely to its "emotional content," but he is unable to state precisely what this content is. The situation has long attracted the attention of aestheticians and psychologists, who have conspicuously failed to come to grips with it, and also that of composers, who, contrary to prevalent belief, do not necessarily understand their art any better than other musicians do, and have from time to time written some pretty silly things on the subject.

Thinkers with a mechanistic approach have occasionally claimed that music does not express anything at all, that it is merely a matter of aural sensations and mathematical relationships—a patent absurdity. Other thinkers have sought for solutions to this murky enigma by drawing analogies with the aesthetic principles of other arts—notably, painting, but these analogies have never proved very fruitful, and have usually demonstrated to the careful reader that music and the other arts do not really have much in common. Clearly, music "says" something, but up to now, as far as I am aware, just what it says has been the subject of romantic reveries, imprecise rhetoric, unsound theorizing, or utter frustration.

I say "up to now" because there has recently arrived on my desk a book that assaults the problem with comprehensiveness and clarity. The book is "Emotion and Meaning in Music," by Leonard B. Meyer (University of Chicago Press), and after reading it I am convinced that it is by far the most important work on musical aesthetics that I have ever encountered. Mr. Meyer, an associate professor of music at the University of Chicago, is obliged to use the languages of the philosopher, the psychologist, and the musical theorist, and his book will make rather hard going for the casual reader, but those who are intrepid enough to follow its complicated trains of thought will find in it the answers to practically all the mysteries that have made musical meaning such a dim and complex business.

Mr. Meyer distinguishes at the outset between what he calls "absolute" and "referential" meanings, the former term designating those meanings that, as he puts it, lie exclusively within the context of a given work, and the latter designating those—love, anger, and the like—that convey concepts familiar in non-musical, as well as musical, thought. Most of his book is concerned with the analysis of absolute meaning, and he traces the various devices that composers have used for conveying it, not only in the music of Western civilization but in jazz, primitive music, and the music of the Orient, thus pointing up the universality of this element of musical communication.

In explaining absolute meaning, he calls attention to a number of psychological phenomena that express themselves in terms of opposites—doubt vs. certainty, insecurity vs. security, expectation vs. satisfaction, incompleteness vs. completion, chance vs. the organizing power of the mind—and that relate to the narrative or kinetic nature of the musical art. The composer, according to Mr. Meyer, uses various formulas to induce these psychological states—inhibiting expected tendencies and thereby producing anxiety in the listener, assuaging this anxiety by trotting out the expected solution, and so forth.

From what Mr. Meyer has written, it is evident that music, like the other narrative arts, relies largely on the factors of suspense and catharsis, and that its methods of embodying these factors are almost limitless in their complexity and diversity. It is also evident that though the psychological states referred to by these terms are simple in the abstract, they actually include a rich range of feeling, and that music is thus enabled to portray, in sublimated form, some of the most powerful and subtle emotional experiences of life. The process necessarily entails a tradition—a frame of reference in which deviations from certain norms may be distinguished from the norms themselves—and this tradition is learned in much the same way a language is learned. Without such an accepted tradition, common musical experience —and, consequently, musical communication of any kind—would prove impossible.

In his final chapter, Mr. Meyer gets around to the more slippery subject of referential meaning—more slippery because referential meaning is to a great extent a matter of association, and different listeners may get different associations from a given musical phenomenon. Nevertheless, referential meanings do exist, and there is enough common ground in the associative habits of people with a common musical culture to make them understandable. Mr. Meyer is comprehensibly and commendably cautious in approaching this area of musical meaning—an area that might be said to constitute the illustrative or metaphorical aspect of the art—but he leaves no doubt that many ideas ordinarily expressed in literature can also be expressed in music, though he is scrupulous about defining the limits of music in this matter. On the subject of death, to take one instance, he notes, "Music does not, for example, present the concept or image of death itself. Rather it connotes that rich realm of experience in which death and darkness, night and cold, winter and sleep and silence are all combined and consolidated into a single connotative complex."

The vast importance of Mr. Meyer's book, to my mind, is that it explains for the first time, and in a thoroughgoing and precise way, just how music is related to human experience. To the critic it offers tools of increased variety and sharpness, to the composer a badly needed clear statement of his purposes, and to the listener an explanation of why music affects him as it does. It will, I think, do a great deal toward silencing the sophomoric prattle of the formalists—including the atonalists—who for a long time have been mistaking the calligraphy of music for its substance. Mr. Meyer, using, among other things, the resources of modern psychology, has succeeded where many a famous predecessor has failed, and as a result the realm of thinking about music will, I feel, never be quite the same again.

January 26, 1957

It seems to me that in the modernization of the elaborate nine-teenth-century stage spectacles of Richard Wagner there is a point beyond which they begin to lose something of their essential character. This point has, I think, been reached in the productions at Bayreuth, where all the papier-mâché props and leafy backdrops of old-fashioned stagecraft have been eliminated, and modern lighting effects, along with a minimum of such in-dispensable utensils as spears and swords, suggest, rather than portray, the details of the Wagnerian wonderland. It is quite true that this simplified method of staging brings Wagner's operas—and the Ring cycle in particular—into better line with what we are accustomed to in the contemporary theatre, but at the same time there is something about the Bayreuth productions —all their stylized spit and polish notwithstanding—that brings them close to being mere concert performances with costumes and tricky lighting added.

Consequently, with all due respect for the ingenuity and the-atrical finish of the Bayreuth performances, most of which I saw last summer, I cannot restrain a certain affection for Wagnerian opera as it is produced at the Metropolitan. The Metropolitan productions of the Ring are unabashedly old-fashioned, and have taken on a period atmosphere that undeniably makes them look a little quaint. I see nothing wrong with this, however. While Wagner's music may be eternal, his theatrical conceptions *are* dated and *do* belong to a period, and when the ancient conventions of this period are, at least in part, observed, his sometimes preposterous fantasies assume an air of nostalgia that I, for one, find distinctly pleasant and often amusing, in a gently sentimental way.

I was reminded of this last week, when the Met trotted out "Das Rheingold" as the opening item of what is to be its first complete Ring cycle in six years. Its Rhine maidens (they were actually ballerinas used as stand-ins for the singers, who sang their lines backstage) dangled, as they traditionally should, way above the stage floor, swinging in and out of the flies like young women on flying trapezes. Alberich magically transformed himself not into a vague lighting effect but into a very large and menacing papier-mâché serpent, which poked its head fearsomely from the wings and flicked its papier-mâché tongue. Erda came out in front of the backdrop at the top of what looked like a dangerously active volcano, and Donner's hammer blow struck prongs of lightning that really appeared to fill the stage. All this was good fun, and if one was in the mood, as I was, to yield to the childlike charm of patent make-believe, it was even, at times, poetically evocative.

I am sorry to hear that in its forthcoming production of "Siegfried" the Metropolitan has decided to dispense with the steam-belching dragon. I think that this is a mistake. "Siegfried's" dragon has always seemed to me one of the most fascinating props of the Ring, and I have invariably looked forward to its Gargantuan maneuvers with mingled glee and apprehension— part of the latter emotion being aroused by the fear that its intricate machinery might stall, or even that the whole contraption might fall apart.

On the musical side, "Das Rheingold" was a long time getting into its stride. Perhaps because of the terribly cold weather that evening, the horns and Bayreuth tubas of Fritz Stiedry's orchestra started off badly, with rather thin tone and frequent lapses from correct marksmanship. But as the evening progressed, the instrumentalists' tone and vigor improved, and the organlike majesty of Wagner's orchestration was finally accorded its full eloquence and smoothness. The singing was, by and large, adequate, and occasionally something more than that, though it never reached any really great heights.

THE THING THAT struck me most forcibly about Prokofieff's ambitious opera "War and Peace," which was heard for the first time in this country when the N.B.C. Television Opera Company presented it on the air a couple of Sundays ago, was the emergence, in certain of its passages, of a different Prokofieff—different, that is, from the brilliant, dry, and ingenious musical satirist who seems to have written the bulk of the composer's work. In these passages, inspired perhaps by the humanity of Tolstoy's novel, Prokofieff has written music of a really moving sort—beautifully melodious, singable, and eminently expressive of the emotions of his characters—and I am sure that they will rank among the finest he ever created. Most of these passages are love scenes—the initial scene between Prince Andrey, Natasha, and Sonia, the scene in which Pierre confesses his love for Natasha, and the scene in which General Kutuzov expresses his love for the city of Moscow. Elsewhere, though, I found "War and Peace" a rather spotty affair—hardly, on the whole, a successful opera. The scenes involving Napoleon are filled with a sort of drumming and gnashing of fiddle strings that obviously expresses the composer's disapproval of that gentleman but fails to give him his due as a major figure, and some of the music of the battlefield sequences hardly rises above the sort of thing that occurs in Hollywood movie scores.

The problem of making an opera out of Tolstoy's lengthy and rambling masterpiece has, I think, been approached much too literally—assuming in the first place that it can be effectively approached at all—and one result of this is that we are scarcely able to become acquainted with any of its twenty-odd major characters before they depart to make way for others; the activities of Pierre, for instance, are reduced to what amounts to three or four walk-ons. Despite the opera's shortcomings, however, it was a fine and enterprising thing for the N.B.C. Television Opera to give it a hearing.

February 2, 1957

WHEN ROY HARRIS'S Third Symphony was first performed here, nearly twenty years ago, it seemed to me to be something rather special among American works of the sort—a work, indeed, of striking individuality and vigor. I was obviously not alone in this view, for the composition has subsequently become the most frequently performed of all American symphonies; even

Mr. Harris himself, as far as I am aware, has not produced anything to surpass, or even equal, it in the rest of his symphonic
output.

Listening to it again when the Philharmonic-Symphony Orchestra, conducted by Leonard Bernstein, played it last week, I
was once more impressed by the originality and dignity of long
stretches of the score—particularly in the second half—and I was
also able to discern just what it was that made the work seem so
exceptional on the occasion of its first performance. It is by no
means a perfect, or even a consistently eloquent, symphony, but
compared with the empty and highly self-conscious works in this
genre that were being turned out by the majority of fashionable
American symphonists at the time of its writing, it has considerable poetic feeling and an unusual sincerity. It seeks—unlike
many symphonies of its period—to convey emotional meaning,
and it achieves this end with an agreeable absence of technical
trickery, using, for the most part, the language of established
musical tradition. Its strongest attribute, one that has contributed to both its initial success and its continuing popularity—is, I
think, the fact that it does not concern itself with the surfaces of
music but goes deeper, utilizing technique, as the works of the
masters do, to express genuine ideas understandably.

The composition that preceded it on the program—Aaron Copland's "Short Symphony"—is, in my opinion, a perfect example
of the sort of empty formalism that once made Mr. Harris's work
stand out, by contrast, as a significant contribution to music. It
was written a few years prior to the Harris symphony and, I am
afraid, bears the worst marks of its period—a period when musical aesthetics were so confused that the penmanship of the art,
so to speak, was often mistaken by composers for the content of
what they were writing. Considered as an exercise in musical
penmanship, Mr. Copland's symphony has its points of very
moderate interest. Its orchestration is expert and its structure in-

tricate, and if you are amused—as I am not—by a contrived effect of incessantly restless and changing rhythm, you may conceivably find it of some purely cerebral appeal. But it has no discernible emotional subject matter, and—to me, at least—it conveys nothing but the tedium that is apt to set in when a composer is bent merely on demonstrating his ingenuity in arranging notes on paper.

The difference between these two compositions has, I must say, been greatly clarified in my mind since I read Leonard Meyer's "Emotion and Meaning in Music," the admirable treatise on musical aesthetics that I mentioned in these columns a few weeks ago. Mr. Harris's musical idiom in the Third Symphony contains many of the complementary elements—action and repose, dissonance and consonance, suspense and catharsis—that, as Mr. Meyer has noted, are capable of gripping the mind of the listener and making him feel that an experience of some sort is in progress.

Mr. Copland's "Short Symphony," on the other hand, is arbitrarily and monotonously dissonant throughout. What propulsion it has is provided by its rhythm alone, and this is so relentlessly eccentric and so lacking in contrasting moments of repose that the work in its entirety has no narrative form whatever. In fairness to Mr. Copland, I must add that he has, in his time, written much better music. But the "Short Symphony" is, to my mind, one of many works of contemporary composers in which notes have been strung together without what Mr. Meyer has defined as meaning.

I WAS DELIGHTED to find that, despite advance reports to the contrary, there was a dragon in the Metropolitan's production of "Siegfried" last week. It was a beautiful dragon, somewhat resembling a thirty- or forty-foot representative of the iguana species of lizard. Its scales gleamed, it belched smoke, and, in its duel with the hero of the piece, it boxed magnificently with its front claws. This was gratifying to me not only as evidence of the Met's continuing respect for the fauna of the Wagnerian world of make-believe but also because in "Siegfried" my sympathies have always been with the dragon, and I have long had to suppress a wish that, in some exceptional performance, justice would triumph and the dragon would eat the beefy *Heldentenor* who so inconsiderately disturbs its rest. This, I realize, is asking too much. Nevertheless, Siegfried remains the least ingratiating of Wagnerian heroes, and in my opinion his egregious lack of charm is one of the main factors that make this opera the weakest, from a dramatic standpoint, of the Ring cycle.

Musically, however, it goes without saying that "Siegfried" contains some beautiful stretches, and, under the experienced direction of Fritz Stiedry, these exerted a great deal of their magic at last week's performance of the opera. I was slightly disappointed in Wolfgang Windgassen's portrayal of the title role, which was, on the whole, sung rather timidly and without the brassy brilliance that some other tenors I remember have given it. I was also disappointed in the singing and acting of Martha Moedl, a German artist who was making her début in the role of Brünnhilde, though I must say by way of extenuation that it is a fearfully difficult role to make a début in, since Brünnhilde appears only during the final half hour of the opera, long after everybody else has had a chance to warm up, and is allotted some of the most taxing phrases that Wagner ever wrote. Elsewhere, it seemed to me the performance adhered to the highest standards.

February 16, 1957

BEING A CONFIRMED admirer of the works of Anton Bruckner, I welcomed as a great occasion the performance of his Ninth Symphony by Bruno Walter and the New York Philharmonic. This was not only because performances of Bruckner symphonies—except, perhaps, for the familiar Seventh—are much rarer in our concert halls than I could wish but because I consider the Ninth one of the finest of them, particularly in its final slow movement, which is, to my mind, the most magnificent of all the magnificent adagios the Austrian Master wrote.

I have found, over a period of many years, that repeated study with the aid of a phonograph is the most satisfactory approach to Bruckner, since of all the composers whose works I am familiar with he is the least likely to reveal the full content of his musical thought on first hearing. The explanation, I think, lies in the complexity of his detail, which at the outset is apt to distract a listener who is trying to apprehend the total organization that constitutes the dramatic continuity of a Bruckner work, and this is undoubtedly why, among the many concertgoers who only occasionally hear one of his compositions, he has a reputation for diffuseness and episodic construction. It is not until one is well acquainted with his music that what appear at first to be episodes fall into place as integral components of a grand and complicated scheme, which—in the greatest of his compositions, at any rate—is rivalled for audacity and creative vision only by certain monumental works of Bach and Beethoven.

The Adagio of the Ninth is one of these grand and complicated schemes. It is filled with technical devices of a sort that appeal to the intellect as well as to the emotions—contrapuntal themes; modulating themes, beginning in one key and ending up in another; inversions, in which Bruckner likes, as Bach did before him, to turn his melodic material upside down; mirror effects, in which themes appear upside down and right side up at the same time; and so on. These, naturally, are sometimes difficult to detect and follow, and I confess that even after the considerable preparation I have had as a student of Bruckner's work, I reach the end of this movement with a feeling of mental fatigue. It is, however, the pleasant fatigue that comes on the heels of a great musical or dramatic experience in which all the involved threads of thought have been finally woven together into a serene and satisfying solution. The listener feels that he has heard a leisurely and profound pronouncement on very basic things—the beauty of life, the finality of death, and the persistence of human aspiration and hope are doubtless among them —and he leaves the auditorium with the conviction that his sense of values has been shaken and then restored in better accord with the deeper realities of existence.

Like Bach, Bruckner was, of course, an intensely religious man, and the message of much of his music is a religious one, but it is not necessary to be religious in any doctrinaire sense to appreciate the majesty and spiritual profundity of what he has to say. All that is needed is an awareness of some of the more splendid mysteries that beset the human psyche, along with sufficient patience to get the many little symphonic details into proper relation.

As for Mr. Walter's interpretation of the symphony, it was very near perfection. His tempos were as correct and appropriately pliant as any I have heard in a performance of this work; he seemed to have identified himself with Bruckner's thought and feeling to a degree that I have seldom encountered; and the Philharmonic sounded better than it had all season.

March 30, 1957

DAVID DIAMOND's Symphony No. 6, which was given its New York première by the Boston Symphony, under Charles Munch, is, I think, possibly the worst composition of its type by a composer of any pretensions to have been heard here since the Philharmonic performed Carlos Chávez' Third, about a year ago. I can only attribute the flutter of polite and tepid hand-clapping that greeted it to the apathy of an audience that has ceased to make the effort required to distinguish good music from bad.

My unfavorable impression of the work is not the result of any jolting departures from conventionality on Mr. Diamond's part, for the symphony contains no trace whatever of technical originality. On the contrary, it is an academic composition in the truest sense of the word. Such technical formulas as it exhibits were invented and exhausted by the late Arnold Schoenberg nearly fifty years ago, and, as far as I am aware, have never contributed much to the progress of musical composition. My objection is simply that the musical language, if it can be called a language, employed by Mr. Diamond in this symphony, as in others, is even weaker than that of most of his formalist contemporaries in those elements of suspense and catharsis that are necessary to the expression of musical meaning—that, in fact, the only skill the work exhibits is a consistent ability to prevent a hundred orchestra players from saying anything musically intelligible.

If I seem a bit intemperate in these remarks, it is not because I consider the perpetration of some twenty minutes of vapid and boring sounds to be, in itself, a crime. The issue, I feel, is larger than that. Mr. Diamond's style of composition has been a more or less fashionable one for a generation. It is a style that is apparently looked on with favor by the small but powerful group of composer-politicians who nowadays are apt to control the awarding of fellowships, prizes, and publishing contracts. It is also, I am afraid, a style that is rapidly reducing the art of symphonic composition to the status of an unimportant and irresponsible little private hobby, about as significant to the music-loving public as knitting or playing marbles. The sinister trouble with the style is not that it wastes the time of composers, performers, and audiences but that the weight of its current prestige and the mass of artistic deadwood it gives rise to are likely to stifle such shoots of living music by younger and better composers as are at present struggling for survival.

The composing of symphonic music is, to my mind, a very serious business, related to a glorious tradition to which many great masters of the past have contributed. Some of the greatest of these have changed and extended the tradition, but their alterations have invariably been made with reference to the established norms of musical communication that it embodies, and have been significant and interesting precisely because they were departures from the expected and universally understood path. It is notable, but scarcely surprising, that virtually all the symphonies by recent composers that have gained any permanent hold on musical audiences—works by such figures as Shostakovich, Prokofieff, Vaughan Williams, and Paul Creston, and that single outstanding composition by Roy Harris, the Third Symphony—have been firmly rooted in this tradition, and have conveyed some degree of meaning for the sole reason that they were related to it. I can only conclude that Mr. Diamond either is ignorant of the tradition or is perversely and fashionably bent on writing as if it didn't exist. In any case, his Sixth Symphony is, in my opinion, not only not a symphony; it is not, even by the most generous definition, music.

April 6, 1957

THE MUSIC of Heitor Villa-Lobos differs from that of a good many of his contemporaries in that it never seems to conform to any formula, either borrowed or original. It is neither violently modern nor in any way old-fashioned. Its technique is not atonal or neo-classical or impressionistic. It does not sound in the least like anybody else's music.

Trying to analyze Villa-Lobos's music is like trying to analyze a torrent one is swimming in. The listener is borne along so rapidly on a current of changing ideas that he has scarcely become acquainted with one idea before he is swept into another. Nearly all the ideas are highly original, and the torrent is nearly always refreshing. Sometimes, especially in the longer works, one wonders where one is going, and even whether Mr. Villa-Lobos knows where *he* is going. But what the composer does in the meanwhile is uniformly notable for its freshness and exuberance, and the listener forgives an occasional suggestion of incoherence in the music because he is continuously fascinated and enchanted by novel touches of melody, orchestration, counterpoint, and other structural elements that he is encountering here for the first time.

Where pure inspiration and musicality of the instinctive—as opposed to the deliberate—sort are concerned, I doubt whether Mr. Villa-Lobos has an equal anywhere today. And though his music may suggest all kinds of things—from the insect-ridden jungles of his native Brazil to memories of Bach—it is never merely decorative. It has strong melodic lines and a compelling sense of propulsion, and these virutes are, after all, basic virtues of genuine music.

Last week Mr. Villa-Lobos celebrated his seventieth birthday, almost a month after it occurred, by taking over the baton of the New York Philharmonic and conducting a program of works by himself and two other contemporary composers—a fellow-Brazilian named Camargo Guarnieri and the Frenchman Florent Schmitt. Though Mr. Villa-Lobos conducted everybody's compositions with equal devotion, the contrast between the efforts of the two other men and his own was so glaring that I could not help wishing he had decided on an all-Villa-Lobos program. As it was, Mr. Schmitt's "Salammbô" Suite No. 2—a tired concatenation of shapeless textures and exotic colors containing all the clichés of Debussyan impressionism—was distinctly tedious, and Mr. Guarnieri's "Abertura Concertante" appeared to be merely a poor imitation of Mr. Villa-Lobos's own music, which I fear is not fruitfully imitable.

The rewarding parts of the program included Mr. Villa-Lo-

bos's "Bachianas Brasileiras" No. 1 for Eight Violoncelli and his
"Chôros" No. 6, both of them highly unconventional items, but
not on that account less appealing. In the former, for reasons
doubtless best known to himself, the composer employed twelve
cellists instead of the eight originally specified, and all twelve
played with exemplary virtuosity. The "Bachianas" proved to be
a powerful and, at the same time, a delicately lyrical composition containing a fine flow of contrapuntal thought, and, in particular, a slow movement of great nobility. The "Chôros," which
is scored for full orchestra, I had heard before. It has, as I think
I have previously remarked, the slightly prolix and diffuse quality that is apt to creep into Villa-Lobos's more extended compositions, and I do not think it is quite as much of a masterpiece as
the "Bachianas." Nevertheless, it has all the torrential facility
and fecundity characteristic of his style, and despite its occasional structural weaknesses, I was very happy to hear it again.

INDEX

INDEX